PROSPER MÉRIMÉE

by Maxwell A. Smith

Once considered a coldly impersonal, objective writer, Mérimée transformed episodes of his own love affairs into the artistic stuff of fiction and twice has given us a "portrait of the author." Above all in the recently published volumes of his *Correspondance* the true Mérimée appears, witty, skeptical, but generous to a fault.

Archaeologist, art and literary critic, linguist and philologist, he thought of himself chiefly as historian, remaining always the amateur in fiction and drama. His essays on Spanish literature did much to create interest in this field but it is especially in Russian literature that he was a pioneer. It is for his creative works in drama and fiction that he is chiefly read today. Like his friend Stendhal he was a forerunner of Romanticism before laying the foundation for the Realism which followed. At least two of his plays have become, like Musset's, the jewels of Romanticism and with his short stories and his one venture into the historical novel have maintained their rank and even gained in popular favor. He is rivalled only by Maupassant—who owes much to his predecessor—as a master of the French short story whose standing he did so much to establish.

By *Deveria*

PROSPER MÉRIMÉE

TWAYNE'S WORLD AUTHORS SERIES

A Survey of the World's Literature

Sylvia E. Bowman, Indiana University

GENERAL EDITOR

FRANCE

Maxwell A. Smith, Guerry Professor of French, Emeritus
The University of Chattanooga
Former Visiting Professor in Modern Languages
The Florida State University

EDITOR

Prosper Mérimée

(TWAS 249)

TWAYNE'S WORLD AUTHORS SERIES (TWAS)

The purpose of TWAS is to survey the major writers —novelists, dramatists, historians, poets, philosophers, and critics—of the nations of the world. Among the national literatures covered are those of Australia, Canada, China, Eastern Europe, France, Germany, Greece, India, Italy, Japan, Latin America, the Netherlands, New Zealand, Poland, Russia, Scandinavia, Spain, and the African nations, as well as Hebrew, Yiddish, and Latin Classical literatures. This survey is complemented by Twayne's United States Authors Series and English Authors Series.

The intent of each volume in these series is to present a critical-analytical study of the works of the writer; to include biographical and historical material that may be necessary for understanding, appreciation, and critical appraisal of the writer; and to present all material in clear, concise English—but not to vitiate the scholarly content of the work by doing so.

Prosper Mérimée

By MAXWELL A. SMITH

University of Chattanooga
Florida State University

Twayne Publishers, Inc. :: New York

To
Our daughters, Marylen and Sylvia

Preface

I am grateful to my colleague, Dr. Nicola R. Pribic, for having
made available to me two rather rare books: Ibrovac's *Claude
Fauriel et la fortune européenne des poésies populaires grecque
et serbe* and especially Yovanovitch's admirable dissertation *La
Guzla de Prosper Mérimée* which has remained for sixty years
the definitive work on this subject, and from which I have often
quoted.

In order to devote more space to Mérimée's imaginative writings I have limited this study to his Illyrian ballads and to his
drama and fiction on which his reputation largely rests today,
omitting his historical, critical, and philological books and essays.
I have, however, read the many volumes of his *Correspondance
générale,* so carefully edited by M. Parturier, from which I have
quoted profusely in regard to the details of his life and works.
Since his life divides itself naturally into three periods—boyhood
and youth, civil administration and work as inspector of historical
monuments, and service under the Second Empire—I have divided his biography into three chapters, each of which is followed
by discussions of his imaginative works produced during those
periods.

Without slighting in any way his better known masterpieces
in fiction and his most successful plays—*Le Carrosse du Saint-
Sacrement* and *L'Occasion*—I have given considerable attention
to *La Guzla, Le Théâtre de Clara Gazul* and his little known
closet dramas *Les Mécontents, Les Deux Héritages,* and *Les
Débuts d'un aventurier,* the latter two of which have been passed
over too lightly, in my opinion, by critics of his work. I have tried
to summarize the work of previous scholars in regard to the
sources for the various writings and their conflicting evaluations
of each, to which I have added my own personal reactions.

In the course of this study it will be found that, partly from a careful reading of his *Correspondance* and partly from an un-expected revelation of personal traits in his imaginative pro-duction, I have been induced to replace my earlier concept of Mérimée as a coldly ironic, blasé, and purely objective writer by that of one whose human warmth and compassion pierce at times the steely armor with which this sensitive man tried to shield himself from public gaze.

Numbers in parentheses after quotations from Mérimée's fiction refer to pages in the Pléiade edition of his *Romans et Nouvelles* edited by Henri Martineau. All translations are my own.

MAXWELL A. SMITH

Contents

Chronology

1803   Born September 28.

1811   Enters Lycée Napoléon (later called Collège Henri IV).

1819   Graduates from lycée and enters law school.

1822   Begins friendship with Stendhal. Writes historical drama on Cromwell.

1823   Graduates from law school.

1824   Writes first of four articles on Spanish drama.

1825   First hoax, *Le Théâtre de Clara Gazul.*

1827   Second hoax, *La Guzla.*

1827–1832   Love affair with Mme Lacoste.

1828   Duel with M. Lacoste. Publication of *La Jaquerie* and *La Famille de Carvajal.*

1829   Publication of *La Chronique du règne de Charles IX, Le Carrosse du Saint-Sacrement,* and *L'Occasion.*

1830   First trip to Spain and meeting with the Montijos.

1831–1834   Career as civil servant and period of dissipation.

1832   Beginning of Mérimée's lifelong friendship with Jenny Dacquin.

1833   Publication of *Mosaïque* and *La Double Méprise.*

1834   Named inspector general of historical monuments. Publication of *Les Ames du Purgatoire.*

1836   Beginning of love affair with Valentine Delessert. Death of his father, Léonor Mérimée.

1837   Publication of *La Vénus d'Ille.*

1839   Trip to Corsica.

1841   Publication of *Colomba.*

1842   Death of his friend Stendhal.

1843   Death of his friend Sutton Sharpe. Election to the Académie des Inscriptions et Belles-Lettres.

1844   Election to the French Academy. Publication of *Arsène Guillot.*

1845   Publication of *Carmen.*

1846   Publication of *L'Abbé Aubain.*

1848   Publication of *L'Histoire de Don Pèdre I.* Revolution of 1848 and temporary exile of Valentine in England. Beginning of Mérimée's Russian studies.

1849   Publication by *La Revue des Deux Mondes* of Mérimée's translation of Pushkin's *La Dame de Pique.*

1850   *Les Deux Héritages.*

1852   Death of Mérimée's mother. Imprisonment in the Libri Affair. *Les Débuts d'un aventurier.*

1853   Marriage of Emperor Napoleon III with Eugénie de Montijo. Mérimée named senator.

1855   Rupture with Valentine Delessert.

1856–   Spends winters in Cannes because of poor health.
1870

1860   Resigns post as inspector general.

1866   Accompanies Imperial family to Biarritz and returns to fiction with *La Chambre bleue* for the empress. Reconciliation with Valentine Delessert.

1869   *Lokis* published in *La Revue des Deux Mondes.*

1870   June, last return to Paris from Cannes. August, last visit to the empress before her flight to England. September, return to Cannes with Miss Lagden and Mrs. Ewer. September 23, death in Cannes.

1871   Burning of Mérimée's home by the Commune.

1873   Publication of *Les Dernières Nouvelles.*

CHAPTER 1

Childhood to Early Manhood: 1803-1829

I *Ancestry*

THOUGH Prosper Mérimée was born in Paris, both sides of his family were of good Norman stock. His paternal grandfather, a lawyer in the *Parlement* of Rouen and manager of the affairs of the Maréchal de Broglie, lived in part of the latter's château where Prosper's father, Jean François Léonor, was born and which ever since has been known as the Mérimée wing. In a letter to Paul Lacroix who was writing a biography of his father, Prosper wrote in 1859: "I believe my father was born about 1758. He died in 1837." [1] In view of Mérimée's lifelong insistence on precision and exact documentation, it is amusing to note that he erred in both dates, for his father was born in 1757 and died in 1836.

Léonor early came to Paris to study painting with Vincent but failed in two attempts to secure the coveted Prix de Rome, receiving only a second and a third place. "He traveled in Holland to see the masterpieces of that country's painters, then he spent several years in Rome and Florence. I have several studies he made from pictures in the Pitti and Uffizi palaces." [2] In Rome, Léonor was allowed to stay in the Mancini Palace, headquarters of the Académie de France where winners of the Prix de Rome dwelt. When the Republic was proclaimed in France, rioters attacked the palace, and Léonor was saved by being hidden by his *inamorata*. "The only romantic adventure I know of my father (I believe he had more than one) was at home where he narrowly missed being assassinated at the same time as Basseville. He was saved by a Roman lady whom I met when she was very old, and who received me in Rome with great affection." [3] We shall notice later the importance of this encounter when we consider the background for Mérimée's story, *Il Viccolo di Madama Lucrezia*.

After imprisonment for a time and the loss of all his possessions, Léonor made his way back to France by the middle of 1793.

Thanks to a growing reputation for wall painting and mythologi-
cal canvases (*Hippolytus Resuscitated by Aesculapius* is still to be
seen in the Louvre), he became assistant drawing master in 1795
at the Ecole Polytechnique and in 1807 permanent secretary to the
Ecole des Beaux-Arts, a post he held until the end of his life. "He
was one of the founders and most assiduous members of the Society for the Encouragement of National Industry. I remember having copied for him many a report for this group. In 1818 he was
sent to England to examine the state of industrial arts." [4] Perhaps
it was his long report on this study for M. Decazes, minister of the
interior, which brought Léonor his nomination as Chevalier de la
Légion d'Honneur in 1820.

Many of Léonor's paintings perished in the fire which consumed Mérimée's house in 1871, including *Innocence Feeding a
Serpent*, of which Prosper was especially fond. Soon he gave up
painting entirely for his lifelong *History of Oil Painting from Van
Eyck to Our Own Day*, published in 1830 and translated into English in 1832, on which his fame largely rests. Léonor was a modest
man with no great faith in his own talent. In the letter already
mentioned, Prosper continues:

He was, like his son, a great idler, curious for learning and lazy for
working. . . . He had made good studies and knew Horace by heart.
He taught me the little Latin I know and the Italian which he knew
and spoke wonderfully well and which I speak very badly. . . . My
father was of the eclectic school but he was horrified by pathos and
could not endure exaggeration. I remember the horrible fright I had
when I read him my short stories. I regret not having always followed
his criticism.[5]

It was while teaching painting at the private school of Mme
Moreau, native of Rouen and widow of the army doctor Nicolas
Moreau, that Léonor fell in love with her daughter Anne. She was
then twenty-seven and he was forty years of age. Anne was the
granddaughter of Mme Leprince de Beaumont, author of the
famous fairy story *Beauty and the Beast* and other tales. Anne was
also a painter, chiefly of portraits and of small children. They
were married in 1800, and three years later their only child Prosper (a name he always hated) was born. There is no record of the
child's baptism, for both parents were agnostics. From her grand-

mother Anne derived her talent for telling stories, which must have been very helpful in keeping her young charges quiet while she painted them. This gift as a raconteuse she passed on to her son, as well as her Voltairian incredulity which her husband shared. She seems to have had great influence in guiding his youth and remained his beloved companion until her death in 1852.

All of his biographers have recounted the significant anecdote, first related by his mother to Sainte-Beuve, which occurred when Prosper was only five. It seems that having committed some minor misdeed for which he had been upbraided, he came to his mother, kneeling and in tears, to beg her forgiveness. When his mother broke out in laughter little Prosper rose to his feet in stupefaction, saying: "Since I'm being made fun of, I shall never again ask forgiveness." Critics have often wondered whether this childhood incident may have had its influence on the later character of Mérimée, with his mask of reserve. It was from his mother that he took the motto in Greek placed on his seal "remember to be always mistrustful."

II *School Days*

At the precocious age of seven, Mérimée experienced the first of many infatuations with the gentler sex which were to be so frequent in his later life. He fell desperately in love with his mother's favorite pupil, a Mlle Dubost, and when she announced her engagement to Dr. Regnier, Prosper was so furious that he refused to speak to her husband for many years. Apparently he relented at last, for we know that he spent several spring vacations with the Regniers in their country home at Colommiers during the early 1820's.

When eight years old, Prosper entered the Lycée Napoléon, later to be called the Collège Henri IV. Because of his elegant dress in the English fashion he was much teased by his schoolmates, particularly by his cousins the Fresnels. As Filon has remarked, these two traits—dandyism and Anglomania—were to become essential features of his personality.[6] English was spoken in his home, and Prosper had many opportunities to meet English artists and writers who frequented the house of his parents. He seems not to have been an especially brilliant student except in the classics, winning only two distinctions, a second prize for Latin *thème* (translation from French to Latin) and a first prize in

Latin *version* (translation from Latin to French).[7] At the lycèe his three best friends were Jean-Jacques Ampère, son of the famous physicist and later professor of comparative literature at the Collège de France, Charles Lenormant who was to become a famous Egyptologist and authority on Greek art, and Victor Jacquemont, destined to die while still a young man, victim of his research as a naturalist in India. His fascination with and for the gentler sex seems to have continued, for both Baschet and Lyon mention a "scandal," a note he received from a neighborhood seamstress, "decorated with two flaming hearts pierced by an arrow" and expressing a most ardent declaration of love. Alas, the outcome of this affair was disastrous for Prosper; his teacher confiscated the note, locked him up and—final humiliation—"the object of this nascent passion consoled herself with my teacher."

More lasting was to be Mérimée's association with two English sisters, Fanny and Emma Lagden, pupils of his mother in painting, whom Mérimée recalled having seen from his earliest days at the Mérimée home. Fanny, born in Abingdon near Cambridge, was seven years his elder and two years younger than her sister Emma, later Mrs. Ewer. Some time before 1822 both sisters had come to live in Paris with their aunt, a Mrs. Beans, in the rue Fleurus. From a passionate letter of Prosper to Fanny which Emma read to a friend after Fanny's death in 1879, then destroyed, we learn that Fanny was probably Prosper's first mistress. She dedicated her whole life to watching over him, and from his letters to her in excellent but very quaint English we know that after 1856 he often sent her on ahead to arrange living quarters in Cannes for his winter sojourns. Faithful, quiet, and self-effacing, Fanny was left most of Mérimée's estate at his death; her body lies in the same grave with his in the cemetery of Cannes.

While at the Lycée, Prosper was allowed by his father to take painting lessons from a family friend, Simon Rochart. Léonor had no great opinion of his son's ability as an artist, but it is important to note that this hobby for sketching and painting remained with Mérimée throughout his life, not only giving him pleasure but also serving him in good stead when he later turned in reports on his archeological missions. At the age of sixteen in August, 1819, Prosper took his "bachot" and the following November was persuaded by his father to enter law school, L'Ecole de Droit, passport to any phase of diplomatic or governmental service. In the intervening months Prosper had thrown himself passionately into the study of magic and the supernatural, a subject to have great influence later on his writing. Along with his legal studies, he found time for a host of other pursuits—Greek, philology, linguistics, numismatics, archeology, while perfecting himself in Spanish and English literature. At seventeen he translated with his friend J. J. Ampère the writings of "Ossian," while preferring the works of Byron, whose *Don Juan* he knew by heart. He also read vociferously in the French eighteenth century, as well as the plays of Shakespeare and the novels of Sir Walter Scott (the latter an enthusiasm he came to denigrate later). In Spanish he was fascinated by Calderón, Lope de Vega, and Cervantes. In May, 1823, Mérimée received his law degree. In view of his lifelong aversion to marriage, it is piquant to note that the subject of his thesis was "De Matrimonio."

III *Stendhal and Other Friends*

In addition to his law courses, Prosper had followed in 1821 the lectures of Joseph Lingay, professor of rhetoric at the Athénée Royal. It was during the summer of 1822 in the garden of his former teacher "in front of good bottles of cool beer" served by Lingay's pretty mistress that Prosper met for the first time Henri Beyle (Stendhal), recently returned to Paris after six years spent chiefly in Italy. Thus began a close friendship which was to last until Stendhal's death. It was when Stendhal introduced Mérimée to the family of the famous zoologist Cuvier at the Jardin des Plantes that Mérimée met the wealthy and brilliant English lawyer Sutton Sharpe, who was to visit him often in Paris and entertain him on many visits to London. At Stendhal's home in the same house, which also sheltered the noted actress Judith Pasta, Stendhal introduced the young Prosper to a more bohemian society, which also included such notables as Cuvier, Léonor's friend the painter Baron Gérard, and Mme de Castellane.

How influential this friendship with Stendhal was for Mérimée's later development as a writer has always been a moot subject for critics. While Sainte-Beuve once stated that Mérimée was Stendhal's only true disciple, Mérimée wrote in *Notes et Souvenirs* in 1855 that "except for a few preferences and a few literary aversions we did not perhaps have one idea in common and there were few subjects on which we were in agreement." [8] Yet three years earlier in a letter of May 31, 1852, he had written his friend Jenny Dacquin: "I spend all my time reading the correspondence of Beyle. That makes me feel at least twenty years younger. It is as if I were making an autopsy of the thoughts of a man whom I knew intimately and whose ideas of things and of men have singularly washed off on mine." [9] The temperaments of these two friends were so far apart in many ways: Stendhal so passionate in his convictions and loves, Mérimée reserved and cautious, on guard against bombast and exaggeration. In the same letter to Jenny Dacquin Mérimée confessed: "We spent our time arguing with each other, with the best faith in the world, each accusing the other of stubbornness and paradox."

Strangely enough, Stendhal's reaction at their first meeting had been most unfavorable, as he admitted many years later. "This young man in grey frock coat and so ugly with his turned up nose had something brazen and extremely unpleasant about him. His small, expressionless eyes had a mean look. Such was the first view of the best of my friends." [10] Despite their differences, including a disparity of almost twenty years in age, there were many traits which the two friends held in common: eighteenth-century irreverence for religious dogma; affection of cynicism; fondness for logical reasoning and factual exactness; sympathy for characters such as bandits and criminals who as outlaws from society embodied energy and violence; and especially, at this early period, an equal penchant for liberalism in government and for the new Romanticism in literature. In any case, Mérimée was the first to put into practice the revolutionary doctrines of Stendhal's manifesto *Racine et Shakespeare* (1823 and 1825) as we shall see when we consider Mérimée's *Théâtre de Clara Gazul* of 1826.

In addition to the salons I have mentioned, during these years of the early 1820's Mérimée encountered in the Friday evening meetings at the home of Viollet-le-Duc (father of his later friend the famous architect) among others Sainte-Beuve, Baron de Mareste, the young publisher Sautelet, and his early friends J. J. Ampère and Albert Stapfer. At the home of the latter's father, Philippe Stapfer, former minister of arts, sciences and cults in his native Switzerland and now Swiss minister to Paris, Mérimée met on Wednesdays such famous travelers and scientists as Alexander von Humboldt, along with Benjamin Constant and Stendhal. Most of these salons represented the liberal-minded middle class, including a Mme Davillier, wife of an industrialist. Her salon boasted the attendance of several great Liberals, such as La Fayette, General Foy, and Béranger. One exception to these Liberal salons was that of Mme Récamier at L'Abbaye-aux-bois, where Prosper was taken by J. J. Ampère, hopelessly in love with Mme Récamier twenty years his senior, and where Prosper was displeased by the spectacle of Chateaubriand presiding in all his glory.

IV *The Early Cromwell*

During the first quarter of the nineteenth century, the life of Oliver Cromwell seems to have fascinated the young Romantic generation. As early as 1817 Villemain had published an *Histoire de Cromwell* which had considerable success.[11] It is interesting to note that three young writers, destined later to achieve fame with more significant works, began their careers with dramas on this subject. While Victor Hugo was to codify the rules for Romantic drama in the *Préface* to his unplayable *Cromwell* in 1827, the youthful Balzac had endeavored as early as 1819 to achieve fame with a *Cromwell* in verse, only to be admonished by a friend to "attempt anything other than literature." We are not surprised therefore to learn that Mérimée tried his hand also at a historical drama on Cromwell which he read in late 1822, either at the home of Viollet-le-Duc or that of Stapfer, to a small group of friends which included Stendhal, Delécluze, J. J. Ampère, and Albert Stapfer.

Since the play was never published and the manuscript presumably perished with other papers in the fire which consumed Mérimée's house in 1871, we are indebted primarily to the *Journal* of Delécluze for information concerning this *Cromwell*: complete rejection of the three unities, frequent changes of setting, mingling of comic and tragic. "The *Cromwell* of Mérimée was one of the first applications of the theory which Stendhal developed in 1823 in his brochure *Racine et Shakespeare*."[12] The only other inkling we possess concerning this drama comes from the somewhat hazy recollections of Stapfer forty years later that the play had the form of a marionette spectacle and that the young impresario broke in from time to time for dialogue with the audience.[13] Delécluze informs us that the little band broke into loud applause, particularly Stendhal, who saw the implementation of his own principles in the work of his friend.

We need not regret too deeply, perhaps, the disappearance of the Cromwell manuscript, for Mérimée himself seems to have taken a very dim view of it even before he finished it. In a letter from Mérimée to Joseph Lingay we read:

Unhappily for me, my tragic fever has subsided. Had I not promised to prepare a finished draft, my *Cromwell* would long since have perished in the flames [curious premonition of its ultimate fate]. You have no idea how painful it is to read with a cool head what one has written with enthusiasm. Now that I am disenchanted I find my tragedy absurd, ridiculous and full of false notes. Neither Cromwell, the King nor Ludlow are interesting, Cromwell's unbounded ambition makes him an unsympathetic figure. The King, depicted as the good hearted fool he really was, will anger the Royalists. . . . Aside from that little fault—the total failure to arouse interest—there is the play's excessive length. I perceive this only too well as I copy it.[14]

V   *The First Hoax—Théâtre de Clara Gazul*

After his early immersion in English history and literature, Mérimée turned next to Spain, in whose language he had become fluent soon after his departure from the lycée. The first indication we have of this new interest is evidenced by his four articles on the Spanish theater which appeared in the *Globe* in the autumn of 1824. In general, these essays glorify the Golden Age of Lope de Vega and Calderón, contrasting unfavorably the decline of the eighteenth-century dramatists such as Moratín, from whom, however, he was to borrow extensively in his own theater. What seems to have inspired his first published volume, *Le Théâtre de Clara Gazul* in 1825, was the invasion of Spain by the Duc d'Angoulême, nephew of Charles X, who had been named commander-in-chief of two hundred thousand men, sent to crush the Spanish Constitutionalists holding the Spanish king Ferdinand VII a prisoner. The Liberal political views of Mérimée were shocked by this repression, and he was furious at the French conquest of Pampelune and the Trocadero, the latter at the cost of thirty-five French lives and millions of francs in bribes.[15] On March 14, 1825, Mérimée read the first two of his six comedies to his friends Delécluze, J. J. Ampère, and Sautelet, according to Delécluze's *Journal*, in the same guttural, monotonous tone he had employed for *Cromwell*. During the next few weeks the reading of the other plays continued, and on April 12 Mérimée posed before Delécluze (with mantilla and gold cross around his neck) for the portrait of the Spanish actress, Clara Gazul, who was supposed to be the original author of these plays. This was the frontispiece when the volume was published by Sautelet in June.

To complete the hoax, Mérimée preceded the play with a "Notice sur Clara Gazul" signed by the pretended translator, Joseph L'Estrange.[16] According to this translator it was in 1813 while in garrison with a Swiss regiment that he had first met Clara when she was only fourteen. Her uncle, commanding a Spanish guerrilla force, had just been hanged by the French, and Clara had become the ward of Father Medrano, inquisitor at the tribunal of Granada. One day she confided in L'Estrange the story of her origin.

I was born under an orange tree on the edge of a road not far from Motril in the kingdom of Granada. My mother's profession was that of fortune teller. I followed her, or rather she carried me on her back until I was five. Then she took me to a Canon of Granada . . . who received us with great demonstrations of joy. My mother said "Greet your uncle." I greeted him. She embraced me and left at once. I never saw her again.

According to Clara, she was the great-granddaughter of the Moor Gazul, so famous in Spanish ballads. Her guardian, a watchful Cerberus, having caught her in the act of writing a love letter, locked her up in a convent from which she escaped in a fortnight to make her debut a few months later at the theater of Cádiz in the role of Doña Clara in Moratín's *Mojigata*. After receiving the inheritance of her uncle, her literary fame began with her little play *Une femme est un diable* and continued until her flight to England at the time of the Restoration. All her works were put on the Index by the Royalists but the translation which follows was made faithfully under the eyes of the author in England.

It does not seem that Mérimée took this first mystification too seriously. It is possible, as Filon has suggested, that Mérimée felt it the part of prudence to assume this mask in order to make the public accept a book which at one and the same time mocked religious piety, dear to half the nation, and the Napoleonic legend, adored by the other half.[17] Mérimée made no secret of his authorship and for several years signed his letters "the author of *Clara Gazul*," just as Sir Walter Scott signed each novel, "By the author of *Waverley*." His father Léonor presented a copy of the book to one of Prosper's old professors at law school. Mérimée's young friend J. J. Ampère gave away the secret in an early review in the *Globe* of June 4, 1825, in which he praised to the skies this young author, one of the first champions of Romantic drama, and proclaimed that a new Shakespeare had appeared. The *Revue Encyclopédique* in June also recognized the purpose of the author "to paint under an assumed name the most salient features of our customs and to allow himself, under the shelter of a Spanish mask, an entire freedom in regard to political prejudices and what he calls literary routines." The *Journal de Paris* in its articles of August 8 and September 21 likewise hastened to make known to the public "that one of our compatriots is hidden under the mantilla of their imaginary Spanish comédienne." Only the stodgy *Journal des Débats* seems to have been taken in by the hoax, praising L'Estrange "for his invaluable service in translating this Theater from the Spanish."

VI   *The Second Hoax—La Guzla*

As early as January, 1820, J. J. Ampère had written to Jules Bastide: "I'm continuing with Mérimée to learn the language of Ossian, we have a grammar. What joy to give an exact translation, with naïvely rendered inversions and images." [18] In 1822 the great French folklorist, Fauriel, published his famous *Chants populaires de la Grèce moderne* which Mérimée read and admired. According to Sainte-Beuve, Ampère introduced Fauriel to Mérimée soon after the publication of this book. The first time Mérimée saw Fauriel, the latter said to him: "Here are two volumes of Serbian poetry someone has sent me; learn Serbian." [19] What whetted the newfound curiosity in France toward the customs and folklore of Dalmatia and Serbia was first the famous *Voyage en Dalmatie* of the Italian, l'abbé Fortis, and then the novels of Nodier, *Jean Sbogar* (1819) and *Smarra* (1821), which were the product of Nodier's stay in Illyria as Napoleon's librarian during the French occupation.

If the mystification produced by *Le Théâtre de Clara Gazul* was easily detected (except outside France as we shall see), *La Guzla* which followed it in late July or early August, 1827 was a more successful hoax, comparable in extent to that of Macpherson's *Ossian*. While Mérimée had read his Spanish plays to various groups of friends, the secret of *La Guzla* was carefully kept, except perhaps from Ampère and Stendhal. The subtitle was *Choice of Illyrian poems collected in Dalmatia, Bosnia, Croatia and Herzegovina*. According to the preface the anonymous translator was an Italian from Spalatro whose love of travel had enabled him to know all the villages, mountains, and valleys from Trieste to Ragusa. He had made these translations of Illyrian folk poetry in French rather than in his native Italian, he explained, because he had lived for a long time in France, a country he dearly loved. He then describes "la guzla," a sort of guitar with only one horsehair string, on which the ragged old bards were wont to accompany their songs, each verse of which ended in a great cry like the howling of a wounded wolf. With typical Mériméean fantasy, this preface is next followed by a carefully documented essay on the chief of these guzlars, one Hyacinthe Maglanovitch, and the volume is provided throughout with apparently scholarly footnotes. So detailed and picturesque was this biography and so many are the learned footnotes that it is little wonder the critics, both French and foreign, were taken in by this hoax.

For the second edition of *La Guzla* in 1842, Mérimée wrote a second preface which we should not accept too literally since, as Filon has pointed out, he may well be adding another mystification to the original one. We should not forget that by this time Mérimée no longer belonged to the Romantic camp and looked back with disdain on his earlier enthusiasms.[20] In this "Avertissement" Mérimée recalls to the reader that in 1827 the avant-garde was infatuated with "local color" which they found in ballads of the Scottish border, romances of the Cid, and the like. He and his friend Ampère planned to visit the area along the Adriatic to learn at first hand the customs and folklore of the primitive inhabitants, but since money for the trip was lacking they conceived the idea of writing up their voyage to earn enough to make the trip later and discover how close their descriptions were to reality. To prepare himself further Mérimée read the *Voyage en Dalmatie* of l'abbé Fortis, together with a statistical account of the Illyrian provinces drawn up by a bureau chief in the department of foreign affairs. He then learned five or six Slavic words and wrote the collection of ballads in a fortnight. If *La Guzla* had little impact in France the hoax succeeded magnificently in the rest of Europe, and Mérimée chuckled at the ease with which he had been able to concoct "local color," the value of which he has now come to doubt.

Rather than rest content with this explanation, we could come closer to the truth by perusing a letter Mérimée wrote in January 1835 to a Russian friend, Sobelevsky, who had been asked by Pushkin to learn more about the "local color" of these ballads, which he had "retranslated" into Russian.[21]

I thought, sir, that La Guzla had only seven readers, including you, myself and the printer; I see with much pleasure that I can count on two more, which makes a pretty total of nine. . . . La Guzla was composed by me for two motives, the first being to make fun of the local color into which we were flinging ourselves headlong around the year of grace 1827. To explain the other motive . . . in that same year 1827 one of my friends and I had formed the project of making a trip to Italy. We had in front of us a map tracing our itinerary in pencil. Arriving in Venice, on the map of course, and bored by the English and Germans we encountered, I proposed to go to Trieste and from there to Ragusa. The proposition was adopted, but we were very short of money and this "nonpareil sorrow," as Rabelais calls it, stopped us in the midst of our plans. I proposed then to write up our trip in advance, sell it to a publisher and use the income to see if we had been greatly mistaken. . . . I was taken at my word. . . . I spent the autumn in the country. We lunched at noon and I rose at ten o'clock; when I had smoked one or two cigars, not knowing what to do before the ladies appeared in the salon, I would write a ballad. The result was a little volume which I published in great secret and which mystified two or three persons.

He then mentioned the sources from which he drew this famous "local color": first a pamphlet of a French consul at Banialouka, his notes; then the chapter on Morlacci customs in the *Voyage en Dalmatie* of Fortis, which included a verse translation of the lamentation of the wife of Asan-Aga, which is really Illyrian. With the help of a Russian friend Mérimée then made a literal prose translation of this ballad. Apparently this was the origin of the feud between Mérimée and Nodier—whose seat, ironically, he was later to take at the Académie Française—for Mérimée continues:

The amusing thing was that Nodier who had dug up Fortis and the Ballad of Asan-Aga and had translated it from the poetic translation of the abbé, making it still more poetic in his prose, Nodier cried out like an eagle that I had robbed him. . . . That is my story. Make my excuses to M. Pushkin. I am proud and ashamed at the same time to have taken him in.

I have quoted from this letter at such length not only because it doubtless comes fairly close to the truth of Mérimée's real attitude in writing *La Guzla* but also because it affords such an illuminating portrait of his own personality—witty, *pince sans rire*, modest and even self-deprecating in his scorn for his early Romantic enthusiasm. I used the term "fairly close" because the letter does not do justice to the young writer's actual fondness for primitive poetry—in his eyes the only true poetry—with its naïve sincerity, brutal cruelty, and unbridled passion, free of the artifice inherent in contemporary civilization. Also, because it makes no mention of the two most important influences Mérimée underwent at this time—the exotic novels of Nodier and Fauriel's *Chants populaires de la Grèce moderne*—nor does it give any indication of the myriad sources found in his vast erudition which he pillaged, exposed so mercilessly by Yovanovitch in his dissertation (to be discussed later).

VII *Mme Lacoste*

Of the various ladies in Mérimée's love life, three were destined to have an important influence on his writing career. Shortly after Mérimée had first met Emilie Lacoste at the salon of Mme Davillier in 1821, the Lacostes left for America where M. Lacoste went into business in New Jersey with the aid and protection of Joseph Bonaparte, Napoleon's elder brother and former king of Spain. For financial reasons M. Félix Lacoste seems to have been indifferent to the fact that his wife became the mistress of Joseph, bearing him her second son, tactfully named Félix-Joseph. On the failure of his business in 1826, M. Lacoste brought his wife back to France, and by early 1827 Mérimée had become her ardent lover, quite unaware at this time of her earlier relationship with Joseph Bonaparte. Early in January, 1828, one of his love letters fell into the hands of M. Lacoste, who promptly challenged Mérimée to a pistol duel. When M. Lacoste asked Mérimée in which arm he preferred to receive his bullets, the latter replied: "the left one, if it is all the same to you," quixotically declining himself to fire and receiving three shots in the left arm and shoulder. Mérimée was thus able to begin writing with his right hand his *Chronique du règne de Charles IX*. After a convalescence of several weeks with his left arm in a sling, he gave several explanations; to one friend he ascribed his injury to a fall from a carriage onto a hard stone, to another a more truthful though witty answer —that the wounds had been caused by a gentleman who did not like his prose.

As Baschet reminds us, in the next few years Emilie Lacoste seems to have played the same role as Egérie or inspirer for Mérimée that Mme Delessert was to play later. We shall see, for example, that Emilie served as the model for the heroine of his first novel, Diane de Turgis of the *Chronique*. Baschet, among other critics, has emphasized their exact resemblance.[22] Another identifying trait is the fact that Mme Lacoste, for all her sensual nature, was extremely pious and often tried to convert Mérimée, just as Diane hoped to convert her lover Mergy in the novel. And when Mérimée later learned of the affair between Emilie and Joseph Bonaparte he was retrospectively jealous, mirroring the attitude of Saint-Clair in regard to Mme de Coursy, another heroine modeled upon Mme Lacoste, in his story *Le Vase étrusque*.

Before Mme Lacoste replaced Mérimée later with another lover, Mérimée himself seems to have conceived in May, 1828, an ardent passion for a visiting Englishwoman of considerable beauty, Mary Wollstonecraft Shelley, widow of the famous poet, and according to Raitt may even have proposed marriage. Though Mary apparently refused his proposal, she no doubt felt extremely flattered, for on returning to England she published a most enthusiastic essay on his *Théâtre de Clara Gazul* and his *Guzla* in the *Westminster Review* of January, 1829, including her translation of three ballads from the latter volume.[23]

VIII *Literary Apprenticeship Ends*

Always fascinated by primitive and fierce emotions, first in Spanish literature then in the folklore of Illyria, Mérimée seems to have conceived the idea of seeking these in French medieval history after witnessing in 1827 the triumphs in Paris of the visiting

Shakespearean actors, among them Kean and Miss Smithson. Medieval history was all the vogue at this time, encouraged by the publication of Froissart's *Chronicles* in the *Chroniques nationales* series of Alexandre Buchon.

We recall Mérimée's habit of reading to a group of friends the various plays which were to compose his *Théâtre de Clara Gazul*. After completing his next manuscript, *La Jaquerie*, he wrote in March, 1828, to Dr. Edwards, who had lent him the nine volumes of Froissart, inviting him to a reading of the manuscript at his home. This letter is typical both of Mérimée's modesty and of his sense of humor. "It's a little Romantic tragedy called *La Jaquerie* by a well-known author. The work is only 300 pages long; in truth they are in-folio. The author charges me to ask you, if you are not too fatigued from your trip, to undergo a worse fatigue Tuesday evening at the home of the above-mentioned author. . . . Tea will be served and sleeping will be permissible, provided one does not sleep too noisely." [24] Though Mérimée in this amusing invitation labeled *La Jaquerie* a "Romantic tragedy" and though it is entirely in dialogue form, it is really an intermediate step toward the historical fiction of the *Chronique du règne de Charles IX* which was to follow it the succeeding year.

In the *Revue trimestrielle* of April, 1828, there had already appeared a fragment of *La Jaquerie*, Scene VI. During the same month Mérimée wrote to a friend, probably Joseph Lingay, concerning the publication of his manuscript, which was to be followed in the same volume by his play *La Famille de Carvajal:* "Here are my two manuscripts. I have no important changes to make, and so the printing could start, if the editor should be in a hurry. I haven't had time to write ten lines of preface for *La Jaquerie*. I must also change the last scene. If you have the patience to glance at this thick folder, make all the changes you want to in it." [25] What a contrast this nonchalance is with the attitude of Hugo toward his own writings. Then Mérimée goes on to grant his friend full powers to make arrangements with an editor, Sautelet, perhaps, the publisher of *Clara Gazul*, though he would prefer to ruin someone else rather than a friend.

The *Chronique du règne de Charles IX*, originally published under the title *1572, Chronique du temps de Charles IX* appeared in March, 1829, when its author was not yet twenty-six years old.

The rivalry between the influence of Shakespeare and that of Sir Walter Scott, evident in *La Jaquerie,* of the preceding year, had been replaced by the triumph of the latter, whose fame and fascination for the French public were now at their height.

CHAPTER 2

Mérimée's Theater

I *Les Espagnols en Danemarck*

THE first and perhaps most successful of the six plays in the original *Le Théâtre de Clara Gazul* was *Les Espagnols en Danemarck*. After the *Avertissement* containing a biographical sketch of the Marquis-General La Romana, Mérimée begins his drama with a witty and amusing Prologue, ostensibly a conversation in the loge of Clara Gazul among the actress, a Spanish grandee, a Captain, and a Poet. Cleverly intermingled in this dialogue is a sort of manifesto of French Romanticism, based on the 1823 *Racine et Shakespeare* of Stendhal. Thus we hear the Poet asking whether the play is divided into acts and the negative reply of Clara (Mérimée has adopted the Spanish custom of *jornados* or *journées*), the rejection of the Classical rules for unity of time and place, to the great disgust of the Poet who admires French Classicism; and the choice of recent French history for the subject, to the great displeasure of the Poet, who would have preferred the characters to have been dead at least four hundred years. In a letter to his friend Lingay, September 21, 1823, requesting information about his hero, La Romana, Mérimée explained in jest that having admired a certain prologue he had just completed he had decided, in order to preserve it, that he would write a play to go with it. "If M. Delille who was a Classicist wrote a poem to enclose his episodes, why should I not make a comedy for my prologue." [1]

The play begins rather slowly with a long monologue by the French *Résident* in Nyborg on the Danish island of Fionie in which we learn that he has been commissioned by Bernadotte, Prince of Ponte Corvo, to watch carefully over the Spanish general La Romana and his Spanish division who, with a number of Napoleon's Danish and German allies, had joined the Emperor in his struggle against England. The *Résident* is soon joined by two female spies, Mme de Coulanges and her venal mother, Mme de Tourville. The young and attractive Mme de Coulanges rapidly falls in love, however, with the dashing Don Juan Diaz, colonel and aid of La Romana, a love which is reciprocated by Don Juan. From the window of the inn where they are all quartered, they look out onto the stormy sea on which a small boat is in peril. Don Juan intrepidly puts out to sea to rescue the drowning boatmen, one of whom turns out to be Wallis, an English agent of the admiral of the English fleet, bearing precious dispatches in a box suspended from his neck.

On the following day, Mme de Tourville expresses to her daughter her suspicions that Wallis, instead of being a member of a group of smugglers, is really an English agent. Her daughter, however, thrilled by the courage Don Juan has shown, and ashamed of her role as paid spy for France, has now decided to change sides and thwart her mother's suspicions, when they see Wallis and Don Juan again put out to sea. On Don Juan's return she enters his room, informs him that she knows of his correspondence with the English, and warns him of his danger from the *Résident*.

On the third day the *Résident* receives a visit from a young French lieutenant, Charles LeBlanc, who advises the *Résident* to invite La Romana and his staff to dinner the next day so that they may be captured and put to death for treason. When Mme de Tourville enters, she recognizes Lieutenant LeBlanc as her son, but the latter spurns her for her disgusting role as paid spy. When she learns that Don Juan has fallen in love with her daughter and has proposed marriage, she realizes that she could profit more by changing sides and therefore informs La Romana of the plot against him. Mme de Coulanges confesses her love to Don Juan but explains her inability to accept his offer of marriage because of the despicable role she and her mother had first intended to play. To her surprise Don Juan forgives her and promises to take her back with him to Spain, offering her mother 10,000 piasters to leave her daughter forever.

In the Conclusion, after a brief ballet on the Place d'Armes of Nyborg we watch the dinner party at the *Résident's* home. Just before the massacre is to begin, the cowardly *Résident* has left the table, ostensibly to seek a more excellent wine. As LeBlanc gives his toast to the emperor (signal for the planned entrance of fifty

French guardsmen), the Spanish soldiers enter instead and disarm LeBlanc. He admits the intended ambush while denying scornfully any role as a spy. Since he faces death so bravely he is pardoned by Don Juan, who is unwilling moreover to have the death of his fiancée's brother on his conscience. Mme de Coulanges then enters, dressed in the costume of a Spanish soldier, while the *Résident* meekly sinks back into the room, ending the play with the expression typical of Spanish drama: "So ends this comedy; excuse the faults of the author."

In the Romantic hero Don Juan, inspired by his patriotic desire to throw off the yoke of the foreign tyrant, it is not difficult to see the liberalism and internationalism of Mérimée, whose espousal of Napoleon's enemies at this time, when the glories of his career were still fresh in the minds of his compatriots, demanded real courage. Equally typical of the young author is his identification with Don Juan's freedom from snobbery and class prejudice, as evidenced by his willingness to forgive Mme de Coulanges (the commoner without prestige or financial resources) and to make her his bride. If *Les Espagnols* is the most successful of these early dramas, the reason is to be found in the realism of character portrayal, particularly in the French protagonists, whom Mérimée understood better than those of an imaginary Spain. Especially vivid is his characterization of those two cynical personages, Lieutenant LeBlanc and his scheming mother, Mme de Tourville. Many critics have pointed out that the real model for the latter was Sophie Gay, accused of being in the service of the police under the empire, who, according to Delécluze, "promenaded her daughter Delphine through the salons of Paris to show her off and sell her if need be or tempt some rich old man." [2] Even more unforgettable is the portrait of the cowardly, pretentious and dull-witted French *Résident*. According to François Michel, this character, suggested to Mérimée by Stendhal who had known him, was in actual life the former auditor at the Conseil d'Etat, Amédée de Pastoret.[3] (Mérimée may have felt that the name of Pacoret given the *Résident* in the play was too thin a disguise for the original, since he changed it in later editions to Achille d'Orbassan.) A final element of realism is to be found in the racy, epigrammatic, sometimes vulgar language employed by the French characters, especially that of Lieutenant LeBlanc and his dastardly mother. As Trahard has so sagaciously observed, "Thus prose takes on an independent gait which defies modesty and verges on the risqué; Mérimée frees it [from constraint] before Hugo frees verse." [4]

II   *Une femme est un diable*

This one-act comedy in three scenes—Clara Gazul explains that "comedy" is taken from Spanish Classicists' use of the term to include any dramatic work, whether farcical or serious—was included along with *Les Espagnols* at Mérimée's first reading in the apartment of Delécluze. The somber setting—the hall of the Inquisition at Granada—shows the influence of "Monk" Lewis and the English "satanic" school on the young author. Two inquisitors, Rafael and Domingo, are awaiting with foreboding the arrival of their new chief Antonio, an austere young man of thirty who to their great displeasure has been placed over them by the Grand Inquisitor. It is easy to gather from their conversation the unholy nature of their character: Rafael has fallen into disfavor because he had converted, then rendered pregnant a young Jewess; Domingo has been accused of not being a Christian because of a chicken thigh found in his room during Lent. "Is it then so necessary to be a Christian in order to be an inquisitor?" is Rafael's shocking query.

When Antonio enters he reveals that his thirty years of austerity have been compromised by his temptation—the subtitle of the play is *The Temptation of Saint Anthony*—at the sight of a lovely Spanish girl evidently sent by Satan to occupy his voluptuous dreams. "I see her everywhere . . . her great black eyes . . . which resemble the eyes of a cat . . . soft and wicked at the same time." (It has been pointed out that this description foretells that of Mme de Turgis, heroine of Mérimée's historical novel *Chronique du règne de Charles IX*.) [5] When Mariquita is now brought in to be condemned to death for sorcery, Antonio recognizes his temptress with dismay, covering his face with his hands in order not to see her during the trial. Though the other two inquisitors favor mercy for this charming young woman whose only crime was dancing, playing castanets, and singing a ribald song, Antonio insists that she be confined to her room while awaiting torture.

In a short second scene we see Antonio in his cell, wrestling in agony with his temptation and finally deciding that since he is already damned he might as well abandon his clerical vows and return to worldly indulgence.

In the third and final scene he goes to Mariquita's cell to proclaim his overpowering passion and promises to flee with her. When Rafael, having locked up Domingo, appears in the cell with the intention of saving Mariquita if she will grant him her favors, Antonio demands that he bless his marriage and on his refusal stabs him with a poignard. As Mariquita prepares herself to leave with her lover, Antonio laments: "In one hour I have become a fornicator, a perjurer and an assassin," while Mariquita addresses the audience: "On seeing this tragic end you will say with us, I believe, that A Woman is a Devil."

This *saynète* of Mérimée has been called by one French critic nothing but the terrifying "Monk" of Lewis compressed into three scenes.[6] The influence of Voltaire and the eighteenth century is also evident in Mérimée's desire to shock the ultrareligious sensibilities of the conservative reaction under Charles X, though his cautiously discreet preface to the play is obviously designed to afford him protection, should the outcries of his enemies become too strident. Lest anyone be scandalized by what may appear sacrilegious, he should realize that the author is not attacking true religion here. Then with tongue in cheek: "Emancipated Spaniards have learned to distinguish true piety from hypocrisy. It is they whom the author takes for judges, confident that they will see only a pleasantry there where the good Torquemada would have seen material for an *auto-da-fe* with many *san-benitos*."

III *L'Amour africain*

The scene of this little "comédie" in one act is laid in Córdoba during the reign of Abdérame. With his servant Baba-Mustafa, Sidi-Nouman is talking of the beautiful slave girl, Mojana, whom he had purchased the day before from the slave merchant Abou-Taber. His best friend the Bedouin Zeïn arrives and requests 5,000 dinars which Nouman is only too happy to procure for him. When the latter learns that Zeïn has sold all his possessions except his beloved steed Abjer in order to purchase a lovely slave girl, Nouman insists on adding another 5,000 dinars to his gift, so that his friend may have money with which to support his coveted purchase. Nouman has not forgotten that when he was dying of thirst on a pilgrimage to Mecca, Zeïn had saved his life by offering him all the precious water of his gourd. After Zeïn leaves, Nouman sends for his beloved slave Mojana, who relates the misfortunes of her family which had made it necessary for her father to sell her, and receives from her adoring master the promise that he will succor her father and marry off her sisters richly.

Zeïn returns at this moment, realizes that the girl for whom he had been willing to sacrifice all his worldly goods is this same Mojana, already purchased by Nouman, and rushes toward his friend with dagger outstretched. As Mojana interposes herself between them, Zeïn reminds Nouman of his promise, at the time his life was saved, that he would grant Zeïn the first request he might make. (Evidently neither he nor Nouman considers the 5,000 dinars in this category.) Nouman offers to let Mojana decide between them, but when she throws her arms around Nouman, Zeïn first intends to return to the desert, calling his friend a perjurer, then wounds Nouman with his saber before the latter kills him. Then Nouman, remorseful for what he has done, stabs to death Mojana who, in his eyes, is responsible for this tragic outcome. The impassivity of the author in the face of this bloody denouement is apparent in the concluding phrases: as B. Mustapha enters with the remark "My lord, supper is ready and the play is over," Nouman replies calmly "Ah, that is different"; the slain protagonists then rise.

Trahard, rather harsh in his judgment of Mérimée's portrayal of Spanish character in *Clara Gazul*, finds these two Bedouin protagonists more credible and approves heartily Mérimée's somewhat jesting statement which Mojana expresses to the audience just before the curtain falls: "You are going to exclaim that these are two noble gentlemen very lacking in gallantry. I admit it and our author was wrong not to give more Spanish sentiments to the Bedouins. He makes bold to answer by claiming that Bedouins are not accustomed to learning their manners in Madrid, and that their love partakes of the heat of the Sahara. What do you think of this argument?" Trahard for one thinks more highly of it than the author and remarks approvingly that critics have compared this play with Othello.[7] In any case, *L'Amour africain* had the honor of being the first of Mérimée's theater actually produced on the stage, at the Théâtre des Nouveautés, July 11, 1827. According to Martino, "half the hall hissed, the other half applauded."[8] There were only ten performances.

IV   *Inès Mendo ou Le Préjugé vaincu*

This one-act play, preceded by a quotation from Don Quixote, is one of those in which Mérimée's imitation of Spanish Classical writers, in particular of Calderón and Cervantes, as well as of the eighteenth-century Moratín, is most apparent. As we are informed in the *Avertissement*, the author's purpose is primarily to furnish a sort of prologue for its successor. The scene is laid in the little town of Monclar in Galicia in the year 1640.

In the opening conversation between the good curate and the peasant Mendo, we learn that the latter laments the sad fate which has made him assume the function of executioner once held by his father. It is true, as the priest reminds him, that no crimes have been committed in the village for many years and therefore few are aware of Mendo's official function; nevertheless, Mendo is assailed by nightmares in which he sees a young man at his feet and the mayor handing him an ax with the command to strike. His daughter Inès enters to confess her love for a neighboring baron, Don Esteban, who wishes to marry her despite her plebeian birth. Don Luis, father of Don Esteban, comes to confirm his son's request, insisting that caste prejudice is ridiculous and that in any case a mésalliance is justified when the suitor is noble and the family name is preserved. Since Don Luis is unaware of Mendo's terrible calling as executioner, it is difficult for him to understand why he balks at such a glorious engagement for his daughter.

In Scene II, Don Esteban encounters in the village an acquaintance, Don Carlos, son of the village mayor, who boasts cynically of his intention to seduce Inès. Enraged by his insolence, Don Esteban slaps him and, when Carlos attacks him with his sword, the duel ends with the death of Carlos. Two peasants observing the flight of Esteban conceive the plan of obtaining a reward from the mayor by reporting the killer of his son.

Scene III contains Mendo's agonized confession of his despised vocation to his daughter, which makes her write a letter to her lover breaking off their relations. On Esteban's entrance she shows him the letter, but her confession has no power to make him abjure his passion. "Stupid prejudices! must I sacrifice my happiness? Shades of my ancestors! I shall break my escutcheon rather than give this girl up." Alas, at this moment the turnkey enters with the armed peasants, touches Esteban with his wand of office, and leads him to prison.

In Scene IV we see Don Esteban in prison condemned to death for murder, making out with the Notary his final will and testament, leaving all his possessions to his beloved Inès.

The fifth and final scene takes place in front of a scaffold in the marketplace of Monclar. As Don Esteban bows his head on the block, Mendo—the involuntary executioner—chops off his own right hand rather than perform the execution. At this magnanimous gesture the peasants rush forward in admiration to drive away the police. Don Luis arrives on horseback followed closely by the King, who makes Mendo kneel to be dubbed a gentleman, and pardons Don Esteban on condition that he marry Inès.

Except for this bloody *coup de théâtre,* the first play of *Inès Mendo* marks a decided contrast with the plays which preceded it. For the first time we have real Spanish character portrayal. However improbable and fantastic the action may be, the depiction of the honorable peasant Mendo, so tortured between his shameful position and his love for his daughter, of the saintly village priest, of the upright lover and his father Don Luis, both imbued with scorn for aristocratic privilege, shows much greater appreciation of true Spanish theater and customs than Mérimée has evidenced in the preceding plays.

V   *Inès Mendo ou Le Triomphe du préjugé*

From a purely technical standpoint, this three-act play must be considered the most Romantic of Mérimée's collection. The unities of time and place are flung to the winds even more than in *Les Espagnols.* Again the author has adopted the old Spanish division into *Jornados* or *Journées* instead of acts, but this appelation, as he himself informs us, is not to be taken too literally, for the time extends over several weeks and perhaps months. As for unity of place, the episodic action moves from the château of Don Esteban in Estramadura to an inn in Portugal before concluding in the Spanish convent of Badajoz. Here again Mérimée's interest in history is evident. Portugal had become a favorite topic at this time, and in the action Mérimée interweaves the revolt of Portugal from the Spanish yoke in the seventeenth century and the placing of Joan de Braganza on the Portuguese throne.

Though this play is the sequel to the Prologue just discussed, its subtitle *Le Triomphe du préjugé* indicates a complete reversal from the earlier theme of prejudice overthrown. In the opening discussion between Don Esteban and his wife, we learn that several months of marriage have begun to cause irritation and misgivings on the part of the husband because of the hostile attitude shown by his noble colleagues toward this mésalliance. To deepen this malaise he receives a letter from a former flame, Doña Seraphine, Duchess of Montalvan, informing him that she is coming to seek refuge from the royal court, at which the new premier Olivarès has accused her of complicity in the revolt of Portugal. On her arrival she manages subtly to discredit in his eyes the awkward naïveté of his peasant bride and to reawaken the passionate memories of his earlier liaison with her. Nevertheless, Don Esteban struggles mightily against temptation, and his sense of honor persuades his benefactor Mendo not to go away to resume his humble existence.

In *Journée* II the *corregidor* with his deputies arrives at the castle to take the Duchess prisoner, but Don Esteban puts them to flight with his sword. Since it is necessary for the Duchess to take refuge in Portugal, Esteban gallantly offers to conduct her, giving his wife the impression, however, that he will accompany her only as far as the orange grove. The *corregidor* returns this time with armed men, only to find that the bird has flown.

Journée III transports us to a Portuguese inn at Elvas where Esteban anxiously observes the affection the Duchess shows to a Portuguese captain, Don César. She is wily enough, however, to allay his suspicions until she can procure for him an order to the commander of the fort at Avis to surrender and retreat to Spain. She bribes the servant Pedro to return to the castle of Mendoza and inform Inès that Esteban has been killed. Then, when Don César returns in triumph from Avis she departs with him to seek new outlets for her ambition at the Portuguese court in Lisbon. Pedro returns with news of the slaughter of the Spanish garrison at Avis and the departure of Inès, escorted by her father, to the nunnery of the Ursalines at Badajoz. Esteban, overcome with remorse for his infidelity, hastens to Badajoz, arriving just in time to receive Inès' forgiveness as she dies in his arms. Mendo, conscious of his previous mistake in sparing Esteban's life, becomes executioner once more as he takes up a pistol in his remaining hand to shoot the faithless husband.

The ironic objectivity of Mérimée is demonstrated once more in the closing paragraph when Inès rises to her feet to thank the audience for their indulgence and congratulate them on the fact that they will not have to endure any third *Inès Mendo*.

VI *Le Ciel et l'enfer*

This short melodrama in two scenes is, like *Une femme est un diable,* a bitter excoriation of religious cant and hypocrisy, though expressed with more subtlety and finesse.

In her home at Valencia, Doña Urraca tries to refuse a kiss to her lover Don Pablo on the ground that since it is Ash Wednesday, such an indulgence would constitute a mortal sin. On his departure Doña Urraca's monologue informs us that she hopes through this liaison to bring Pablo back from atheism to the Catholic belief. As she takes up her guitar and begins a rather blasphemous song she is visited by her confessor, the inquisitor Fray Bartholomé. The materialistic and sensual nature of this worthy ecclesiastic is soon evidenced by his delight in the delicious cakes and preserves she has prepared for him. After thanking her for the basket of Bordeaux wine she had sent him, he suggests that next time she might send it in a box for books, since the prior had seen the basket and the reverend fathers had not left a drop with which to sustain himself during his nocturnal prayers. She now confesses the sins committed last Saturday: a fit of impatience against her maid for not lacing her up tightly enough, a momentary distraction during divine service at the sight of a soldier in red and blue uniform, some malicious gossip concerning her friends, and excessive tenderness toward her pet dog. To all these sins Fray Bartholomé shows himself indulgent except toward the latter, for the dog has bitten him in the legs and must therefore receive one hundred blows of the stick, or at least fifty, or at least be deprived of sugar for three days. Now in an episode which seems inspired by Molière's *Tartuffe,* Doña Urraca confesses having swallowed a fly in her chocolate, involving thereby the possibility that she has eaten meat in Lent. With Jesuitical casuistry the priest opines that since this was only a little fly, not a big one, she cannot be guilty of this sacrilege.

But what about her amorous liaison with Don Pablo? At her admission of guilt he insists that she break off relations even though she still hopes to convert him. Yet when she promises the

Church the silver candelabra the priest had admired so much, he admits that such alms constitute "a powerful method of doing penance" and agrees to modify his stern demands, providing she say her *pater* and *ave* conscientiously. Then her confessor tries to learn from Doña Urraca whether Don Pablo was the author of a certain scurrilous pamphlet going the rounds. She denies this vehemently. The crafty ecclesiastic lets fall from his pocket a portrait of Don Pablo which he claims to have received from his repentant mistress, Doña Belisa. Furious at what she considers her lover's infidelity, Doña Urraca now confesses that Don Pablo is indeed the author of the pamphlet.

In the second and final scene, which takes place in a prison of the Inquisition, Don Pablo, condemned to death on the morrow, receives a visit from Doña Urraca who has been authorized to announce his pardon providing he do public penance and enter a monastery. On his refusal she reveals that she is the one who has betrayed him and upbraids him for being unfaithful to their love. After Pablo proves to her, however, from the uniform in the picture, that his liaison with Doña Belisa had occurred several years ago, before he had met Doña Urraca, her fury now turns against her confessor who had torn from her the secret by his duplicity. Unable to persuade her lover to kill Fray Bartholomé, she stabs him herself, throws his robe over Pablo, and leads him forth from the prison.

This play, with its mingling of Byronic passion and Voltairian skepticism, is the last of the six plays in the original version of *Le Théâtre de Clara Gazul*, though we shall soon see that two more were added in the 1830 edition.

VII   *Foreign Reception of Clara Gazul*

Though the reception of Mérimée's first volume, in spite of the favorable publicity we have seen, was rather tepid—it took five years for the first edition to sell out—the repercussions were not long in spreading abroad. Stendhal, delighted by this illustration of his own dramatic theories by his young friend and disciple, in May and July, 1826, sent two articles from Paris to the *London Magazine* in which he eulogized this new work. "All these plays are of perfect originality and copy in no wise the work of others. . . . No book, since the *Chansons* of Béranger, has given us so much pleasure." Again in the *New Monthly Magazine* of August

1, Stendhal praised the author for his naturalness, lack of senti-
mentality, depth of observation, and knowledge of the passions.
"Without contradiction that is the most remarkable work which
has come from French presses in many years." [9] An English translation of *Les Espagnols en Danemarck* appeared in the *London
Magazine* as early as July, and a complete English translation appeared a little later. If the German translation had to wait twenty
years, nevertheless Goethe is supposed to have commented:
"There is a little rascal hiding under the genius of a woman; but it
is in truth the genius of a strong man, destined to go far" and in a
contemporary article praised Mérimée as a young independent
seeking to practice and perfect his fine talent by applying it to
poetic subjects and genres of diversified nature.[10] The reader of
Mérimée's *Correspondance* will observe that in his later years, at
least, he was far from reciprocating this admiration.

VIII   *La Famille de Carvajal*

In June, 1828, Balzac's printing press issued a new volume of
Mérimée which contained *La Jaquerie* followed by a one-act
melodrama, *La Famille de Carvajal*. The latter was received with
almost unanimous condemnation by contemporary reviewers,
who were scandalized by its atmosphere of cynicism, savage cruelty, and attempted incest. Even the *Globe,* usually the ardent ally
of the young Romanticists, found it ignoble, ugly, and monstrous.
It is generally agreed by most critics today that this mystification
misled Mérimée's critics into taking the drama seriously instead of
recognizing in it a parody of Pixérécourt and the melodrama of
the boulevard theaters so popular at this time. Mérimée's satirical
intention is evident from his letter of May 15, 1831, written to
Stendhal.[11] "In the year of grace 1829 [he meant 1828] I edified
the public with the *Famille de Carvajal,* a moral work if ever
there was one, and inspired by the frequentation of bureau chiefs
and their spouses." The proof that Mérimée was thumbing his
nose here not only at the inanity of pseudo-Classical drama but
also at the excesses of Romantic melodrama can be found in a
perusal of the *Préface* and the two "letters" from correspondents
which precede the drama proper (or improper).

First we find in the *Préface* a long historical quotation from
"the unfortunate Usteriz's volume on New Granada," which forms
the basis for the tragic story of Don José, his wife and daughter.

(No one has ever discovered anything to make us believe that Usteriz was any more real than Clara Gazul.) The first "letter," from a Spanish privateer Don Diego, requests the author to write a play for the sailors to act out on shipboard, "not anything insipid, on the contrary nothing will be too hot or too spicy for us. We are not prudes and we fear nothing but languor." The second "letter," from a fifteen-year-old girl, forbidden by her mother to read Romantic novels or dramas and who has exhausted on the sly her papa's library of such works, wonders if Mérimée could not make for her "a little drama or a little novel very black, very terrible with lots of crimes and love à la lord Byron. . . . P.S. I would like to have it end badly and especially to have the heroine die unhappily. Second P.S. If it's all the same to you, I would like the hero's name to be Alphonse. It's such a pretty name." How faithfully the young author followed the prescriptions of his fictitious freebooter and little girl admirer can be seen in the following résumé of this horrendous melodrama to end all melodramas.

As the scene opens in the South American province of New Granada in the seventeenth century, Don José is discussing the terrible punishment and death to be meted out to a Negro poisoner, to the dismay of his wife Doña Augustina and daughter Catalina. The latter informs her mother of her cruel father's incestuous passion and asks her mother to escape with her when her lover, Captain Alonso, is to come to abduct her. The second scene shows us Don José practicing alchemy with his assistant Mugnoz in an unsuccessful effort to transmute base metals into gold. This is followed by a blasphemous interview of Don José with his despised Almoner, whose suggestion that Don José might achieve absolution for his crimes by building a chapel is met with derisive laughter. Don Alonso arrives with his Indian allies to storm the dwelling but, wounded, is driven off by Don José and his servants. Don José then accuses his wife of infidelity and, with a dagger at her heart, forces her to sign a false confession that Catalina is the daughter of a certain Don Diego Ricaurte. When he shows this letter to his daughter she tears it up, unwilling to believe any immorality of her mother, threatening to kill herself rather than respond to his incestuous passion. Don José has Mugnoz poison Doña Augustina, who dies in terrible, protracted agony. Realizing that the house is besieged by Don Alonso with two hundred Indians and sixty white followers, Don José knows that his death is near, but would give anything for an hour of "diabolical bliss." He concocts an "infernal beverage" for his daughter to make her unable to resist him, but in her piety she refuses to take nourishment on this fast day. When he rushes to embrace her, she seizes his dagger and kills him as he raises his bloody hand to curse her.

At this moment, Don Alonso and his comrades break in. Seeing Catalina standing over the dead body of her father, they recoil in horror from this parricide. Don Alonso prevents the Indian chief from cutting off her head and accedes to her wish that she be taken to the forest where she will probably be devoured by tigers. "Rather tigers than men," she exclaims before falling unconscious on her father's body. "And so ends this comedy and the Carvajal family," ejaculates the Indian, Ingol. "The father is stabbed, the daughter will be devoured; excuse the faults of the author." With what sardonic mirth Mérimée must have greeted the scandalized outcries of critics who took this melodramatic buffoonery seriously.

IX Le Carrosse du Saint-Sacrement

Far more important are the two plays Mérimée wrote in 1829, which he incorporated in the second edition of Le Théâtre de Clara Gazul in 1830. First published in the Revue de Paris in June, 1829, Le Carrosse du Saint-Sacrement is a charming and sparkling saynète, with the scene laid in South America like its predecessor and successor—in this case Lima, Peru, of the eighteenth century. It is likely that Mérimée's interest in South America had been aroused by the stories brought back from that continent by Dr. François Désiré Roulin, a friend of his family.

In the cabinet of the Viceroy this vain and pompous official, afflicted with a severe case of gout which he insists is only a swelling in his foot, is debating whether to attend in his new coach from Spain the official baptism of the young Indian prince at the Cathedral. In his mail he finds a letter from the Countess of Montemayor beseeching him to punish the famous actress la Périchole (his adored mistress) for having satirized her in a comedy she is now playing. In a delightfully comic scene reminiscent both of Molière and of Lesage, the Viceroy asks his secretary Martinez to tell him whether there is any truth in the rumors of la Périchole's infidelity. After much urging and with great misgivings, Martinez finally admits that she has at least two other lovers, Captain Aguirre and a dashing young matador—perhaps the prototype of the future lover of Carmen. True to human nature, the Viceroy, instead of being grateful to his secretary for his frankness, turns on him in a rage, banishing him to a distant post in the country.

Now la Périchole enters and, before the Viceroy can reproach her, brazenly requests that he give her his magnificent new carriage so that she can drive to the Cathedral in state and humiliate her jealous rivals. When he upbraids her for her duplicity, she haughtily refuses to disculpate herself and apparently is about to leave in a huff until her remorseful protector humbly beseeches her to stay and dispel his suspicions. (One is reminded of the famous lovers' quarrel in Molière's *Bourgeois Gentilhomme*.) The artful minx has little difficulty in alleging plausible circumstances to justify her behavior, and the grateful Viceroy is only too happy to give her the carriage.

As he watches her triumphal progress toward the Cathedral, the Viceroy is horrified to see her carriage collide with that of the Marchioness, who is thrown out into the street. The Licencié comes to the Viceroy to protest the scandal and threatens to leave the Church unless la Périchole is forced to make amends to the powerful Marchioness; he is placated only by the promise of a Murillo picture for the Marchioness and a promotion for his nephew.

The crowning irony of the play is now afforded by the arrival of the Archbishop who announces that la Périchole has generously donated the magnificent carriage to the Church, along with a pious foundation for its upkeep in perpetuity, so that it will now serve to carry the holy sacrament to the dying and thereby save many souls from damnation. The Bishop and the Licencié are happy to accept the Viceroy's invitation to dinner with him and la Périchole, who will sing for them with a voice capable of converting an infidel—pious songs of course.

In 1848 Mérimée wrote that this play was written "at a time when it took a little courage to make fun of viceroys and bishops." [12] Indeed, the play aroused cries of scandal among the conservatives—the devout, the royalists, the ultras, and defenders of the *Congrégation*. The Duchess de Berry gave up her subscription to the *Revue de Paris*, a gesture followed by other reactionary

salons. Even two decades later when the play was performed by
the Théâtre Français, furious cries of indignation arose. "Mérimée
feared he would be burned as a heretic and Théophile Gautier
regretted not having put on his red waistcoat." [13] Yet today it is
difficult to understand why the play caused so much more consternation in conservative circles and jubilation among young rad-
icals than the preceding plays in Le Théâtre de Clara Gazul. The
satire of Le Carrosse is lighthearted and gay, without malice or
deep anticlerical propaganda. The setting is skillfully outlined, the
action is rapid and unified, and the characters are delightfully
drawn—in particular the stupid and vainglorious Viceroy, reminiscent of the Résident in Les Espagnols, and the capricious and
seductive la Périchole, in many ways a prototype for Carmen. Le
Carrosse du Saint-Sacrement, almost a masterpiece, has become
the most enduringly popular of Mérimée's theater.

X L'Occasion

Like its predecessor, L'Occasion appeared first in La Revue de
Paris (autumn of 1829) before being added to the 1830 edition of
Le Théâtre de Clara Gazul; its setting is also placed in the New
World, this time in a convent garden of Havana. Here the resemblance ends, for mockery and irony are for the first time subdued
in Mérimée and are replaced by poetic reverie and a moving
study of jealousy in the hearts of two young girls. Not all readers
will agree with Trahard who considers it Mérimée's masterpiece,
superior even to Le Carrosse, but it shares with the latter play and
with Les Espagnols the honor of joining the repertory of the
Comédie Française.

In the convent garden fifteen-year-old Doña Maria is thinking
aloud of her hopeless love for the young priest who serves as father confessor. Should she give him the letter she has rewritten so
many times to confess her passion? At the entrance of the servant
Rita there ensues a discussion of a poison flask recently added to
the convent pharmacy—a premonition of the tragic ending to
come, as is Maria's gift to Rita of a precious string of gold beads
by which to remember her. The handsome young priest Fray
Eugenio, unaware of her presence, removes a letter from a hollow
in the orange tree, replacing it with one of his own. When he sees
her and reproaches her gently for her melancholy, caused he imagines by some childish infatuation, she replies: "At fifteen can

one not suffer as much as at thirty?" And after some hesitation she hands him her letter, not to be read until later. Her perturbation in which are mingled religious scruples, fear of being scorned, and hope that Eugenio may share her love, is transformed in the next scene into bitter jealousy of her best friend, Doña Francisca aged eighteen, who with unconscious cruelty confides her delicious happiness in her love for Eugenio, passionately reciprocated by the young priest.

Emboldened by a previous sojourn in England where she had seen "priests" happily married and with children, she wishes she had the means to escape with Eugenio to Jamaica. With a Cornelian effort of the will Maria insists that Francisca accept her diamonds, taking pride like a soldier or a Roman in the glory of her stoic sacrifice. Taking the bottle of poison from the pharmacy, she asks Rita to bring her some lemonade. At this moment Fray Eugenio arrives to reproach her hypocritically for the sacrilegious passion evinced in her letter; informing him that she now knows his guilty secret, she offers money to escape the country, a gift which Eugenio rather ignominiously accepts. Rita returns with the lemonade into which Maria pours a few drops of poison, but before she has the courage to drink it Francisca arrives to request the use of her room that night so that her lover can climb up a rope ladder to rejoin her. Maria grants this request and then, outraged perhaps by this last humiliation, allows Francisca to drink the poisoned lemonade without warning her. As Francisca dies in horrible suffering, Maria rushes off in remorse to drown herself in the well of the convent.

Following as usual his Spanish models, the author has Fray Eugenio come forward to conclude the performance: "Don't blame me too much for having caused the deaths of these two likable young ladies and deign to excuse the faults of the author."

Trahard is quite justified in comparing this charming and sincere painting of virginal passion and jealousy with the plays of Musset, *A quoi rêvent les jeunes filles*, *Il ne faut jurer de rien* and especially *On ne badine pas avec l'amour*.[14] We find here the same comic relief—in the amorous dispute between the lightheaded girls Doña Irène and Doña Ximena over the relative merits as husband of a sea captain and an officer of the dragoons—and the same delicate blending of natural setting with sensual passion as in the following passage: "We would sigh from time to time, looking up at the starry heavens. We could see the Southern Cross bending slowly in front of us, and from time to time a slight sea breeze made orange blossoms fall upon our heads." Even more similar to Musset's plays is the delicate portrayal of feminine jealousy, reminding us of Camille and Rosine. Poujet finds in Fray Eugenio the only priest in Mérimée's theater who is not frankly odious "because he entered holy orders through a spirit of sacrifice to save his dying mother, and because a sincere passion has erased in him all stains of the priesthood." [15] (M. Poujet has forgotten, I think, the worthy curate in the first part of *Inès Mendo*.) It is hard to believe that Mérimée was only twenty-six when he completed these two gems of dramatic art, far removed from the youthful bravado of his six earlier pieces, equally far removed in quality from his play *Les Mécontents* of the following year.

XI   *Les Mécontents*

Most critics have given scant attention to this play, published early in 1830 in *La Revue de Paris,* and on the whole it is difficult to blame them. *Les Mécontents* is a one-act drama, partly historical since its events took place under Napoleon I in 1810, partly a *comédie de salon* which at times degenerates into broad, heavy-handed farce. At the château of the Count and Countess des Tournelles near the province of la Vendée a group of provincial aristocrats have gathered to discuss a conspiracy to overthrow the regime of the usurper-emperor and restore the royal government which existed before the revolution. They are joined by the dashing young aristocrat, Lieutenant Edouard de Nangis, soon converted to their cause by love for his cousin the Countess, and by the sturdy peasant Bertrand, former major in the royal army of the Vendéeans.

Either because he was still a liberal at this time or because, as Trahard has suggested, he had been bored listening to the long-winded speeches of elderly aristocrats in the salons he attended, Mérimée caricatures these aristocrats unmercifully. First the Countess is terrified by a spider, then the group shows its egotism by voting each one for himself as president, then they show their shameful cowardice by fleeing from the château as a messenger from the prefect arrives. The latter brings, however, a letter notifying the Count that he has been appointed chamberlain to the empress, at which all desire for conspiracy evaporates, each noble whispering in his ear a request for preferment through his influence at court.

Eugène Marsan in his *Préface* to the Divan edition of *Mosaïque* which includes this play calls it the only work of Mérimée which is truly insignificant, adding that only two Mériméean passages spoken by Bertrand give him the courage to reread it; Trahard is a little more generous in adding to the brave Bertrand—a truthful depiction of the Chouan patriots—the dashing, witty and gallant figure of the young Lieutenant Edouard de Nangis (who reminds him of Hulot in Balzac's *Les Chouans*) as the two portraits giving value to *Les Mécontents*.[16] It is difficult to take issue with these rather unflattering judgments; although a reading of this play is not really boring, it is hard to conceive how Mérimée could have descended so far from the heights he was reaching this same year in the short story. As for Mérimée's two later closet dramas, they resemble fiction in dialogue form rather than drama per se and hence will be reserved for later discussion.

XII   *Evaluation of Mérimée's Theater*

The scholarly and painstaking study of Merimée's theater by Pierre Trahard has left all later commentators deeply in his debt.[17] With his wide knowledge of Spanish as well as French and English literature he has indicated the sources Mérimée pillaged: Lope de Vega, Calderón, Cervantes, Ramón de la Cruz, Moratín, Molière, Lesage, Voltaire, Diderot, and the English "satanic" school of Ann Radcliffe and "Monk" Lewis. He enumerates in several pages the mistakes—historical, psychological, and linguistic—of which the young dramatist has been guilty, opining that Mérimée's endings, "Please excuse the faults of the author" are only too appropriate. Though Trahard like most critics is severe in pointing out that Mérimée's characters are not well developed, that his *parti pris* in depicting most ecclesiastics as possessed of the devil is scandalous, and that his local color is superficial and conventional, he nevertheless finds it more picturesque and truthful than that of Lesage.

Since *Le Théâtre de Clara Gazul* was for the most part not brought to the stage, its influence on the development of French Romantic drama was of course less decisive than that of Hugo or Dumas père, for its success was limited to literary circles and was scarcely known to the general public. Nevertheless, it did crystal-

lize in concrete form the Romantic theories first advocated by
Stendhal: the mingling of comedy and tragedy; the departure
from the Classic unities of time, place, and action; the use of national history both medieval and contemporary; and the abundant
flavoring of exotic color—Portuguese, Spanish, and colonial.

Aside from the relative impact of Mérimée's theater on the historical development of Romantic drama, what is its intrinsic
worth as viewed today? No critic was ever more harsh to
Mérimée's theater than the author himself, for in a letter to Mlle
Brohan, September 16, 1848, he wrote that he felt himself "particularly unsuited for writing for the theater." The failure of
L'Amour africain in 1827 and of Le Carrosse du Saint-Sacrement
at the Théâtre Français in 1850 must have convinced him that he
was right. Yet in addition to numerous editions from 1842 to 1882,
and a large number since the 1920's when Mérimée's copyrights
expired, there have been many performances of his plays, beginning with Jacques Copeau's production of Le Carrosse at the
Vieux Colombier, followed by that of L'Occasion at the Atelier in
1922 and 1924 and that of L'Amour africain by Pitoëff's company
in 1926. More recent performances have been that of Le Carrosse by the Théâtre Antoine in 1946–47 (and as The Golden Carriage, one of Jean Renoir's best films in the 1950's) and of Le Ciel
et l'enfer at the Théâtre des Champs Elysées, and in 1947 simulta-
neous performances of Les Espagnols en Danemarck by the
Théâtre de la Poche and Le Théâtre Français. The libretto of the
famous light opera La Périchole is of course inspired by Le Carrosse of Mérimée.

In the light of this popularity it is easy to agree with the para-
doxical assertion of M. Baschet: "these plays, just like those of
Musset which were also not written for the stage, turn out to be,
of the entire theatrical production of the Romanticists, the most
naturally dramatic." [18] Mérimée's reputation, like that of his
friend Stendhal, has been steadily rising in public favor. His dramatic faults are easy to forgive today in favor of his concision, his
realistic and natural expression, his brilliant wit, and his efferves-
cent irony.

CHAPTER 3

La Guzla

I *Biography of Hyacinthe Maglanovitch*

WITH tongue in cheek, Mérimée begins *La Guzla* with a biography of the chief of the Illyrian *guzlars,* one Hyacinthe Maglanovitch, purported to be the result of actual interviews by the "translator." Born in Zuonigrad the son of a cobbler, he apparently never learned to read or write. He was carried off at the age of eight by bohemians who converted him to Islamism. While in the service of the Turkish mayor of Livino he was converted to Catholicism by a Christian monk with whom he managed to make his escape, carrying with him his master's cloak, saber, and a few sequins. Arriving in Dalmatia under the protection of the Venetian government, Maglanovitch lived for some time off the charity of the natives in return for singing on the *guzla* old ballads he knew by heart, and later some he composed himself for marriages and funerals. At twenty-five, a handsome young man already famous as poet and musician, he eloped with Helen, daughter of a rich Morlaque, thereby arousing the jealousy of a rival, Uglian, who tried to prevent the abduction but was shot by the favored suitor. Then to escape vengeance from the deceased's family he was obliged to flee to the mountains with his beloved. Later he left the mountains, purchased some cattle, and settled down with his wife and children near Smocovich at the edge of a little stream.

It was at Zara in 1816 that our "translator" first met Maglanovitch and sketched this picturesque portrait of him (which reminds us of the German *reître* in Mérimée's first novel two years later):

Hyacinthe was then about 60 years old. He was a tall man, vigorous and robust for his age, with broad shoulders and remarkably big neck. His prodigiously tanned face, his little eyes slightly raised in Chinese fashion, his aquiline nose, somewhat reddened by the use of strong liqueurs, his long white moustache and his big black eyebrows formed an ensemble difficult to forget when once seen. Add to that a long scar extending over the eyebrow and a part of the cheek. His head was close shaven according to the almost universal custom of the Morlaques, and he wore a bonnet of black lambskin; his clothing was rather old but still neat.

Agreeing to sing only when copiously provided with meat and drink, he suddenly dropped down on a carpet near the fire and slept so soundly that it was impossible to awaken him. Next time, taught by this lesson, the "translator" let him imbibe more moderately and was rewarded with several of the ballads in this collection. Five days later Maglanovitch left him, taking with him his host's pair of English pistols but not his purse or watch. In 1817, the "translator" spent two days in Hyacinthe's home, received joyously by him, his wife, children, and grandchildren, one of his sons serving as mountain guide for several days without accepting any reward. So plausible and detailed is this "biography," it is small wonder the critics were taken in.

II   "L'Aubépine de Veliko"

The opening ballad, "L'Aubépine de Veliko," like all the others in prose rather than verse, is one of the most moving in its tragic cruelty. The bey, Jean Veliko, whose house has been burned by his enemies after he had lost ten sons in battle and one in prison, with his one remaining child had sought shelter with his friend George Estivanich. Three of his enemies with their brigand followers come to demand that George deliver up to them Veliko and his son Alexis and, on his refusal, split his head with a saber. Mistaking Estivanich's son for that of Veliko, they kill him along with Veliko. Ten years later the son Alexis grown to robust manhood is shown the bloody robe belonging to his dead father and that of his martyred protector and announces his identity to the three assassins, whom he kills one by one, completing his vengeance.

The last paragraph is especially effective. "Take away, take away these bloody robes. The beys of the East are dead, Jean and George are avenged. The hawthorn [aubépine] of Veliko has blossomed again; its stem shall not perish." Though Yovanovitch feels that the subject is reminiscent of Nodier's "Bey Spelatin," the story is borrowed from a Chinese drama *Tchao-Chi-Con-Ell* or *The Little Orphan of the House of Tchao,* which in French translation had been the principal source for Voltaire's tragedy, *L'Orphelin de la Chine.* Yovanovitch points out the superiority of Mérimée's version—imbued with fierce energy and concentrated on the passion of vengeance in which the future writer of *Carmen* and *Mateo Falcone* can be glimpsed—over that of Voltaire, in which an amorous intrigue and a happy ending detract from the exotic emotion.[1] It was from *Le Voyage* of Fortis, according to the Yugoslav scholar, that Mérimée borrowed the superficial local color and also the detail of the bloody robes, which he will later use so powerfully in *Colomba.*

III King Thomas II

Four of the twenty-eight ballads in *La Guzla* are devoted to Thomas II, King of Bosnia, a character unknown in popular tradition. Most interesting of these to the modern reader is "La Vision de Thomas II" which Yovanovitch declares to be a preliminary sketch for Mérimée's later tale, *La Vision de Charles XI,* founded on a story of Colonel Gustafson, dethroned king of Sweden.[2]

IV The Bandit Ballads

Two of the ballads, "Chant de mort" and "Les Braves Heiduques," are devoted to the patriotic bandits of Illyria (*heiduque,* according to the "translator's" note, means "highway man"). The former with its message to father and loved ones from the dying warrior lying in the moonlight on the plain reminds me somewhat of Leconte de Lisle's "Le Coeur de Hialmar" in *Poèmes barbares.* The latter leaves an impression of horror mingled with poignant sadness. Christich Mladin with his lovely wife Catherine and their two brave sons have been besieged in a cavern for three days by the *pandours* (according to the note, soldiers scarcely better morally than the bandits themselves). Without food or water except what they can find in the hollow of a rock, their tongues have become black and swollen. Catherine dies and when on the fourth day even the water in the rock has dried up, the elder son, grown mad, draws a knife and looks at his mother's corpse "with eyes like those of a wolf who sees a lamb." The younger son, horrified, pierces his own arm, inviting his brother to drink his blood rather than commit a crime. Mladin rises, tells his sons that a bul-

let in the head is preferable to the agony of hunger, and the three
rush forth like mad wolves to receive ten bullets in their breasts
but not before each has killed ten men.

Mérimée's debt here to the story of Ugolin in Dante's *Inferno*
was noticed by at least three contemporary reviewers. Yovanovitch points out that he has taken from Dante the tragedy of hunger, transforming it into a tragedy of thirst, as well as the silent
and terrifying glance, so easily deciphered on the corpse. "Nothing more impersonal than this poem. The author has wished to
give us first an impression of horror; then to make us admire the
savage grandeur of these men for whom death costs but little; in
no wise has he tried to move our pity. A dramatic breath animates
the whole tale. . . . So many horrors are accumulated on purpose
with cynical coldness. Hyacinthe Maglanovitch frightens us; who
could not recognize the hand of Mérimée in this story?" [3] Our
Yugoslav critic, while admitting that this ballad is not without
resemblance to the real Serbian poems, thinks it lacks, however,
the patriotic feeling of the Serb poets, "that national and social
hatred against Turks and merchants which transforms the cruel
bandits of the Turko-Venetian frontier into true heroes of the entire race."

V *Ballads of Domestic Life*

Least successful in Yovanovitch's eyes are the ballads dealing
with domestic life. Especially misleading, he thinks, is the treatment of women, as in "L'Amante de Dannisch," based entirely on
Mérimée's reading of Fortis. This short ballad describing the infatuation of three lovers for the heroine seems to our critic out of
harmony with true Serbian poetry because of the sensuality and
naïve cynicism with which the girl extracts presents from her
various suitors, more like a Spanish sister of Carmen than a Serbian.[4]

The men in these ballads ring more true than the women, particularly in their exaltation of masculine friendship. Thus in "La
Flamme de Perrusich," for instance, Janco, after he has acciden-
tally slain his boon companion Cyrille Pervan during a festival,
"drinks no more wine or brandy, eats only roots and runs here and
there like an ox frightened by a gadfly." Finally he returns to the
church to pray for an entire day, his arms outstretched like a cross
on the paved floor, returns home, sups, and goes to bed. He calls

his wife to ask if she can see the church from the window, but when she answers that it is veiled in fog he prays again for the soul of Cyrille. The same question then brings her reply that she can see a pale and trembling light. After saying his rosary he receives from his wife an answer to his third question: "I see in the middle of the river a brilliant light coming rapidly toward us." Then she heard a great sigh and something falling on the floor. Janco was dead. (A footnote informs us of the Serbian superstition that a bluish light fluttering around tombs announces the presence of the dead.)

A second example of fraternal union is "Les Pobratini," in which two men, Jean Lubovich and Cyrille Zborr, have sworn before a priest eternal fidelity. In battle with the enemy they capture goats, precious arms, rich material, and a beautiful Turkish slave girl whom each desires. They agree to sleep off their intoxication and settle this rivalry on the morrow. Sober on awakening, with tears streaming from their eyes they take the hand of the slave girl, seize their daggers, and plunge them into her breast. "Let the infidel perish rather than our friendship." Then they clasp hands and never cease to love each other. (In a curious footnote, which one would have thought sufficient to dispel the hoax and reveal Mérimée as the real author, we read: "I suppose that this song . . . furnished the author of *Le Théâtre de Clara Gazul* the idea for *L'Amour africain*.")

The third ballad on this theme "La Querelle de Lepe et de Tchernyegor," much gayer and lighter in tone, according to Yovanovitch is a parody not only of the preceding ballads but also of the famous quarrel between Agamemnon and Achilles in the *Iliad*.[5] Two devoted friends, Lepe and Tchernyegor, have each married a beautiful girl. One day they capture a rich barque, containing among its spoils a lovely dress which each one demands as a present for his wife. Tchernyegor tries to shoot Lepe but kills his page instead. An old *guzla* player springs forward to end the dispute by tearing the dress into little pieces. Instead of shaking hands, each of the two friends withdraws in anger, vowing vengeance. Lepe goes to his friend's home, abducts his wife Nastasia, and sells her to a slave ship at anchor near the shore. In the meantime his friend does the same thing with Lepe's wife asking 600 pieces of gold but accepting 500 when the merchant says that is all he paid for an even lovelier slave. When Tchernyegor realizes

that the other is his own wife, he rushes ashore and makes common cause with Lepe; as friends once more they attack the cara-
vel to recapture their wives, forgetting, however, to refund the
money. Yovanovitch is quite shocked by the levity of this imbroglio, which he finds more appropriate for vaudeville than for epic
poetry, but most readers may find it more amusing than shocking.

VI Montenegrin Ballads

The collection includes two ballads on the Montenegrins, the
first of which, "Hadagny," was inspired by *Lettres sur la Grèce,
notes et chants populaires extraits du portefeuille du Colonel
Voutier*, published in Paris in 1820. In the tribal war between
Ostrowicz and Serral, the latter city sends out the chief's wife
Hélène to spy upon the enemy. Young Hadagny, observing her
approach in the distance, kills her with a shot from his gun only to
discover with shame that he has fired on a woman. His father, old
Bietko, feeling that his son has dishonored the tribe, sends him
away into exile. Returning much later to the district, now desolate
and destroyed, he finds only a single goatherd who informs him
that Serral has avenged Hélène's death by killing all the warriors
of Ostrowicz, devastating the crops, and selling the children to the
infidels. On learning that his father has been killed and pushed off
the precipice, Hadagny rolls over the same precipice in expiation.

The second of this group, "Les Monténégrins," glorifies the
courage of these mountaineers in their struggles against the army
of Napoleon, which has come to subdue their land and carry off
their women and children. Each man hoists a red bonnet on a
stick, and when the twenty thousand soldiers fire on them, the five
hundred Montenegrins rise to their feet, kill twenty-six of the in-
vaders, and put the rest to inglorious flight. It is interesting to
observe that Mérimée shows himself here much more sympathetic
to the Montenegrins than to Napoleon's French soldiers. Perhaps
this is one reason Yovanovitch admires this ballad, more concise
than anything Mérimée ever wrote, closer perhaps to his later
story "L'Enlèvement de la redoute" than to primitive folk poetry.[6]

VII Ballads of Lyrical Contrast

An entirely different poem, "Barcarolle," apparently interpo-
lated by Mérimée for variety and quiet relief between ballads of
violence and tragedy, is a short, graceful evocation of the Illyrian

boatmen, chanting in unison on the blue sea. It is reminiscent of the rhythmic cadence of the "Volga Boatman." Two other ballads, "L'Impromptu" and "Le Morlaque à Venise," form a gentle contrast also with the ballads of cruelty and terror; they were praised by the *Gazette de France*,[7] which found the former a graceful imitation of the *Galatea* of Theocritus. "Le Morlaque à Venise" is the melancholy plaint of the Illyrian persuaded to go to Venice to seek his fortune but "like a tree transplanted in summer" wasting away with homesickness for his native land. Yovanovitch finds the beginning a direct reflection of Idyl XIV of Theocritus and the end inspired by the *Chants populaires de la Grèce moderne* of Fauriel.[8] Mérimée also borrows various images from Homer and others from Virgil and Aeschylus.

VIII *Vampirism*

Two-thirds of *La Guzla* consist of ballads inspired by superstitious beliefs of the Illyrians either in the existence of vampires or in the dreaded capacity of those with "the evil eye" to cast spells leading to misfortune or death. A large part of Mérimée's essay on vampirism in *La Guzla* is a quotation from a famous eighteenth-century writer on this subject, Don Calmet, whose *Dissertations sur les apparitions des anges, des démons et des esprits, et sur les revenants et les vampires,* published in 1746, had a tremendous vogue for over a century, and was well known to Mérimée, who had made a special study of magic.

According to Yovanovitch the word "vampire" came into European languages around 1830 from the Serbian. Goethe, inspired by Calmet's work, was the first to use the theme in literature with his *Braut von Corinth* and long maintained his interest in vampires, mentioning them twice in *Faust*. Gautier later took up the subject in his poem "Les Taches jaunes" and in his vampire story "La Mort amoureuse." Byron alludes to this superstition in his *Giaour* (1813); and when three years later a Romantic society was formed in Geneva including Byron, Mrs. Shelley, Dr. Polidari, and "Monk" Lewis, Byron recounted a terrifying tale he had intended to write under the title "The Vampire." Polidari wrote it down and published it under Byron's name in the *New Monthly Magazine* in April, 1819; it was such a success that Goethe called it Byron's best work, and Amédée Pichot, including it in his French translation of Byron's works, asserted that it had contributed as much as his most famous poems to Byron's fame in France.[9] In 1820 Nodier's *Le Vampire* was all the rage at the Théâtre de la Porte Saint-Martin, was imitated at other theaters, and was still attracting crowds three years later. The English "satanic school" of Lewis, Mrs. Radcliffe, and Maturin exploited this taste for the uncanny, the monstrous, and the horrible; and in 1818 Collin de Plancy published his *Dictionnaire infernal,* one of the five books on which Hugo was to draw for his *Notre-Dame de Paris.* Mérimée was following, then, this Romantic infatuation with his ballads in his search for local color since these superstitions were rampant particularly in the primitive folklore of the Balkans.

The first of the five ballads devoted to vampirism in *La Guzla,* "La Belle Sophie" is in dramatic form with lyric effusions on the part of the actors. While gay crowds are celebrating the imminent marriage of lovely Sophie with the rich bey of Moïna, she sees advancing toward her on his black mare a pale young man, Nicephore, her earlier lover. The latter gallops off "to the valley of tears" and a hermit, hearing a shot fired, discovers his dead body which he buries in the sand near the torrent. In the atrocious conclusion Sophie calls out in agony as the bey of Moïna presses down upon her like a cadaver of lead, bites her in the vein of her neck, and sucks her blood. As usual, Mérimée borrows the local color as the material for his notes from the *Voyage* of Fortis as well.

In the next ballad, "Jeannot," Mérimée seems to be making fun of vampirism. Jeannot "more cowardly than a woman" returning through a cemetery trembles with fright as he hears something gnawing, which he takes for a vampire eating in his tomb. As he tries to protect himself by eating the earth of the grave, he is bitten by a dog which had been gnawing a bone. Yovanovitch considers that this introduction of a coward in a volume concerning heroes evidences lack of taste on the part of the author.

"Le Vampire" is a fragment consisting merely of the description of the vampire who in real life had been the cursed Venetian who had led Marie astray from the path of virtue. His throat pierced by a bullet, his heart by a dagger, he has been lying on the ground for three days, his blood still flowing warm and red. His beard and nails have continued to grow (evident signs of vampirism), and his bloody mouth smiles like that of a man tormented with a hideous love.

"Cara-Ali le Vampire" is the story of Juméli's desertion of her husband Basile—"for who is the woman who resists much gold?" —to follow the rich Moslem Cara-Ali, who puts her on his white horse and rides off with her. Her husband runs to the yellow river, sees the two escaping, and shoots Cara-Ali. In his last gasp, the latter tells Juméli to take from his saddle box the Alcoran and open it to page 66 which will enable one to command all the spirits of earth and water. As Basile rushes up to kill his wife, she obtains his pardon by giving him this precious talisman. But when that night Basile opens the impious book to page 66, the earth trembles with a frightful sound to let emerge a bloody specter, Cara-Ali, who seizes the unlucky man, bites him in the neck, and sucks all the blood from his veins.

In the fifth and final ballad dealing with vampirism, "Constantin Yacoubovich," the hero by that name is approached by a young man whose hair is white, whose eyes are dull, whose cheeks are hollow, and whose gait is uncertain. Demanding brandy and milk, he detaches his belt to show a bloody wound caused the preceding day by an enemy bullet, then dies after requesting burial on this knoll exposed to the sunshine. Constantin obeys without considering whether this Christian cemetery would be disturbed by the body of a schismatic Greek. When Constantin's son becomes pale and feeble a week later, a holy monk, noticing a red spot on his neck, affirms that it has been caused by the tooth of a vampire. On opening the stranger's grave, they discover his body still fresh and rosy, with beard still growing and nails as long as those of a bird's claws. Before Constantin can pierce it with a spear, the corpse utters a cry and flees into the woods. The hermit rubs the body of the child with blood and earth taken from the grave. A giant enters the house, fascinating Constantin with his diabolical glance until the hermit throws a bunch of rosemary on the fire and with his breath directs the smoke toward the specter, in the name of Jesus. The gigantic specter rushes out of the door like a wolf pursued by hunters. Next day at the same hour a man enters in the appearance of a soldier, again fascinates Constantin with "the evil eye," and is put to flight by the hermit. A third day the vampire reappears, this time in the shape of a dwarf with eyes gleaming like torches until, exorcised by the hermit, he flees, never to return.

The Yugoslav critic finds this the best of the five ballads from the standpoint of composition: "Mérimée makes us pass without our realizing it from reality into the domain of the marvelous; from the domain of things possible . . . we have passed by clever transitions and almost without being aware of it into complete fantasy." [10] Yovanovitch points out that if Mérimée in his "Notice sur le vampirism," inspired by Calmet and Fortis, correctly interprets the true spirit of vampirism as hallucination or madness, in his ballads on the other hand he gives us Romantic vampires in the manner of Nodier or Byron, types of the accursed "héros fatal" having nothing in common with the superstitions of traditional and popular vampirism." [11]

IX   The Evil Eye

Somewhat similar to these ballads of vampires are those concerning the tragic fascination of the "evil eye," the caster of spells. This ancient superstition, mentioned in antiquity by Theocritus, Pliny the Elder, and Ovid, was taken up by Nodier and recurs later in Gautier's *Jettatura* (1857). As in the case of the ballads on vampirism, Mérimée precedes these ballads with an essay on the superstition of the "evil eye" in which, after a long quotation from the learned treatise of Jean Baptiste Porta's *Magiae naturalis* containing a whole chapter on this subject, he mentions several experiences of his own in this regard. Especially amusing is his recital of the little child he had fondled and praised to the skies, only to have the child's mother insist that he spit on the child's forehead to remove the baleful influence which his eulogy of the child might cause.

"Le Mauvais Oeil," evidently inspired by this experience, is the poignant lament of the mother whose child, flattered by the praise of a stranger, has pined away, his hair grown white, his eyes dull. His uncle has gone to Starigrad to bring back earth from the tomb of a saint, and his cousin the bishop has brought a relic to hang around the child's neck in a vain effort to cure him. If only that cursed stranger were in her power, the mother would compel him to spit on the child's pretty brow!

"Maxime et Zoé" relates the tragic story of two lovers. Maxime comes every night to serenade beautiful Zoé on his *guzla* under her window, but he never shows his face because at dawn he rushes off to the forest. One night Zoé asks him to come tomorrow at noon so she can ride off with him, carrying her loveliest clothes. At first he tries to persuade her to wait until night, but at her insistence he arrives at noon on his white horse with a velvet cushion on which she can sit. His forehead, however, is covered with a thick veil, leaving only the mouth and moustache visible. Soon she requests him to stop his horse and remove his veil so that she may embrace him. When he implores her to wait until night she accuses him of scorning her, threatening to leap from the horse even if it should kill her. Then the stranger stops his horse, removes his veil and when he turns to kiss her she sees that he has two eyeballs in one eye! As she falls lifeless to the ground, Maxime in despair tears out his own eyes with his dagger. After Zoé's burial Maxime enters a cloister, but soon her tomb is opened to place Maxime by her side. In a note to this ballad Mérimée writes: "One observes here how the fable of Orpheus and Eurydice has been travestied by the Illyrian poet, who, I am sure, has never read Virgil."

X *Other Ballads of the Supernatural*

Yovanovitch assures us that neither vampirism nor the evil eye was considered a subject worthy to be exploited by the true Illyrian *guzlars* and singers of folk ballads. There are, however, other examples, of the miraculous and the supernatural to be found in *La Guzla*. "L'Amant en bouteille," according to a note of the "translator," was evidently inspired by a somewhat similar tale he had found in *Le Monde enchanté* (1691) of the Dutch theologian Balthasar Bekker, a man persecuted for his defense of Descartes and praised by Voltaire for his attack on superstitions. In this ballad the beautiful Khava had turned down all offers of marriage and wore suspended from her neck by a golden chain a glass flask which she called her dear lover. Everything she wishes he is able to furnish her, whether it be a pearl from the ocean depths or sequins to place in her hair. The bishop, hearing of this marvel, seized this bottle and, to drive away this "black demon," made the sign of the cross and dealt a great hammer blow to the glass. As blood spurted forth, fair Khava uttered a cry and died. "'Twas a great pity that so great a beauty should thus have been the victim of a demon." That Mérimée must have smiled to himself while concocting this fabulous story may be guessed from his opening paragraph: "Young ladies who listen to me while weaving your mats, you would be very content if, like the fair Khava, you could hide your lovers in a bottle."

In "La Belle Hélène" fair Hélène has married the bold and handsome Theodore Khonopke in preference to the ugly and wicked Piero Stamati. When Theodore leaves to spend a year in Venice, Piero tries to seduce her, offering a velvet dress and a handful of sequins for her black hair. She rejects him angrily, pushing him so hard that he falls on his back and returns home weeping in rage. An "impious Jew" whom he consults for vengeance advises him to seek under the stone of a tomb until he can find a black toad to bring him in an earthen pot. They give the toad the name of John the apostle, pierce it with daggers, gathering up in a flask the venom issuing from its wounds; then they make the toad drink it and lick a beautiful fruit. This fruit is brought to Hélène who, after eating it, has the impression that a serpent is moving about in her belly.

In Part II Hélène's belly swells little by little until the women begin to say that she must be pregnant. Poor Hélène, afraid to leave the house, weeps day and night in shame, wondering what she can say to her husband on his return. Unable to believe her protestations of innocence, he draws his saber and cuts off her head. Opening her bosom he draws out not a child but a black toad; realizing that his wife had not been unfaithful he kisses her severed head, which opens its eyes and declares that Piero aided by a wicked Jew had bewitched her in vengeance. Theodore kills Piero and the Jew, then has thirty masses said for the repose of his wife's soul. This ballad reminds us of the famous medieval legend of Geneviève de Brabant, which had come down the ages to be made the subject of French novels in 1805 and 1810 that Mérimée must have known. The enchantment by a toad came to Mérimée doubtless from Porta's *Magiae Naturalis*.[12] In a footnote Mérimée mentions also an English king who was poisoned by a monk with ale in which he had drowned a toad (a detail borrowed from Sir Walter Scott's *Minstrelsy of the Scottish Border*).

"Le Seigneur Mercure" like "La Belle Hélène" has the same theme, fidelity of the spouse, but this time the treatment is exactly the reverse. When Mercure leaves for battle he gives his wife a rosary of amber beads, telling her that if she is faithful the rosary will remain intact; otherwise, the string will break and the beads will fall. His cousin Spiridion returns with bloody, torn garments to announce that Mercure has been killed but that he can console her. Drying her tears, Euphémie sleeps that same night with the traitor Spiridion.

In the meantime Mercure, very much alive, had come to a lake covered with fog; when the mist lifts in the moonlight, he sees galloping on the lake an army of little dwarfs, who on reaching the shore take on gigantic proportions. One of their number on a black steed challenges Mercure to a duel and, when he is vanquished, gives Mercure, as payment of ransom, the advice not to return home where death would await him. Heedless of this prophecy, Mercure nevertheless returns; passing by the cemetery, he sees priests and mourners at an open grave beside a corpse with saber at his side and a black veil over his head. Laughing with derision on being told that the dead man is he himself, Mercure goes home to embrace Euphémie and demand the magic rosary—which had broken and been replaced with one poisoned by his wife. "Count the beads," she says to him, "you know there were 67." As the poison enters his skin, at the sixty-sixth bead he utters a great sigh and falls dead. Unable to determine the exact source for this ballad in Mérimée's readings, Yovanovitch declares that here for once we have an incontestable folklore theme.

XI   *"Ballade de la noble épouse d'Asan-Aga"*

We have now come to the only authentic Serbian ballad in the entire collection. We are indebted to the Yugoslav's scholarly treatise for a detailed history of its many translations.[13] First revealed to European scholars in 1774 by the *Voyage* of Fortis, it had many adaptations in Germany and the Slavic nations as well as in England and France. The most famous German translation was by Goethe in 1775 or 1776; the most notable of seven English translations was Sir Walter Scott's "The Lamentation of the Faithful Wife of Asan-Aga," composed in 1798 or 1799. Of thirteen French translations the best known before Mérimée's was that of Charles Nodier in 1821, included in his *Smarra ou les démons de la nuit*. There were also translations into Italian, Latin, Hungarian, Czech, with two each in Spanish and Russian. Let us now attempt a résumé of Mérimée's translation before comparing it with others.

The whiteness on the green hills is not snow or swans but the tents of the wounded aga Asan-Aga. Come to care for him are his mother and sister but not his beloved wife, detained by her timidity (in keeping with the Moslem custom that a wife must never present herself before her husband without being summoned). Irritated by her absence, Asan sends word to his wife that she is never to look at him in his house or in front of his relatives. Saddened and crushed, she shuts herself up in her room until her brother arrives with a red silk purse containing her divorce. Snatching her from her children, even from her fifth child still in the cradle, her brother takes her to his home where she is soon sought in marriage by many noble lords of the country. In spite of her entreaties, her brother destines her for the cadi d'Imoski, to whom she sends a letter imploring him to cover her with a long veil so that in passing before her old home she will not see her orphaned children. Her sons and daughters recognize her as she passes in the wedding procession, and she is allowed to halt in order to give her two sons shoes embroidered in gold, her two daughters robes of many colors, and her little child in the cradle a chemisette. Asan-Aga, who has been watching all this from his hiding place, calls the two sons to him and demands that they leave "this mother who has abandoned you." The last paragraph differs as we shall see from earlier translations. "The poor mother grew pale, her head struck the ground, and at once she ceased to live, from sorrow at seeing her children orphans."

In a note to this ballad, the "translator" (really Mérimée) informs us that instead of following the poetic version of Fortis he has preferred to give a literal translation. Another note states that his exact and literal translation was made under the eyes of a Russian friend who gave him the meaning, word by word; this affirmation is corroborated as we have seen in Mérimée's letter later to Sobolevsky. With his customary concision Mérimée, by eliminating most of the florid adjectives of Fortis, had reduced the 991 words of Nodier to 629 without omitting anything of the original. Yovanovitch with the original Serbian version before him asserts categorically that Mérimée's translation is more faithful than those of Goethe, Nodier, and others, which had all been based on that of Fortis.[14] His translation of the final paragraph, so important for our understanding of the true spirit of the ballad, is the only one which is correct. Whereas Fortis, followed by Goethe,

Nodier, and the others had translated the last line "seeing her orphans leave her" (a calumny of filial love) Mérimée gave the correct meaning, "from sorrow at seeing her children orphans."

XII Success of the Hoax

Unlike his treatment of *Clara Gazul*, Mérimée took every precaution to keep secret his identity as author of *La Guzla*. He commissioned Joseph Lingay to get him as publisher F. G. Levrault of Strasbourg, with the condition that the latter would "publish an edition without receiving anything or paying anything," which would seem to refute the legend that Mérimée sold the manuscript to obtain money for his trip to Illyria.[15] The book appeared without any advertising and according to Mérimée sold only a dozen copies: "My heart still bleeds when I think of the poor publisher who had all the expense of this mystification; but if the French did not read me, foreigners and competent judges did me full justice."[16] Yet even in France *La Guzla* seems to have been praised by almost all the literary reviews of the day, completely taken in by their impression that these were authentic translations of true Serbian folk songs.

Mérimée was quite justified in his boast that his hoax had been acclaimed widely throughout Europe. Four months after the publication of *La Guzla* in France a German poet and friend of Goethe, M. W. Gerhardt, published a two-volume edition of Serbian folk songs in German translation, including all the ballads of *La Guzla* except the one authentic one, since he did not want to compete with the famous translation by Goethe. In the *Avertissement* Mérimée showed his amusement at the fact that Gerhardt, after sending him this translation, remarked in his preface that under Mérimée's prose he had discovered the meter of the Illyrian verses. "The Germans discover many things as we know, and he asked me for more ballads to make a third volume."[17] Gerhardt was not the only German to be fooled by *La Guzla;* among the others was a young professor, Leopold Ranke, later to become a famous historian, who in his *History of the Serbian Revolution* (1829) cited Mérimée's "Les Pobratini" as a faithful picture of Serbian customs.[18]

The only German who seems not to have fallen victim to Mérimée's hoax was the great Goethe who on March 28 in an article for the magazine *Über Kunst und Altertum* (*Art and Antiq-*

uity) pointed out that in the word *Guzla* the word *Gazul* was hiding, and concluded: "M. Mérimée will not object, therefore, if we declare him to be the author of *La Guzla,* and if we seek to know, for our pleasure, all the clandestine children which it will please him thus to produce." Mérimée, while grateful to Goethe for his article, could not conceal his resentment for Goethe's taking credit for piercing the true identity of the author: "What lessens his merit at guessing the author of *La Guzla* is that I had sent him a copy, with signature and dedication, by a Russian passing through Weimar. He put on the gloves of discovery in order to show himself more shrewd." [19]

Even more striking was the success of Mérimée's hoax in England. As Mérimée wrote in the *Avertissement* for the 1842 edition, "Two months after the publication of *La Guzla,* Mr. Bowring, author of a Slav anthology, wrote me to ask for the original verses which I had so well translated." Since Mérimée, probably on the advice of Stendhal, had sent review copies to various English periodicals, as early as November, 1827, the influential *Monthly Review* gave him a twelve-page article, solemnly discussing the preface and the biography of Hyacinthe Maglanovitch, quoting in prose translation "Le Chant de mort," "Les Braves Heiduques" and the first part of "Hadagny," and in verse the "Barcarolle," and paying homage to the extreme modesty of the French "translator." Yovanovitch gives us also the article of June, 1828, by Thomas Keightley in the *Foreign Quarterly Review* which contains the biography of Maglanovich, translates "L'Aubépine de Veliko," and goes into dithyrambic praise over "Les Braves Heydukes": "We do not hesitate to consider it one of the greatest efforts of the greatest poet that the world has ever known." Especially interesting to the English reviewer were the ballads on vampirism and the "evil eye."

Finally in the *Avertissement* Mérimée chuckled over the fact that Pushkin "translated into Russian several of my little stories and that is comparable to *Gil Blas* translated into Spanish and the *Lettres d'une religieuse portugaise* translated into Portuguese." We recall the famous letter Mérimée wrote to Sobolevsky and particularly his apology to Pushkin: "Make my apologies to M. Pushkin; I am proud and at the same time ashamed of having taken him in." Even after having learned the fictitious character of Hyacinthe Maglanovich, Pushkin, reprinting the "Notice" of

Mérimée, wrote: "I do not know whether Maglanovich ever existed. Whatever the case may be, the writing of his biography has an extraordinary charm of originality and resemblance." But Pushkin was not the only Slav to have been duped by Mérimée's hoax. Yovanovitch reminds us that three years before, a young Polish poet who was later to teach Slavic languages at the Collège de France, Alexandre Chodzko, had translated three of Mérimée's ballads into Polish verse and at the same time the famous author Mickiewicz translated "Le Morlaque à Venise."

XIII *Evaluation*

Ever since the massive documentation of Mérimée's borrowings in Yovanovitch's scholarly dissertation, it has been impossible to see in *La Guzla* an accurate interpretation of Serbian customs and folklore. In his Introduction to this study, Filon, one of the earliest and most devoted writers on Mérimée, poses the question: has the former done Mérimée's reputation an ill-service by this work? His answer is a vigorous negative, for he feels that Yovanovitch "has rendered a distinguished service to our author by confronting his material with his work, and that no one, before him, had so well exposed the incomparable talent with which the great artist transformed material often poor in itself"; he cites, for instance, "L'Aubépine de Veliko" taken from a cold Chinese apologue and an even colder tragedy of Voltaire and transformed by Mérimée into a true masterpiece whose emotion seizes us by the throat.[20]

Admitting that *La Guzla* is not truly one of Mérimée's great works, Yovanovitch nevertheless insists on its considerable influence over the evolution of Romantic exoticism and its gradual transformation into contemporary realistic exoticism.[21] Among later "mystifications" based on Serbian poetry after publication of *La Guzla,* an expert on Claude Fauriel, M. Ibrovac, mentions *L'Uscoque* of George Sand, *Les Monténégrins* a play by Nerval, *Yanko le Bandit* of Théophile Gautier, and François Coppée's drama *Pour la couronne.* Yet in view of the fact that popular reception of *La Guzla* in France, in spite of favorable critical notices, was even slighter than that of *Le Théâtre de Clara Gazul,* I feel inclined to agree with Trahard who finds Yovanovitch's claims for the influence of *La Guzla* excessive.[22]

Mérimée contributed more than anyone else to the initial lack of esteem for *La Guzla.* As early as 1831 he called it "une drogue

et une vieillerie" (worthless and old-fashioned) and in his preface
for the 1842 edition he concluded sarcastically: "Strengthened by
the testimony of Messrs Bowring, Gerhardt and Pushkin, I could
boast of having created *local color;* but the process was so simple,
so easy that I came to doubt the merit of *local color* itself and I
forgave Racine for having polished the savage heroes of Sophocles
and Euripides." We must not forget, however, that Mérimée had
long since broken with his Romantic colleagues and that this
scornful appreciation is far from reflecting his real infatuation
with Romantic legends and primitive folklore at the time of composition. If *La Guzla* is inferior as a work of art to some of his
plays, which enjoy renewed popularity in our own day, nevertheless the student of Mérimée will find it full of dramatic action,
terrifying realism, vivid colors, simple but picturesque characters
—all this expressed in a style which is nervous, concise, lucid, here
and there impregnated with tender emotion all the more poignant
because of the cold objectivity of the author. These characteris-
tics, adumbrated in this early work by a youth of twenty-four
years, we shall find again soon in the more mature productions of
our writer.

CHAPTER 4

Historical Fiction

I Background sources for La Jaquerie

WE recall that in 1827 Mérimée had been fascinated by the
success in Paris of the visiting Shakespearean actors. Trahard has carefully documented all the influences which led to *La
Jaquerie*. Mérimée himself mentions Froissart in his short *Préface*,
though seeming to reduce the importance of this influence when
he writes: "In Froissart one finds only a few details and much
partiality." From Froissart, however, Mérimée borrowed not only
many details from Froissart's four short chapters on the peasant
uprising of the Jaquerie but also from his entire work.[1] Equally
important, perhaps, was the influence exerted on Mérimée by his
fondness for Shakespeare and Sir Walter Scott, whose Waverly
novels were so popular in France at this time. To Scott Mérimée
owes much of the picturesque color of his scenes—costumes,
armor, and Romantic setting.[2] Hesitating between the manner of
Scott and of Shakespeare and full of admiration for the latter's
historical plays—*King John, Richard III, Henry IV,* and *Henry
VI*—Mérimée borrows from them his structure and his use of the
chronicle in dialogue form.[3] In the second part of *Henry VI*
Shakespeare shows us an English *jaquerie* or peasant rebellion led
by Jack Cade; Trahard goes so far as to call *La Jaquerie* "an exact
but pale copy of the second part of *Henry VI*." Because of its
many melodramatic touches, Trahard sums up this work of
Mérimée as a sort of *Quentin Durward*, arranged in the manner
of Shakespeare according to the procedure of Pixérécourt, owing
something also to Goethe's medieval drama, *Goetz von Berlichin-
gen*, which also includes a peasant revolt.[4]

II The Narrative

As the curtain rises on the first scene in the forest, Le Loup-
Garou (Werewolf) and his fellow brigands are receiving a new

recruit into their band, which is pledged to attack lords, gendarmes, and monks, with the single exception of Friar Jean. The scene changes to a Gothic hall in the abbey of Saint-Lenfroy, lighted by torches, where the chapter has gathered to elect an abbott. Though they recognize the leadership qualities of Friar Jean, they are persuaded by a letter from their feudal lord, Gilbert d'Apremont, to choose his cousin, Frère Honoré, a pious ignoramus. Transported now to the Gothic hall of the castle, we observe the contempt of nobles for vassals which underlies the approaching revolt of Jacques Bonhomme, as peasants were called (origin of the name Jacquerie, or Jaquerie as Mérimée writes it, given to the rebellion).

Conrad, son of Lord Gilbert d'Apremont who delights in beating peasants with his stick, rejoices the next feast day at the spectacle of the hanging of Girart, seized by Gilbert in the abbey where he had sought sanctuary. The greater sensibility and gentleness of his sister Isabelle are evidenced by her unsuccessful plea to have her father spare a poor village woman unable to pay her feudal taxes. A group of English cavalry under Siwart attempts to capture Gilbert and Isabelle, who is saved by the intervention of her valet Pierre and of Friar Jean, but when the peasants retake the cattle which the English were driving off, the wicked seneschal seizes most of them for his master. Simon's wife, eight months pregnant, forced to work by the seneschal, dies with her unborn child from a kick the seneschal has given her in the stomach.

Friar Jean, horrified by this oppression of the peasants, resigns from the abbey and puts himself at the head of the revolt, which is joined by Le Loup-Garou and his outlaw band. Pierre, the savior of Isabelle, is angrily dismissed from her service when she realizes that he, a mere commoner, is in love with her. He joins the revolt. Renaud, brother of the murdered woman, kills the seneschal in revenge, then gives himself up at the castle to prevent indiscriminate slaughter of the villagers in retaliation. As he is about to be hanged on the village square, the peasants, armed by Friar Jean and joined by the bandit troop to rescue Renaud, kill Conrad, and drive Gilbert back into his castle, taking prisoner the Englishman Siwart, who is only too glad to put his English archers at their service. Le Loup-Garou and his bandits enter the abbey, kill the abbot Honoré, seize the treasure, and hold the rest of the eighty-two monks for ransom. Thanks partly to disagreement concerning tactics among the nobles, their army is ambushed by the peasants and the English archers, whose arrows take as deadly toll of the mounted knights as previously at the battle of Poitiers. In the nearby city of Beauvais the humble workmen, long oppressed by the rich burghers, seize control and offer the keys of the city to the uprising. In the castle, d'Apremont though wounded bravely refuses to surrender, but when he tries to escape into the forest with Isabelle he is killed by an arrow, and Isabelle is captured by Siwart. After being violated by him she insists on having a priest unite them in marriage to save her virtue, then plans to depart to a convent, leaving him all her lands as a dowry.

Now dissension begins to spread among the insurrectionists. Pierre, furious at learning what Siwart has done, tries to attack him but is killed by Le Loup-Garou. The peasants, anxious to return to their fields, grumble at the order of their leader, Friar Jean, to march on Meaux. Emissaries of the Duke of Normandy arrive, promising to grant all the demands of the peasants and proposing a truce, eagerly accepted by the peasants. Siwart and his English companions, learning that the *captal* de Busch has raised a large army to put down the rebellion, change sides once more. After a disastrous battle, Le Loup-Garou decides to flee with his remaining bandits. The peasants, reproaching Friar Jean bitterly for having led them into this danger, kill him with an arrow from the rear, then flee with the cry "Sauve qui peut" as they are attacked by the gendarmes of the king. The "jaquerie" is over.

III   *Evaluation of La Jaquerie*

If this résumé leaves an impression of confusion and lack of unity and connection among its various scenes and characters, it is because *La Jaquerie* itself makes this impression on the reader. Yet this adverse criticism to be valid would rest upon the assumption, based perhaps on Mérimée's own characterization of the book as "a Romantic tragedy," that *La Jaquerie* is a drama. Trahard is misled, I believe, when he says it proceeds directly from *Le Théâtre de Clara Gazul*, in relation to which it represents a step backward.[5] On the contrary, we should keep in mind

Mérimée's subtitle, *Scènes féodales*. It is obvious that unlike the
plays of his *Théâtre*, several of which as we have seen have been
successful on the stage, *La Jaquerie* was written with no dramatic
purpose in mind but only to be read under the lamp like a novel.
Mérimée's aim was not the creation of unified action or carefully
delineated characters as in a drama, but a broad picture of feudal
customs at a time when the feudal system was beginning to decay.

If modern criticism has shown some of the historical details to
be inexact, this is a criticism which can be leveled at all historical
fiction of the French Romantics, whether it be that of Vigny,
Hugo, or Dumas père. It may be true as Trahard has claimed that
Mérimée seeks to achieve a spurious "local color" by inserting 97
words and 43 oaths borrowed from the Middle Ages, and that he
resembles Pixérécourt in his fondness for melodrama—19 murders
in addition to the mass carnage of several battles.[6] Yet Trahard is
too harsh, I think, when he states that the reader, in spite of realistic and truthful details, is left with the general impression of falsification of the truth and a feeling of boredom.[7] *This* reader at
least never felt his interest waver at this picturesque evocation of
medieval chivalry in its decline. Cruel and bloody as it may be at
times, I am inclined to believe Mérimée's assertion in his *Préface:*
"I have tried to give some idea of the atrocious customs of the
fourteenth century, and I think I have rather softened than dark-
ened the colors of my picture."

The chief adverse criticism often made against *La Jaquerie* is
that Mérimée, far from being impartial, leans heavily in favor of
the peasants. It is true that Mérimée in his *Préface* protests
against the partiality shown by Froissart in favor of the nobles. To
some extent this attitude of Mérimée has contemporary political
overtones, for *La Jaquerie* was written at a time when French
Liberals were reacting against the Conservative monarchy of the
Bourbon, Charles X, soon to be overthrown. In addition to his
sympathy for underdog and victim, it was only natural for the
Liberal Mérimée to place himself on the side of the insurrection
against the oppression of church and state. Yet we should remember that even here Mérimée retains a certain balance. Besides the
lack of gratitude shown by the peasants for their benefactor, Friar
Jean, even among the nobles Mérimée gives us as his two principal protagonists a wounded Gilbert d'Apremont heroic in his
preference for death rather than surrender, and his daughter Isa-

belle, who despite her aristocratic prejudices is warmhearted and commiserates with the poor.

In his admirable introduction to his edition of *La Jaquerie*, M. Marsan was perhaps the first to recognize the progress Mérimée has made here in his transition from historical drama toward his later fiction. "We find in *La Jaquerie* as it were the points of bearing or of culmination of a vast novel. . . . It is in truth a historical novel in dialogue form." Yet Marsan in his effort to rehabilitate the reputation of *La Jaquerie*—so long unjustly under a cloud, little appreciated by its contemporaries including strangely enough Stendhal—goes too far, I believe, when he places it above its successor, the *Chronique du règne de Charles IX*, partly because Mérimée has avoided here the temptation to bring in great historical personages.[8] (But the same tendency in the main we shall find in the *Chronique*.) *La Jaquerie*, picturesque and colorful as it may be, is too scattered and confused to rank as a true masterpiece; its interest for the modern reader is primarily that of apprentice work leading by a natural transition to Mérimée's first and only attempt at the historical novel in his *Chronique* the following year.

IV *Background and Sources for the Chronique*

Mérimée, for whom the sixteenth century was always one of his favorite epochs, tells us in his *Préface* the source of his inspiration for the *Chronique du règne de Charles IX*, his longest work. "I had just read a great number of memoirs and pamphlets relating to the end of the sixteenth century. I wanted to make an excerpt from these readings, and here is this excerpt." Among these he mentions with others Montluc, Brantôme, D'Aubigné, and La Noue. Martineau has pointed out also that the Liberal and anticlerical nature of Mérimée was bound to observe a striking similarity between this period of the Ligue and the Guises with the pretensions of the ultra-Conservatives in the closing days of the reign of Charles IX, though he adds that Mérimée's novel is in no wise intended as a political pamphlet.[9] In addition to these literary sources, one must include another purely personal inspiration for Mérimée's narrative, his love affair with Mme Lacoste already discussed. As we have seen, Emilie Lacoste was the model for his heroine, Countess Diane de Turgis, the devout Catholic whose endeavors to convert her lover Mergy paralleled the efforts of

Mérimée's own mistress to combat his agnosticism. Like his hero, Mérimée had also been wounded in a duel over his mistress, as we have noted.

V   The Plot of the Chronique

Bernard Mergy, a young Protestant gentleman on his way to Paris, encounters in the hotel near Etampes a group of German cavalry commanded by the famous Dietrich Hornstein, a veteran of many campaigns under Coligny the Huguenot leader. The soldiers are accompanied by two attractive young women, one of whom, the soothsayer Mila, predicts from a reading of Mergy's palm that he will have happiness and unhappiness and that he will shed his own blood. Awaking on the morrow, Mergy discovers with disgust that the Germans have gone, leaving him in place of his noble steed a broken-down nag and but two of the 25 gold pieces he had had in his purse. Fortunately on his entrance into Paris he encounters in a group of gay young blades his beloved brother George, who to the great sorrow of his stern Huguenot parents had embraced the Catholic cause, not from any profound religious convictions, but merely to make his way at court. He had gained thereby a position as captain in the royal *chevau-légers*. Provided by his brother with a new mount, money, and lodging, Mergy enters the service of Admiral Coligny (under whom his father had been a courageous fighter), falls in love at first sight with the attractive young countess, Diane de Turgis, awkwardly allows the professional duelist Comminges to push him aside as he is about to pick up the glove Diane had dropped, and then is persuaded by his newfound friends that he must challenge this redoubtable adversary to a duel on the following day.

Before the duel occurs, both Mergy and the hated Comminges accompany Diane on the royal hunt; Diane makes it clear by her dismissal of Comminges that she favors Mergy, to whom she sends a sacred relic to hang around his neck for protection in the coming duel. A thrust from Comminges which would have been fatal to Mergy was turned aside as it met this gold relic, leaving only a glancing wound in the shoulder. Before Comminges had time to withdraw his sword Mergy was able to pierce his skull with his poignard. Recovered from his wound as a result of ministrations of the famous surgeon, Ambroise Paré, Mergy soon succeeds in making Countess Diane his adoring mistress since she feels absolved from guilt by her pious design for converting her lover to the true faith.

The central episode in the book, the massacre of Saint Bartholomew's Eve, now approaches. George, indignant on learning that his company has been ordered to take part in the massacre, renounces his command and tries to warn his brother. Mergy, on his way to his nightly rendezvous at the home of the Countess, encounters many soldiers en route to what they call "le divertissement" at the Louvre. He also meets George's friend Béville who tries to hide his martial accouterments and warns Mergy "to cross over the Seine before midnight." Heedless of the warning, Mergy proceeds to his rendezvous, where he is joined by his brother just before the outbreak of the bloodshed and terror begins. Fortunately, the home of the pious Diane is above suspicion and with some difficulty she persuades Mergy not to rush out to certain and useless death.

A few days later occurs the amusing confrontation of Mergy and Captain Hornstein, both disguised as monks as they await the ferry at Beaugency on their way to the Huguenot stronghold of La Rochelle, which is soon to be besieged by the royal army of Catholics, including George. La Noue, the great Huguenot general and friend of the murdered Admiral Coligny, has been sent by the king to urge the defenders to surrender, but he decides instead to take command of his fellow religionists. In a successful sortie Mergy gives the command to fire on the leader of a Catholic detachment coming as reinforcement and to his horror learns that the man brought down mortally wounded is his own brother George. The prediction of the sorcerer Mila has alas come true. As George is embraced with poignant despair by his brother, his last words are "Mme de Turgis has charged me to tell you that she still loves you." At this point, Mérimée breaks off his narrative with a quizzical, offhanded indifference we shall meet again in many of his short stories: "Did Mergy become consoled? Did Diane take another lover? I leave this to the decision of the reader, who thus can always end the story to his own liking."

VI *Evaluation of the Chronique*

"In history I care only for anecdotes, among which I prefer those in which I imagine I find a true painting of the customs and characters at a given period," Mérimée remarks in his *Préface*.

What a contrast to the idealistic philosophy of a Vigny, with his fondness for abstract symbols and his disdain for historical accuracy! Mérimée is indeed at the opposite pole from Vigny's *Cinq-Mars* in his cold objectivity and impartiality. In this rapid, fascinating evocation of the events leading up to the massacre of Saint Bartholomew's Eve, Mérimée remains ever the impressive bystander, excoriating in equal measure the somber asceticism of the Huguenots and the naïve superstitions of the Catholics. The astonishing realism of this story comes indeed from this very fact; we feel that it is a cross-section of the age, presented primarily as a picture with no intention of illustrating any theory of the author.

Yet it would be incorrect to infer from this that Mérimée feels no revulsion against the fanaticism of this massacre, or that he does not have his own interpretation of the events he describes so vividly. In the *Préface* he tells us that he is convinced, from a careful analysis of historical sources, that the massacre was not a carefully planned, deep-laid conspiracy of the king but rather an almost spontaneous uprising of the bourgeois of Paris, goaded into fury by the threats and urging of the Guises. Filon has pointed out that Mérimée does not follow this interpretation in the novel, in which Charles IX seems to represent the incarnation of cruel villainy and secret cunning.[10] But Filon has perhaps exaggerated this disparity between the *Préface* and the actual conduct as presented in the novel; Mérimée had himself pointed out that the earlier attempt on Coligny's life at the instigation of the king proved the lack of conspiracy at that time for the general massacre of the Huguenots who were put on guard by this attack. In any case, we are disarmed by the indifference which Mérimée holds for his own interpretation since he ends his *Préface* with a mocking smile, in the words of Lord Byron: "I only say, suppose this supposition." Abhorring the naïve enthusiasm of the polemist, Mérimée always retains the casual tone of the skeptic, the well-bred gentleman.

Significant likewise is the contrast between Vigny and Mérimée in their choice of character. Mérimée is closer to Scott than to Vigny in his method of introducing historical personages chiefly as background, reserving his romantic interest exclusively for fictitious characters of his own invention. That this technique is not accidental but carefully planned is evident from the famous Chapter VIII with its flippant "Dialogue between reader and author" in which Mérimée seems to be satirizing not only Vigny's penchant for historical portraits but also the long-drawn-out settings of Sir Walter Scott.

Ah, sir author, what a fine chance you now have to make some portraits for us. And what portraits! You are going to take us to the Château of Madrid, in the midst of the court. And what a court! You are going to show it to us, this Franco-Italian court? Show us one after another all the historical personages who are distinguished in it, How many things we are going to learn! and how interesting must be a day spent in the midst of so many great personages!

Alas, sir reader, what do you demand of me? I wish I had the talent to write a History of France; then I wouldn't relate stories. But tell me, why do you want me to introduce you to people who are to play no rôle in my novel?

But you are quite wrong in not having them play a rôle. What! you carry me back to the year 1572 and you intend to skip the portraits of so many important men. Come now, no hesitation. Begin; I'll give you the first sentence: *The door of the salon opened and one saw appear . . .*

But, sir reader, there wasn't any *salon* in the Château of Madrid.

And the airy persiflage of the author continues in a similar vein for several pages in which he refers those interested in the appearance of Charles IX to the latter's bust, number 98, in the Angoulême museum, depicts Catherine de Médicis as a fat, sleepy woman with a big nose and lips puckered up as if by seasickness, and avoids entirely a portrait of Marguerite, since the latter "was a little indisposed that day and kept to her room." Yet the reader should be on guard against taking this amusing badinage too literally. It is true indeed that we have no further mention of the sinister queen mother, that Coligny's murder on Saint Bartholomew's Eve is scarcely mentioned, and that the Guises never even appear. Nevertheless, in the portrait of La Noue, the indomitable old commander of La Rochelle, in the scene at the residence of Coligny, and in the attempt of Charles IX to persuade George to murder the Admiral, we have glimpses of historical personages which contribute powerfully to the atmosphere of reality.

The *Chronique,* although the longest of Mérimée's fiction works, is still one of the briefest of historical novels. It is likely that its continued popularity comes partly from this fact, together with its swift action, stirring adventures, and abundance of bloodshed.

Whereas Vigny's *Cinq-Mars* had contained a number of nature descriptions, in Mérimée this poetic quality is almost entirely absent. On the tragic eve of the massacre we learn only that "the night was beautiful, a gentle zephyr had tempered the heat; the moon appeared and disappeared in the midst of light, white clouds. It was a night made for love." The reader of Hugo cannot fail to be struck by the simplicity of this passage. The only other reference to the world of nature in the entire novel is a description, excellent of its kind, of the fog and rain which concealed the sortie of the soldiers from La Rochelle.

Almost equally concise and restrained is the description of the court, Paris, and the life of the period. Although the book gives us an uncanny feeling of acquaintance with the times, it seems to be almost entirely in dialogue and action rather than in description. While the subject matter—the passionate love affair of Bernard Mergy with Diane and the frenzied horror of the massacre—is highly Romantic, the sobriety of style is almost Classical in its pellucid simplicity. In this connection Trahard has shrewdly pointed out the influence of the eighteenth-century *Jacques le fataliste* and *La Religieuse* of Diderot on Mérimée's style and particularly on his dialogue with the reader.[11] It is not by elaborate descriptions but by picturesque flashes and revealing anecdotes that Mérimée gives us the sensation of real life. Among the former the most vivid are the meeting of Mergy with Hornstein and his motley crew of *reîtres*, the eyewitness account of the massacre, and the capture of the bastion of La Rochelle; among the latter, the haunting silhouette of Charles IX at his window in the Louvre, sniping at the Huguenot fugitives with his crossbow, or the tragically cruel episode of the Catholic knight at La Rochelle, caught on the window ledge and burned to death as he hung suspended in full armor.

Another reason for the popularity of the *Chronique* is its abundance of wit and humor. Terrible as the religious wars may appear, Mérimée has relieved his somber pages by passages of brilliant mockery in the best Gallic tradition, such as the satirical account of the Catholic sermon in which Père Lubin wins the wager that he will not dare use four oaths in his address, or the confrontation of the two make-believe monks at the inn where each is trying to get the other to pronounce the benediction which neither one knows. There is a constant source of irony in the action of the austere Huguenot Mergy, faithfully attending mass to be near his sweetheart, and in Diane's excuse that though she is commiting mortal sin in her passion for Mergy she may achieve absolution by winning him over to the Catholic faith. Sometimes, however, Mérimée's humor becomes a little grim for the average taste, as for instance the manner in which Béville cancels his debt with the Huguenot moneylender or the squabble between priest and minister for George's soul on the latter's deathbed. From Mérimée's correspondence we now know that he was not really the cold-blooded cynic he showed to the world but a man of tender feeling and kindly benevolence. The only outlet he ever allowed himself for his emotion was restrained irony, and it is by reading between the lines in these grim and ghastly passages that we can detect Mérimée's own horror of injustice and fanaticism.

To some readers the harrowing scenes of the *Chronique* will seem all the more moving because of their almost callous tone, reminiscent of Hamilton and the sophisticated gentlemen of the eighteenth century. The choice of the colorless title, *Chronicle,* is of course typical of Mérimée in this respect, as well as the conclusion, to be paralleled in some of his later short stories, in which he almost contemptuously invites the reader to finish the story for himself. To others, the impartiality with which Mérimée satirizes Catholics and Protestants alike, imparts a certain coldness and cynical indifference to the novel. So well indeed has Mérimée preserved his urbane serenity amidst the shocking cruelties of both sides that it is dangerous to ascribe his preference to either faction. There is one character, however, George the agnostic, happy-go-lucky, daredevil brother of the hero, sharing the dogmatic beliefs of neither side and dying with serene indifference to the fanaticism of priest and minister, who seems to typify more than any other character the ideal of the author.

Except for the unsatisfactory denouement and the lack of unity in these somewhat disparate and disconnected episodes—a criticism which Mérimée has largely avoided by terming his story not a novel but a chronicle of the period—the chief criticism which has been directed at the *Chronique* has been certain historical inaccuracies. It may be, as Trahard has pointed out, that the picture it gives is more appropriate to the early years of the following century than to that of 1572,[12] that rapiers did not appear until the

seventeenth century, that hunting swords rather than hunting
knives were used in the sixteenth century, and that it was the left
arm of La Noue rather than the right which had been replaced by
an iron cramp. For most readers such errors will seem venial indeed, and posterity has been kinder to Mérimée than his own
pejorative appreciation of his work, when he wrote to his friend
Albert Stapfer December 16, 1828, "I'm making a poor novel
which bores me." More perspicacious was the judgment of Sainte-
Beuve, expressed in a letter to a friend, April 23, 1829: "Mérimée,
author of *Clara Gazul* and who is one of my very great friends,
has published a charming book, half-novel, half-chronicle, on the
court of Charles IX in 1572." [13]

Marsan, as we have seen, is the only critic who judges the
Chronique inferior in artistry to the earlier *Jaquerie*. Even the
generally hostile Trahard observes great progress here over the
earlier book and perceptively points out the influence it will exert
over historical-realistic novels toward the end of the century, such
as *Les Dieux ont soif* of Anatole France.[14] Raitt reminds us that
Walter Pater called the *Chronique* "Mérimée's one quite cheerful
book"—he must have forgotten *Le Carrosse* and some of Mérimée's short stories such as *L'Abbé Aubain* and even *Colomba*
—and Raitt concludes, while quite rightfully refusing to place it
among the very greatest novels of Balzac, Stendhal, and Flaubert,
"it remains nevertheless one of the outstanding successes of its
notoriously difficult genre and by its keen observation and telling
use of detail it looks forward both to mid-century realism and to
Mérimée's own later distinction as a historian." [15] Most critics
agree that the *Chronique* should be classed at least as the last and
best apprentice work of Mérimée and in Martineau's words, "of a
workman who is on the point of becoming a master." [16] I am
tempted to go a step further and suggest that the *Chronique* in
some respects marks the beginning of Mérimée's masterworks.
We may well regret that henceforth Mérimée was to abandon the
historical novel for history, attacking severely his former master
Sir Walter Scott; the *Chronique* has maintained its popularity and
has perhaps more readers today than in its own time.

CHAPTER 5

Maturity: 1829-1853

I *First Trip to Spain*

IN a letter of December 16, 1828, to his friend Albert Stapfer Mérimée wrote: "I am working to a degree which is extraordinary not only for a lazy person like me but even for a man of letters. God willing, I shall blacken a lot of paper in 1829." [1] This prophecy was magnificently fulfilled. Not only did Mérimée write during this productive year three Illyrian ballads to be included in later editions of *La Guzla,* two of his most significant plays (*L'Occasion* and *Le Carrosse du Saint-Sacrement*), but also most of the remarkable short stories to be combined later in *Mosaïque.*

In the midst of his creative vigor in the years 1829–30, Mérimée conceived the idea of a trip to his favorite country, Spain. The direct motivation for this decision seems to have been an unhappy love affair, as we learn from a letter he wrote two years later to Jenny Dacquin.

I was about to fall in love when I left for Spain. This is one of the good actions of my life. The person who caused my trip never knew anything about it. If I had remained, I should perhaps have committed a great stupidity: that of offering a woman worthy of every happiness one can enjoy on earth, of offering her, I say, in exchange for the loss of all the things which were dear to her an affection which I myself felt very inferior to the sacrifice that she would perhaps have made. You remember my motto: "Love excuses everything," but one must be really sure that it is love.[2]

The identity of this woman has aroused much speculation among critics. Raitt has made a strong and I think unassailable case for Mélanie Double, daughter of Dr. François-Joseph Double.[3] Because of the great financial gulf between this family and Mérimée's, discreet soundings in regard to an engagement had a negative result, for the doctor wanted assurances of a stable position in society and considerable wealth for his daughter. Mérimée could have eloped with Mélanie, but with great suffering he renounced this alternative, which explains his statement just quoted that this should count as one of the good actions of his life. Our interest in Mélanie is enhanced by the fact that twenty years later Mérimée was to come gallantly to the defense of her second husband, the notorious M. Libri.

Realizing the struggle going on in Mérimée's heart, his parents got together enough funds for his trip to Spain, made possible by Léonor's invention of cartridge paper for the navy. Prosper left Paris June 25, 1830, for a three-month trip, prolonged for six months, partly perhaps because of the July Revolution in France. To please his father he spent some time in museums doing research on Spanish painting and copying works by Velásquez, Goya, and Murillo. Most of his time, however, was spent crisscrossing Spain, making the acquaintance of picturesque types of the lower classes—gypsies, smugglers, bull fighters, and the like. He sent back four Letters to the *Revue de Paris*, later included in *Mosaïque;* the first, dated October 25 from Madrid, gives a vivid account of his first attendance at a bullfight, at which he felt more enthusiasm for the bull than for its tormentors; the second, dated Valencia November 15, a realistic and gruesome description of an execution he had witnessed. To his disappointment, he did not meet any bandits but in his third letter, dated Madrid, November, he related anecdotes he had heard about the famous José Maria, the Robin Hood of Spain and destined to be the prototype later for the Don Garcie of his *Carmen*. The fourth letter from Valencia also dated November is a fascinating series of anecdotes concerning Spanish sorcerers. Trahard has pointed out that the story of the wedding of Andujar was later utilized by Mérimée in his *Vénus d'Ille*. On one occasion Mérimée persuaded his guide, much against his will, to enter a little inn where they were served cool water and *gazpacho* by an attractive dark-skinned beauty called *Carmencita* whose portrait he sketched and who later became the inspiration for his Carmen.

But the most important event of Mérimée's stay in Spain was his encounter in a stagecoach with a middle-aged aristocrat, Count de Teba, who had lost an eye and suffered wounds in his right leg and left arm in the service of Napoleon. Returning in 1830 from exile because of his Liberal opinions, this gentleman was so taken with Mérimée that he invited him to his home in Madrid to meet his wife, Manuela, a lovely woman of mixed Belgian (Walloon) and Scottish descent, and their two children, Francesca (Paca) and Eugenia, aged five and four, respectively. Soon Mérimée became a great favorite of these children, giving them French lessons and riding them playfully on his back. Little did he realize that his friendship with the Countess de Teba, later the Countess de Montijo on the death of her brother-in-law, was to endure throughout his life, and that one day he would see his little pupil Eugenia become empress of the French. The countess was a delightful storyteller, relating among others the tale of a Gypsy girl stabbed to death in Málaga by a jealous lover—the foundation later for Mérimée's *Carmen*. To her he owed also his historical account of Pedro I, and perhaps, according to Trahard, his *Ames du Purgatoire*.[4]

II   *Civil Servant and Man-About-Town 1831–34*

Soon after Mérimée returned from Spain, he was called for duty in the National Guard, summoned to quell the disturbances which occurred during the trial of Charles X's ministers. Here in the fourth artillery battery, called the "Killer" because it contained so many doctors, he made the acquaintance of Alexandre Dumas. With characteristic irony Mérimée wrote to a friend, December 29, 1831: "You have probably learned how I . . . saved the fatherland, last Wednesday, from five or six hundred street urchins, most of them pastry cooks and hunchbacks, who wanted to turn it into a republic. As the price of my heroism I caught a cold like ten wolves and I have a nose as big as a cucumber, but of a very different color."[5]

The change to the constitutional monarchy of Louis Philippe brought with it promotion for all the Liberal dissenters of the previous regime, among them Mérimée's friends Stendhal, Baron de Mareste, and Lenormant. Mérimée had previously refused the offer of Mme Récamier in 1829 to have him appointed embassy secretary in London. His father was growing old, and though he had always hoped to see his son enter the diplomatic service he was delighted when Prosper took a position as secretary to Stendhal's friend, Count d'Argout, thereby interrupting his literary career for civil service "where he will acquire new ideas that will later serve him in good stead." Mérimée's promotion was rapid:

February 6, 1831, he became bureau chief in d'Argout's Ministry of Marine, in March cabinet chief, and in May he received the cross of the Legion of Honor. In March, 1832, he followed d'Argout to the Commerce Ministry and to that of the Interior in December of the same year. During the terrible cholera epidemic of 1832 Mérimée was appointed special commissioner in charge of sanitary measures and showed great courage in visiting the patients in the hospitals.

Though he performed his duties with conscientious efficiency, Mérimée was bored and depressed by the monotony of civil administration. He sought relief in dissipation along with such cronies as the painter Delacroix, Musset, Hoffmann's friend the German Jew Dr. Koreff, Baron de Mareste, Stendhal when on leave in Paris from Civitavecchia, and the English lawyer Sutton Sharpe, who spent in two months of riotous living in Paris the amount he had earned in ten months of brilliant law practice in London. Among Mérimée's acquaintances in the group of chorus girls of the opera and music hall there was one, Céline Cayot, who remained his mistress until 1836 and was the model for his appealing heroine in *Arsène Guillot*. Concerning this period so barren of literary activity except for his short novel *La Double Méprise* (1833) and *Les Ames du Purgatoire* (1834), Mérimée was to write later:

The strange thing in my life is that, having become a great scamp I lived for two years on the good reputation I had before, and that, now that I am very moral again, people still take me for a scamp. The truth is that I don't think I was one for longer than three years, and I didn't do it from the heart, but solely out of sadness and perhaps out of curiosity.[6]

A fortuneteller had predicted that Mérimée would experience many misfortunes in 1833. This was indeed a most unhappy year for him. Early in the year he received the sad news of the death in India of his dear friend, the naturalist Victor Jacquemont, concerning whom he wrote a very moving essay. In April occurred his seriocomic liaison of one night with George Sand which ended in a fiasco though Raitt, unlike André Maurois, insists that she remained his mistress for several weeks before the affair ended in mutual recriminations and hostility.[7] She was writing *Lélia* at this time, before her passionate liaison with Musset, and Mérimée was composing *La Double Méprise* whose situation Raitt finds paralleling many aspects of this distressing "misunderstanding." This same year saw the deaths of an aunt and uncle and the breakup of the friendship between Hugo and Mérimée. On June 23 Mérimée told his friend Edouard Grasset: "A woman I loved has dismissed me and another that I loved still more has been taken from me." [8] It seems probable that the first was Mme Lacoste who broke off her liaison with Mérimée at this period, and the second may have been Mme Delessert, whom Mérimée had been courting for some time and whose long liaison with him beginning in 1836 will be discussed later. In any case, the entire direction of Mérimée's life was to be changed for the better by his appointment in 1834 as inspector general of historical monuments, but before discussing this new vocation let us consider the beginning of his lifelong friendship with the *Inconnue,* Jenny Dacquin.

III *Jenny Dacquin*

On October 31, 1831, Mérimée had received a very flattering letter, in English, from a person signing herself Lady Algernon Seymour, saying she had been greatly impressed by his *Chronique* and desired his autograph. Intrigued by this mystery, Mérimée responded, and a lively correspondence ensued. In the fall of 1832 Mérimée was in England again, entertained as usual by his friend Sutton Sharpe. Unable to arrange a meeting with the mysterious "Lady Seymour," he learned that he could receive further information from a Mme Lambert (or Mme Lemaire as Raitt calls her) in Calais where he stopped off on his return to France in January, 1833. Here he learned that she was not English but a young French girl named Jenny Dacquin, living with her mother in Boulogne-sur-mer. In a letter to Sutton Sharpe January 29, Mérimée shows himself greatly impressed at their first meeting. "We chatted; she had a very agreeable voice. We spoke of a hundred things. She seemed to me a little timid but witty. I saw then a very beautiful person about twenty years of age, brunette, with beautiful dark eyes à la French; admirable eyebrows, black hair etc. Add to that a foot like a finger in a satin slipper." He concluded this letter with the information that Jenny would come to Paris in a few months; "my virtue will then need to make many efforts to resist."

Thus began a correspondence and friendship destined to last thirty-seven years, for it was to her that Mérimée wrote his last letter only two hours before his death. She was a person of both charm and intelligence with whom Mérimée could discuss literature, politics, and the fine arts. In 1873 she decided to publish his letters, with an interesting preface by Taine, still keeping her identity a secret. According to Félix Chambon[9] the originals of Jenny's letters to Mérimée were probably burned by her instructions after her death in 1895. So well did she keep the secret of her identity that it was only in 1892 that her real name was revealed by a family friend. Born in Boulogne, November 25, 1811, as Jeanne-Françoise, she had early been a *dame de compagnie* to Lady MacDonald in England. Whether this long friendship with Mérimée was only a platonic one has intrigued critics to this day. To strengthen the affirmative we know that she was a woman of fine character who expected at first to lead Mérimée to the altar; his many letters expressing impatience and frustration would seem to indicate that she was unwilling to yield herself to him. The evidence for the contrary is equally convincing: why did she rearrange and delete his letters—we possess none for the period 1834-40—and have the originals burned at her death? What did Mérimée mean in his letter to her October 24, 1842 when he wrote: "We began to write each other making witticisms, then we did what? I shall not remind you of it." In any case this durable friendship in which Mérimée watched over her intellectual development, called on her for assistance in locating manuscripts and historical facts, and relied on her judgment and taste in regard to his writings, exerted a stabilizing and beneficent influence over his life for almost four decades.

IV *Inspector General of Historical Monuments*

In April, 1834, through a shuffle of ministries Thiers became minister of the interior and promptly appointed Mérimée to the new post of inspector general of historical monuments. This fortunate event changed the whole course of Mérimée's life. He wrote to his friend Sutton Sharpe in London: "Thiers has been very kind to me. . . . He is offering me the position of Inspector General of Historical Monuments. . . . It is wonderfully suited to my tastes, my indolence, my ideas of travel. Thus everything is for the best in the best of worlds." [10] Realizing that he had much to learn in the

two months before his trip of inspection, Mérimée studied
diligently everything he could find concerning archeology and architecture. All his life he had been interested in art and history;
his experience in governmental bureaus had taught him adminis-
trative procedure; and he already possessed qualities of diplo-
macy, patience, and capacity for hard and exacting work which
stood him in good stead in his new position.

Until the Romantic movement, architects and the general
public had felt only disdain for Gothic architecture, the very term
signifying "barbaric." Mérimée was soon to find the architectural
treasures of France in sorry state—partly because the Protestants
had destroyed so much in their fury against Catholicism, partly
because the terrorists during the French Revolution had vandal-
ized the churches, but even more because the state had transformed religious edifices for its own use (the Abbey of Saint
Michel into a prison, the Palace of the Popes into a barracks).
Even worse had been the restoration of medieval buildings by
municipalities and the clergy, painting over priceless friezes or
allowing the construction of buildings on the side of churches and
arches. For eighteen years Mérimée was to react against these
abuses: selecting the buildings to be classified as historical monuments, struggling with municipal and ecclesiastical authorities
and with the various ministries in Paris to obtain necessary funds
for restoration. In 1837 he became secretary of a new Commission
for Historical Monuments, which is still in existence today.

The energy which Mérimée gave to this new passion in his life
can be seen from the fact that his first inspection trip to the south
of France lasted from July to December 14, after which he left
almost at once for Fontevrault to make a report on the tomb and
remains of Richard the Lionhearted. Then for the next three
months beside his fire he worked diligently on the first of his long
reports, published the following summer, *Notes d'un voyage dans
le Midi de la France*. Similar trips followed in 1835 to Brittany
and the west of France and in 1836 to Alsace and eastern France.
With the aid of his friend and protégé the brilliant young architect Viollet-le-Duc, Mérimée succeeded by 1849 in classifying
four thousand structures as historical monuments and increasing
the funds from the state for their upkeep and restoration tenfold
during his administration.[11]

To sum up the contribution made by Mérimée during his long

career as inspector general, Filon quoted an anonymous art critic:
"If Victor Hugo had not written *Notre-Dame de Paris* and if
Mérimée had not organized the Commission of Historical Monuments, all of our old edifices would have been razed to construct
Madeleines and Bourses [Stock Exchanges]." [12] To Filon's list of
historical monuments whose preservation was owed to Mérimée
—Vézélay, the theaters of Orange and Arles, the churches of St.
Savin, St. Martin of Tours, and the cathedral of Lyon—Raitt has
added the following: the Palace of the Popes at Avignon; the ca-
thedrals of Laon and Strasbourg; the abbeys of St. Denis, Cher-
roux, and Fontgombault; and the castles of Blois and Chinon, besides the restoration of relics in such cities as Poitiers, Saintes,
Angers, Caen, Bourges, Loches, and Saumur. No one will dispute
P. Léon's tribute to Mérimée: "He deserved well of the France of
olden times; he has a right to the gratitude of France today." [13]

V   *Mme Delessert*

If Mérimée had broken off with Céline Cayot and "turned over
a new leaf" it was because he had met the great passion of his life,
one which was to last for almost a quarter of a century. Valentine,
daughter of Count Alexandre de Laborde, had married at eighteen Gabriel Delessert, son of a banker and twenty years older
than Valentine. He descended from an old Protestant family of
Lyon, and his gravity of temperament, combined with his ad-
vanced age, made the marriage an unhappy one. Valentine herself
was witty and gay, beautiful and full of coquetry, and possessed
of great intelligence and refined culture. Stendhal was to copy her
in his portrait of Mme Grandet in *Lucien Leuwen*, just as he was
to incorporate some features of his friend Mérimée in Lucien himself. [14] Mérimée had first met her in 1830 when invited to dinner at
her home and, fascinated by her combination of wit, coquetry and
beauty, began a courtship of six years, quite unusual for the Don
Juan nature he had shown up to this time.

Learning that her husband had been made prefect at Carcas-
sonne, Mérimée arranged to include this town in his first southern
journey of inspection, only to find that M. Delessert had been
transferred to Chartres as prefect of Eure-et-Loir. Since Chartres
was full of architectural treasures, Mérimée contrived visits to the
prefecture at New Year's 1835 and again the following summer
but it was not until February 16, 1836, that she finally became his

mistress. Every year thereafter he celebrated this anniversary by giving her precious gifts. As early as January 12 he had written his friend Requien in Avignon: "I am madly in love with this pearl of women, happy because I am loved, very unhappy because I cannot prove my love to her as often as I would like." [15] And to Stendhal he wrote on July 5: "I am greatly and profoundly in love." [16]

When M. Delessert was made prefect of police in Paris later in 1836, Mérimée became a frequent visitor to Valentine's salon, acting as unofficial "uncle" to her children Cécile and Edouard. Time lent to this relationship a sort of respectability. It is not clear why her husband permitted this liaison—was it blindness on his part, indifference, or confidence that Valentine's discretion would always avoid an open scandal? For many years Mérimée wrote only for her, presenting his stories first to her for approval and criticism —the result of which can be seen, for instance in the changes she suggested for his *Vénus d'Ille* in 1837 and his *Colomba* in 1840. If he lost interest in writing fiction after *L'Abbé Aubain* in 1846, the reason can be sought in the gradual dissolution of this liaison, though the final break, as we shall see, did not occur until 1853.

VI *Trip to Corsica*

On September 27, 1836, occurred the death of Mérimée's father, Léonor, at the age of seventy-nine. Anyone who has the false idea that Mérimée lacked affection and warmth should read the letters he wrote at this time expressing deep sorrow at his loss. One effect was to bring Mérimée even closer to his mother, with whom he lived until her death. It has been said that she was the only one he allowed to lay his fire, feeling that she alone knew how he liked to have it done. The presence of several cats, one of which she allowed to sleep on his feet to keep them warm, adds a further touch of bourgeois domesticity to this period of his life.

In July, 1835, his good friend the Countess de Montijo (formerly Countess de Teba) had arrived in Paris with her daughters Paca and Eugenia, now aged eleven and ten, respectively, in order to place them in convent boarding school the following autumn. The count's elder brother had died, leaving him a considerable fortune and the title Comte de Montijo. Mérimée devoted himself to the children, bringing them to shooting galleries and correcting their French accent. When Stendhal came to Paris on furlough in 1838 Mérimée introduced his friend to the Montijos, and Stendhal also became a great favorite with the children, telling them stories of the Napoleon he admired. When in 1839 the count's death recalled the Montijos to Spain, Mérimée was almost inconsolable at the girls' departure.

On August 15, 1839, Mérimée embarked from Toulon to Bastia on an official tour of investigation, anxious to see whether this Corsica which he had described from purely literary sources in his *Mateo Falcone* corresponded with reality. Here he spent seven weeks, disappointed by the absence of architectural monuments but fascinated by the picturesque customs and character of the people. As he wrote to his friend Requien, "What I liked best was pure nature . . . I mean the pure nature of Man who in these parts is a very curious mammal. . . . Here local color is almost as. common as fleas." [17] His most fortunate encounter was with the sixty-eight-year-old Colomba Bartoli who "excells in the manufacture of cartridges and manages very well to send them against people who have the misfortune to displease her" (an allusion to her vengeance on the Durazzo family for having killed her son). This lady had a lovely daughter, "a heroine also, . . . beautiful as Cupid, with hair falling to the ground, thirty-two pearls in her mouth, lips like the thunder of God, five feet three inches and who at the age of sixteen gave a most elegant thrashing to a workman of the opposing faction. She is called la Morgana and she is truly a fairy, for I am bewitched by her." [18] From a combination of these two ladies Mérimée was to create his immortal Colomba.

On October 7 Mérimée took a ship from Bastia to Leghorn, picking up Stendhal at Civitavecchia and departing with him for Rome, Naples, and Pompeii. He shared his friend's enthusiasm for Italy, but this voyage seems to have brought about a certain cooling in their friendship; instead of using his favorite term, "Clara," Stendhal now addresses his friend as "Academus" or "pédant Academus," disconcerted by Mérimée's new seriousness and pedantry in archeological matters. Returning to Paris in December, Mérimée published his *Notes de mon voyage en Corse*, April 5, 1840, and his *Colomba* in July of that year in the *Revue des Deux Mondes*.

VII   *Twice an Academician*

Finding himself in Bayonne on August 16, 1840, on an inspection trip to the Southwest of France, Mérimée could not resist the

temptation to visit the Montijos again in Madrid and Carabanchel, country home of the countess. In August the following year
with his friend Charles Lenormant and the Belgian scholar Baron
de Witte, Mérimée went to Greece, joining J. J. Ampère in
Athens. Here the Russian wife of the French ambassador, Theo-
dose de Lagrené, inspired Mérimée with the desire to learn Russian, a study which was to have great influence later. Greek architecture fascinated Mérimée and confirmed his passage from
Romanticism to Classicism. With Ampère he went on to Asia
Minor before returning to Paris.

As early as 1838 Mérimée had conceived the idea of writing a
life of Julius Caesar but first decided to prepare the background
with an *Essai sur la guerre sociale,* finished in February, 1841.
Already he had begun to hope for election to one of the French
Academies, urged on by the desire to please Valentine Delessert.
He restricted the edition to 150 copies, distributed among arche-
ologists, historians, and members of the Academy of Inscriptions
and Belles-Lettres, no doubt to further his image as a learned
scholar of antiquity rather than as a writer of popular tales. Its
sequel, *La Conjuration* [Conspiracy] *de Catalina* dealing with
Caesar's early political career, joined to the earlier volume, was
published March 23, 1843, under the title *Etudes sur l'histoire ro-
maine.* The life of Caesar, which was to have been the third
volume in the series, was never completed, and many years later
Mérimée was to turn over his notes to Napoleon III for his work
on this subject.

On March 23, 1842, Mérimée suffered the loss of his friend
Stendhal, a victim of apoplexy in Paris, and the following year an
equally distressing blow, the death in London of his old crony,
Sutton Sharpe—as Mérimée was to say later, "from working too
hard and excessive lovemaking."

Unable to decide whether to campaign for the Académie des
Inscriptions or for the Académie Française, Mérimée was persuaded by his friends that election to the former would be a step-
pingstone rather than an obstacle to the latter. Sending his letter
of candidacy on September 21, 1843, to Thiers, he spent two
months calling on the members and alerting all his influential
friends. His chief rival was a long forgotten minor historian Ter-
naux-Compans, whom Mérimée called "the truffle man" because of his lavish hospitality to members. "People can rarely re-

sist a good dinner. On the other hand it is in my favor if they happen to get indigestion." [19] Mérimée blamed his rival also for a notice appearing in a Paris newspaper a week before the election, stating falsely that Mérimée had just had a five-act comedy accepted by the Théâtre Français; this rumor would obviously detract from his serious image as a scholar of antiquity. Mérimée need not have worried, for on November 17, 1843 he was elected with twenty-five votes to eleven for his rival and entered the Académie des Inscriptions November 24. The day after his election Mérimée wrote to Mme de Montijo in Spain, with a typical mingling of humor and impiety: "Yesterday I was elected triumphantly at the Academy, 38 voters. I received 25 and M. Ternaux 11. Two votes wasted. There are 27 who claim they voted for me and there were only 25 ballots with my name. Our Lord found one traitor among the 12 apostles, I found myself better off than he since I count only 2 out of 27." [20] Equally amusing is Mérimée's account of his "triumphant reception" a week later: "The permanent secretary, having put on gloves, which he wears, I believe, only for this occasion . . . led me by the hand as if I had been his dancing partner to the midst of the august assembly which rose to its feet like one man, I bowed forty times. I sat down and all was finished." (Critics who cite these remarks seem to have been bothered by the fact that Mérimée made forty bows instead of thirty-nine.) Was he bowing also for himself?

The winter of 1843–44 must have been a severe one, for Mérimée wrote to Mme de Montijo "the Academicians are dying off like flies." Despite this slight exaggeration there were soon three empty chairs to fill at the Académie Française: those of Campenon, Casimir Delavigne, and Charles Nodier. Mérimée's letters of this period express his disgust at having to begin again the humiliating and hypocritical visitation of members to request their support. Mérimée and Sainte-Beuve had decided to pool their resources and aim, the former for the chair vacated by Nodier, the latter for that of Delavigne. On March 14 Mérimée waited in Sainte-Beuve's apartment for the result of the elections. The latter won easily on the second ballot, but since there were several candidates for Nodier's seat—including Vigny who had just lost to Sainte-Beuve—a total of seven rounds was necessary before Mérimée finally triumphed with nineteen votes, to thirteen for the minor dramatist Casimir Bonjour, and three for Vigny (who was to be elected the following year). Now according to the ritual Mérimée had to make visits to all the members, "to thank friends and enemies, in order to show that one possesses grandeur of soul."

But the most amusing part was still to come. The following day there appeared in the *Revue des Deux Mondes* Mérimée's shocking story *Arsène Guillot*, purely by chance as he claimed, though critics have concluded that he had carefully arranged the timing, either to mock his enemies in case of a reversal in the election or to assert his own independence from convention in case of nomination. The result was a chorus of indignation which first angered, then amused, Mérimée, as we can see in the following letters, the first to his friend Requien, the second to Mme de Montijo.

Half of the academicians who elected me voted for me in hopes that the election would be postponed, and to prevent my competitors from entering. Among the others more than one repents having given me his vote, especially the devout and moral people who have just read *Arsène Guillot*, novella of your humble servant which excites general indignation. . . . I persist in thinking that there is not enough with which to whip a cat in my novella and yet the good souls cry scandal opening their eyes and mouths as wide as porte-cochères.[21]

And even more caustically Mérimée wrote the following day to Mme de Montijo:

. . . my election was rather popular, however, but the next day fortune would have it that a novella of mine appeared in the *Revue des Deux Mondes* and caused a great scandal. It was found to be impious and immoral. Three or four women, notorious adulteresses, uttered cries of fury which their lovers repeated in chorus. Each vied in casting the first stone against me. . . . All this unchaining of hypocrisy at first made me angry, but now amuses me. I have nothing more to fear and can snap my fingers at them.[22]

In still another letter four days later Mérimée remarks that three of his backers at the election, M. Molé, M. de Barante, and M. Ballanche "feel their false hair standing on end and declare that they would not have voted for me, were it to be done over again."[23]

In keeping with tradition, Mérimée had to pronounce a eulogy of his predecessor the same day that another member saluted his own election. What made this an uncongenial task for Mérimée was his ill-concealed dislike for Nodier, ever since the latter had attacked his *Guzla*. As he told his friend Albert Stapfer, he felt that Nodier was "an infamous liar," but the problem was to translate this into polite academic terms. The result was the following passage in his Discourse: "Whether it concerns him or others what does the rigorous exactness of facts matter to M. Nodier? For him everything is drama or novel." (Coming from the mystifier of *Clara Gazul* and *La Guzla* such a reproach may seem rather amusing.) When the day for his reception arrived, February 6, 1845, Mérimée described his entrance into the French Academy in these terms to Mme de Montijo: "I was scared stiff and they told me I looked exactly like someone being led to the scaffold for hanging. My face was the same color as the green embroidery on my uniform. I read my speech quite well, in a firm decisive tone. People seemed pleased." [24] Evidently Mérimée flattered himself, for two days later *La Quotidienne* mentioned his monotonous voice which put everyone to sleep, but at least Mérimée's ordeal was now over and he could enjoy the prestige of his safe arrival among the "40 immortals."

VIII *Two Novellas and a History*

As early as November, 1843, Mérimée had been planning to work on a history of Don Pedro, for at that time he reminded Mme de Montijo of her promise to get him a manuscript on this "poor devil of a king." However, soon after his reception in the French Academy, he interrupted this work to write his *Carmen*, which she had also inspired. On May 16, 1845, he wrote her:

I have just spent eight days shut up writing, not the deeds and gestures of the late Don Pedro, but a story you related to me fifteen years ago and which I'm afraid I have spoiled. It concerned a Jacque of Málaga who had killed his mistress who devoted herself exclusively to the public. After *Arsène Guillot* I have not found anything more moral to offer our fine ladies. As I have been studying the gypsies for sometime with much care, I have made my heroine a gypsy. [25]

It was perhaps not to offend his Spanish friends that he had chosen to do so, for he had also made Don José Basque rather than purely Spanish. Returning to Paris from a three-month inspection tour, he wrote his friend Requien that "poverty, inevitable result of a long trip," had induced him to give his *Carmen* to Buloz for his *Revue des Deux Mondes,* and with typical disdain for his own masterpieces he told Vitet that his "petite drôlerie" would have remained unpublished had it not been for the need to buy himself a pair of trousers.

On October 30, 1845, Mérimée wrote Charles de Rémusat that he had written "an immoral novella" and that he "allait la manger" (that is, employ the receipts) on the other side of the Pyrenees. Apparently Mérimée was still unaware at this time that Rémusat was gradually replacing him in Mme Delessert's affections, for he innocently invited him to accompany him to Spain without realizing how important it was to get him away from Valentine.[26] By the following spring his suspicions may have been aroused, for although to please her he had helped Rémusat get elected to the French Academy in January, 1846, she seems to have become Rémusat's mistress shortly thereafter.[27] At any rate, Mérimée's letters to Mme de Montijo that spring express melancholy and foreboding: "I am tormented by all the *blue devils.* If I were in Madrid I would tell you about a lot of things that are happening to me and you could give me some good advice."[28]

About this time Mérimée was writing his ironic short story, *L'Abbé Aubain,* which first appeared in the *Constitutionnel* on February 24 without his signature. He explains the reason in a letter to Mme de Montijo: "I am sending you a little story that I wrote without signing it, because I have only to speak of priests for all the devout old ladies to cry out 'irreligious.' The adventure is a true one and I could name the persons."[29] Another story written the same year, *Il Viccolo di Madama Lucrezia* was not published until 1873.

For four years Mérimée seems to have devoted most of his free time to painstaking research on a *History of Don Pedro,* finished July 1, 1847, and dedicated to Mme de Montijo who had helped him with her aid and inspiration. This was first published in the *Revue des Deux Mondes* from December, 1847, to February, 1848, and in book form in September, 1848. Alas for Mérimée, this work of four years remained almost unnoticed because of the Revolution of 1848, although it did receive acclamation in Spain

which resulted in Mérimée's election to the Spanish Historical
Academy.

IX   The Revolutions of 1848

Though Mérimée had little enthusiasm for the regime of Louis
Philippe with its increasing corruption, he was nevertheless
shocked by the revolution of February 22 which sent the king
ingloriously into exile. With Léon de Laborde, Valentine's
brother, he helped prevent the Tuileries from being looted. On
February 24 Gabriel Delessert had resigned as prefect of police
and joined his family at Laborde's home on the Quai Malaquais,
from whose windows Mérimée could see the angry crowd milling
about in the Tuileries. Feeling that things were unsafe for M.
Delessert, he took him around the corner to his own home, rue
Jacob, gave him his own room for the night, and slept on the floor
outside to protect him. On the next day he took him and Valentine
across the Tuileries to the Hotel Bedford where Alexis de Vilon,
son-in-law of the Delesserts, was staying. In a letter to Mme de
Montijo he wrote that Valentine had shown herself extremely
brave in the midst of the shooting. The following day Charles de
Rémusat joined them to say farewell to the Delesserts as they de-
parted for exile in England. According to Alexis, Rémusat's features were contracted in anguish, and Mérimée himself "sobbed
like a child." To Mérimée's sorrow at the possibility of losing Valentine forever was added the fact that he could not even be sure
which of her two lovers she most regretted leaving.[30] She did not
write him from England, and though she came back to Paris
briefly on one or two trips before her final return in June, she
appeared more concerned with Rémusat than with Mérimée. The
following December Mérimée remarked sadly to Laborde that
Rémusat was seeing a great deal of Valentine.

Donning his National Guard uniform Mérimée in May aided in
dispersing a mob which was threatening the Chamber of Deputies and took part in suppressing the terrible four-day revolt in
June. He gave Mme de Montijo a graphic picture of the atrocities
committed on both sides. Wondering what would happen to his
old mother if he should resign or be dismissed, he received from
Mme de Montijo an offer to place him as archeologist, but gra-
ciously refused on the ground that it was his duty to remain. Seeing only chaos and destruction for France in the future, he had

written: "If only there were a Napoleon, all might yet be saved; but where is there such a man?" [31] Little could he foresee at this moment that such a man did in truth exist, that December 4, 1848 Louis Napoleon would be elected prince president, biding his time for the coup d'état of December, 1852, which would make him Emperor of the French—and change the entire life of Mérimée.

X   *Russian Studies*

As early as 1829 Mérimée had began a long friendship with the Russian Sobolevsky, and on his visit to Greece in 1841 he had been introduced to the charming and vivacious wife of the French consul in Athens, Mme de Lagrené, née Barbe Doubenski, a former demoiselle d'honneur of the Grand Duchess Marie, daughter of Emperor Nicholas I. In 1847 Mérimée's cousin Henri Mérimée had published his account of several years' stay in Russia. In the autumn of 1848, discouraged by the changes in French government and saddened by the growing coldness shown him by Valentine, Mérimée at the age of forty-five had thrown himself into a study of the Russian language, which he considered the most beautiful in Europe. Aided by Mme de Lagrené, he was able in less than a year to present to the *Revue des Deux Mondes* in July, 1849, a translation of Pushkin's *La Dame de Pique* (The Queen of Spades) which at first was taken for his own work, so great was his reputation for literary hoaxes. It will be recalled that Pushkin had once translated part of Mérimée's *Guzla* and that he considered Mérimée the greatest French author of his time. There was indeed a curious affinity between the two authors, and Mérimée felt that Pushkin was the greatest Russian poet of the century. So successful was this first translation—from which Scribe wrote a three-act libretto to music by Halévy—that from now on Mérimée devoted most of his intellectual activity to Russian literature and history; it has been truly said, "for over twenty years Mérimée went into a literary emigration to Russia."

In 1851 Mérimée translated Pushkin's prose poems *The Bohemians* and *The Hussard* and also wrote a long study on Gogol for the *Revue des Deux Mondes*. In 1853 he published a translation of Gogol's *Dead Souls* and *The Inspector General*. It should be noted, however, that Mérimée never fully appreciated Gogol, who, he felt, gave undue prominence to violence and sordidness in his work. In 1856 he published one of his best translations, that of Pushkin's *Coup de Pistolet* (The Pistol Shot) often included in editions of his own short stories. Not until 1854 did he come to know personally Turgenev, whose warm friend and translator he remained until his death. As for Mérimée's interest in Russian history, this had first been aroused by his reading of Pushkin's *Boris Godunov* and later Oustrialov's *Contemporary Memoirs on the False Demetrius*. Fascinated by the personality of the first of three impostors posing as the son of Ivan the Terrible, Mérimée wrote two works: a closet drama of the impostor's early years, *Les Débuts d'un aventurier* (1852) and a more conventional history of his public career, *Les Faux Démétrius* (1853). These works, together with *Les Cosaques d'autrefois* in 1865, appealed to Filon as Mérimée's most attractive writings outside of his novels and short stories.[32]

Mérimée's appreciation of Russian literature was not without some inequalities and prejudices—his failure to understand Gogol's true genius, for instance, and his dislike for Dostoevsky, who he felt owed more to Hugo than to Pushkin.[33] Nevertheless, he was almost alone in his day to call the attention of the French public to Russian literature and history. As a pioneer in this field he had a great influence in bringing about the later "invasion of French literature by the Russians" as Hemming has so aptly stated.

XI *Mérimée in Prison—The Libri Affair*

The year 1852 was a very sad one for Mérimée. This was the year Valentine became Maxime Du Camp's mistress, and although Mérimée discovered this only several years later he was conscious of her growing coldness to him. On April 30, his mother died in his arms, keeping to the very last "the calm feature and the gentle air habitual to her," as he wrote Jenny Dacquin. This was a terrible blow to Mérimée, but at least his mother was spared the sorrow of seeing her son condemned to prison.

In 1850 his friend Guglielmo Libri, a naturalized French scholar and inspector general of libraries, had been accused of appropriating several rare books and had escaped to London with several boxes of such treasures before being condemned to ten years in prison for theft. Mérimée was convinced that Libri was being persecuted by the clerical party for his liberalism; his zeal for defending Libri may have been due in part to the fact that Libri had married Mélanie Double, Mérimée's old flame of 1829, after the death of her first husband. He shared a belief in Libri's innocence with many others at the time, including Victor Cousin, Paulin Paris, and Buloz; Panizzi, director of the British Museum, had even offered Libri a place on his staff. In the April, 1852, issue of the *Revue des Deux Mondes* Mérimée published a vitriolic attack on the judges who had condemned Libri, for which he was sentenced in May to pay a fine of 1,000 francs and spend two weeks in prison. Mérimée thereupon turned in his resignation as inspector general of historical monuments, which, however, was not accepted.

In spite of his fury at what he considered punishment for an unselfish act, Mérimée took his misfortune with his accustomed irony, writing to Mme de Lagrené:

Five minutes after the sentence I had persuaded myself that they had stolen from me a thousand franc note and that I had had the imprudence of entering a pesthouse, two incidents for which I consoled myself immediately. I shall profit from the second by learning the irregular verbs of the Russian language which I have too much neglected and which but for this opportunity I would risk never knowing. Thrice blessed be these gentlemen.[34]

In the torrid days of July Mérimée was allowed to serve out his sentence (July 6–30) in the cool Conciergerie prison—an ironic location for the inspector of medieval monuments—being permitted to take with him two cushions, a Persian carpet, and a great quantity of books and notes to work on his study of the False Demetrius. As luck would have it, Valentine's brother-in-law Edouard Bocher was condemned to a light sentence in prison at the same time for having distributed Orleanist tracts, and was allowed to share his cell which had a view over the courtyard; many friends came to see them in their confinement, including Mérimée's early flame Mme Lacoste—so many indeed that their visits interfered with his Russian studies.

CHAPTER 6

Mosaïque

T HE first volume of Mérimée's short stories, *Mosaïque*, was published in 1833, but all of these had been written within fourteen months and published in magazine form, chiefly in the new *Revue de Paris*, in 1829 and 1830.

I *Mateo Falcone*

Even while correcting the proof sheets of the *Chronique*—"a wretched work which bores me," the author too modestly said—Mérimée was bidding farewell to the historical novel and his early favorite Sir Walter Scott to find his true vocation in the contemporary, realistic short story, of which *Mateo Falcone* marks the first dazzling success. Received with almost universal praise from his day to the present, this brief tale condensed into a dozen pages was sufficient to confirm the literary reputation of the author.

In his scholarly preface to the Pléiade edition of Mérimée's fiction (pp. xvi–xvii), Martineau mentions as possible sources *L'Histoire des révolutions de Corse* by l'abbé de Germanes; a story by Robert Benson in *Sketches of Corsica*, London 1825; and the *Novelle storiche corse* of Renucci of 1827. He gives credit, however, to M. Gustave Charlier[1] for having indicated as probable source the *Revue Trimestrielle* directed by Mérimée's friend Alexandre Buchon, in the July, 1828, issue of which can be found a study entitled "Les Devoirs de la Corse envers la France" containing the story of a shepherd who for money betrayed two deserters and was executed by his own relatives. The same study mentioned Gabriel Feydel's *Moeurs et coutumes des Corses* from which Mérimée evidently borrowed. Richard reminds us also that the *Globe*, to which Mérimée often contributed, had published six articles in 1826 and 1827 on Corsican honor and hospitality.[2]

The famous marksman Mateo Falcone had four children—three daughters happily married and a son Fortunato, aged ten, the apple of his eye. One day when Fortunato had been left at home dreaming tranquilly in the sunshine, he was startled by several distant gun shots, and soon appeared a bearded bandit covered with rags and dragging his leg because of a wound in the thigh. Offered a 5-franc piece to grant him shelter from the militiamen, Fortunato hid him in a pile of hay on top of which he placed a cat with kittens before covering with dust the traces of blood in the path. On the arrival of the pursuers, the adjutant Gamba, receiving only evasive answers from Fortunato, threatened him to no avail with imprisonment and execution. Trying another strategy, he dangled before Fortunato a shiny gold watch. "Fortunato, eyeing the watch out of the corner of his eye, resembled a cat presented with an entire chicken" (201). Convinced that the offer was real, he pointed to the pile of hay, which the militiamen then searched to find the bandit and take him into custody.

At this moment Mateo and his wife returned. His cousin, the adjutant, came forward to inform him of the capture of the bandit, thanks to the aid from his son. At the sight of Mateo the bandit spat on the doorstep with the bitter ejaculation, "house of a traitor," and, refusing a jar of milk from the lad, he repulsed him scornfully, accepting instead a water flask from a soldier.

When Fortunato confessed that his gold watch was a gift from the adjutant, Mateo seized it to smash it against a stone, lamenting that his son was the first of his race to commit a treacherous act. Taking Fortunato to a little ravine where the soil was soft and easy to excavate, he made him recite all the prayers he could remember, then shot him dead. Without glancing at the corpse, he strode back to the house to get a spade with which to bury his son. To the anguished query of his wife, alarmed at hearing the shot, he replied that he had done justice. "He died as a Christian; I shall have a mass sung for him. Tell my son-in-law Tiodoro Bianchi to come to live with us" (207).

The tragic loneliness of Mateo after the sacrifice of his beloved son is subtly evoked by this last sentence. It would be difficult indeed to express more tense emotion than that aroused by this concentrated narration compressed into a dozen stark pages, "perhaps the cruelest story in the world" as Walter Pater has called it.[3] It is rendered all the more poignant by the absence of commentary on the part of the author. In fact, the latter's intervention is apparent only by a few flashes of tragic irony: the choice of the

name Fortunato for this pitiful victim; the remark that "the em-
ployment of a good housewife, in case of combat, is to load the
firearms of her husband" (203); and the comment of the adjutant
concerning the broken arm received by his corporal Chardon,
"no great harm was done, he was only a Frenchman" (204). The
realistic setting of the wild maquis of Corsica is so vivid and accurate that although Mérimée had not yet been to this island he
found only a few retouches necessary in later editions after his
visit there in 1839.

Though extended character analysis is out of the question in
this compact narrative, the personages reveal themselves clearly
in dialogue: the proud bandit in his scorn for his betrayer; the
wily adjutant substituting flattery and temptation when he realizes that threats are useless; the despairing mother, praying fervently before the image of the Virgin, unable to restrain the cruel
vengeance of her husband. Mateo achieves tragic grandeur in his
subordination of parental love to his sense of honor and hospitality, but the greatest psychological triumph is Mérimée's subtle de-
lineation of little Fortunato. Precocious and wary in his reception
of the wounded bandit, greedy like a child in his acceptance of
the 5-franc bribe, he shows himself evasive and cautious in his
answers to the militia, next, through filial pride in the prowess of
his father, mocking the menaces of the adjutant, then little by
little overcome by temptation for the glittering watch and finally,
moved by a sense of shame for his treachery, throwing back to the
bandit the money acccepted for hiding him.

We shall find this theme of honor reappearing in later stories of
Mérimée, in particular in *La Partie de trictrac*. Richard has
pointed out the resemblance to the *point d'honneur* of Corneille
and has mentioned as lineal descendants of *Mateo Falcone* "La
Vendetta" of Balzac and later "Deux Amis" of Maupassant and
"L'Enfant espion" in Daudet's *Contes du lundi*.[4]

II   *Vision de Charles XI*

This second story in *Mosaïque*, first published in the *Revue de
Paris* of July, 1829, seems far removed from the realistic *Mateo
Falcone* because of its atmosphere of supernatural terror and mys-
tery. It reminds us of some of the bloody otherworldly evocations
among the ballads of *La Guzla,* presaging likewise some of
Mérimée's later fantastic tales. It may seem strange to learn that

Mérimée was inspired here by an authentic document, well known in Sweden during the eighteenth century, which had been published in a German periodical in 1810.[5] Amusingly enough, the Swedish court felt obliged to lodge a protest against the *Revue de Paris* for printing Mérimée's story, under the curious title, "Denial given to a phantom." Even here in this evocation of mystery Mérimée seeks credibility by the vividness and precision of the setting; twenty years later, he was to encourage his friend Edouard Delessert to multiply the details of materialistic realism when writing of the supernatural. "It is the great art of Hoffmann," writes Billy.[6]

Mérimée's close acquaintance with English literature and particularly Shakespeare is evident once more in the English quotation from Hamlet, Act I, Scene V, with which this tale is preceded:

> There are more things in heaven and earth, Horatio,
> Than are dreamt of in your philosophy.

Charles XI of Sweden and Norway, morose and taciturn after his wife's death, was sitting one autumn evening in dressing gown and slippers before his office fire in the palace at Stockholm, accompanied by his chamberlain, Count Brahé, and his doctor, Baumgarten. Suddenly he noticed in the vast hall of the States-General opposite his office a strange illumination which could have come neither from the torches of his servants nor from a conflagration. Despite the protests of his companions, he has the janitor awakened to bring the keys and enters the anteroom whose walls, formerly paneled in oak, were now covered with black drapes. Pushing on into the great hall he found the tapestry replaced by black hangings, the German, Danish, and Muscovite flags captured by Gustavus Adolphus along the walls, and in their midst the banners of Sweden covered with funereal crêpe. In the benches were a vast multitude of the four classes—nobility, clergy, bourgeois, and peasants, all dressed in black—and on the throne a bloody corpse, bearing the insignia of royalty. At his right stood a child, crown on head and scepter in hand, while at his left, leaning on the throne, was an elderly man, attired in the mantle of the former Administrators of Sweden. In front of the throne were several men, dressed in long judicial robes, seated before a table full of massive volumes and parchments. Between the throne and the benches one could see an execution block covered with black crêpe beside an ax.

When the oldest judge struck three times against one of the volumes, several young men, their hands tied behind their backs, entered from the other side. As the one in front stopped in front of the block, the corpse on the throne trembled convulsively while fresh red blood flowed from his wound. The young man kneeled to place his head on the block, the ax descended, and a rivulet of blood sprinkled the platform as the head rolled down, tinging the king's feet with blood. At this horrible spectacle Charles, addressing the Administrator, pronounced the customary formula: "If thou art from God, speak; if thou art from the Other, leave us in peace." The phantom's reply was slow and solemn: "King Charles, this blood will not be shed during thy reign, but five reigns later. Woe, woe, woe to the blood of Wasa." Then the forms of this strange assembly became indistinct and melted away, the fantastic torches were extinguished and the old tapestries reappeared, waving gently in the wind. All that was left to remind the king of this weird apparition was the bloodstain on his slipper. Once back in his office, the king wrote down what he had just seen, adding to his signature those of his companions.

In the concluding lines of this story the author points out the prophetic nature of this vision: the corpse was that of the murdered King Gustavus III; the young man decapitated was his murderer Ankarstroen; the child, his successor Gustavus Adolphus IV; and the old man, the Duke of Sudermanie, uncle of Gustavus IV, regent of the kingdom and later king, after his nephew had been deposed.

What lingers in our mind after reading this hallucinating tale, in which mysticism and vivid realism are mingled, is that stroke of genius on the part of the author, bringing into high relief that dramatic touch, the stain of blood on the slipper of the king.

III *L'Enlèvement de la redoute*

This brief tale, *The Capture of the Redoubt,* was published in the bimonthly *Revue Française* of September-October, 1829. For its origin we have no definite information, other than the opening sentence: "A military friend of mine . . . told me one day of the first affair in which he was engaged. His story struck me so deeply that I wrote it down from memory as soon as I had leisure" (215). Since the hero's name begins with P, it has been conjectured that this stood for Pasquier, nephew of Chancellor Pasquier the lover of Mérimée's good friend Mme de Boigne whose initial and dwelling are indeed mentioned in the story. It is likely also that Mérimée may have read Ségur's *Histoire de Napoléon et de la Grande Armée*, published in 1824, which contains an account of the Russian campaign of 1812 and the famous capture of the redoubt of Schwardino or Chevardino (called Cheverino by Mérimée).[7]

The narrator, a young lieutenant fresh from officers' training school, has just arrived on the front to replace the lieutenant killed the day before. Despite his courage, his superstitious nature is affected greatly by the sight of the full red moon on which the enemy fort is outlined in black, like the cone of a volcano. "It's very red," said a soldier, "that's a sign that it will cost us dear to take it, this famous redoubt." The following day three battalions were ordered to attack, one of these to slip around the fortress to the rear, the other two, including our lieutenant, to make a frontal assault. Protected by an intervening hill, the soldiers received few casualties at first until arriving at the foot of the barricade.

I raised my eyes and never shall I forget the spectacle I saw. Most of the smoke had risen and remained suspended like a dais twenty feet above the redoubt. Through a bluish vapor one could see behind their half-destroyed parapet the Russian grenadiers, guns held aloft, motionless as statues. I can still see each soldier, his left eye fixed on us, his right hidden by the raised gun. In an embrasure, a few feet from us, a man holding a *lance à feu* was near a cannon. I quivered and thought my last hour had come. "And now the dance is about to begin," cried my captain. "Good night." Those were the last words I ever heard him speak. (218–19)

After a horrible explosion followed by cries and groans, the lieutenant found himself surrounded by dead and dying, among them his captain, his head crushed by a cannon ball. Only six men of his company were upright besides himself. After a moment of stupor the Colonel, his hat on the end of his sword, mounted the parapet, crying "Vive l'Empereur" and followed by the survivors. In the midst of the smoke the lieutenant heard him shout "Victory," and when the smoke lifted two hundred men in French uniform and eleven Russian prisoners were visible among the corpses which covered the cannons.

A fitting conclusion to this recital of heroism, terror, and carnage is found in the laconic dialogue between the sergeant and the wounded colonel. To the latter's request for the oldest captain, the sergeant replied with a significant shrug of his shoulders. "And the oldest lieutenant?" "This gentleman who arrived yesterday," said the sergeant in a very calm tone. The colonel smiled bitterly. "Well sir," he said to me, "you are commander in chief; have the rear of the redoubt fortified with these carts, for the enemy is in force; but General C—will come to your support."

"Colonel," I said, "you are gravely wounded."
"Done for [euphemism for the colonel's "sublime obscenity" as Filon calls it], my dear fellow, but the redoubt is taken." (219–20)

The heroic simplicity of this conclusion reminds us of that famous Cornelian line in *Le Cid*, "Et le combat cessa faute de combattants," or of the laconic report of an American pilot in World War II, "Sighted sub, sank same." Filon observes that Mérimée has given us here a summary of the entire imperial epic. "The lieutenant who arrived the preceding evening and who finds himself commanding a regiment as 'le plus ancien' symbolizes in a terrifying manner that race of extraordinary men, that pursuit of glory, that terrible lottery in which they staked their lives and in which the survivors gained thrones or marshal's batons." [8]

In this concentrated action there is little room for description, yet once more the author, as in the evocation of the bloodstain on Charles XI's slipper, has immortalized for all time the gory vision of the redoubt before the battle. What a stroke of genius was this symbol of the bloody massacre to take place on the morrow!

Yet more than in tenseness of narration and in symbolic choice of setting, Mérimée has shown his interest above all in the human equation. With a few deft strokes he makes us see the gigantic, grumpy, and superstitious captain, the intrepid and stoic colonel, and most of all, the young lieutenant-narrator. Susceptible in his pride to the disdain of his captain, superstitious after the prophecy of the old soldier in regard to the gory moon, filled with natural vanity at the thought of recounting later in a ballroom his exciting adventure, moved only by his apprehension that he might

give the impression of lacking courage, able to call forth a witty
jest when a shot removes his shako, Lieutenant P is a lifelike creation who always rings true. As Faguet has so well expressed it,
"All Mérimée's imagination is employed in evoking soul states,
and in combining events which set off in dazzling light the course
of the passions." [9]

IV Tamango

Tamango, published on October 4, 1829, in the *Revue de Paris*,
longer and more episodic than the earlier stories, expresses a more
subjective attitude on Mérimée's part in his protest against the
cruelty of the slave trade. Officially outlawed by the Congress of
Vienna in 1815, this commerce still persisted illegally for many
years. Among the philanthropic societies organized in France to
combat this trade was the Société de la morale chrétienne
founded by Baron de Staël and the pastor Stapfer, whose son Albert was a close friend of Mérimée. As early as 1820 Victor Hugo
in his novel *Bug-Jargal* had given an eloquent arraignment of the
injustice meted out to slaves in the West Indies. Among the works
Mérimée may have read to document his protest were a pamphlet
by Clarkson and *Le Précis historique de la traite des noirs* of
Morénas in 1828.[10] The maritime vocabulary was probably furnished by Mérimée's reading of James Fenimore Cooper, and by
conversation with his cousin Jean-Auguste Marc, a naval captain.[11]

Captain Ledoux, after commanding a privateer until peace was
made with England, had equipped a new ship, *L'Espérance* for
the slave trade. Deceiving the marine inspectors of Nantes with
papers calling ostensibly for a trip to Sénégal to acquire wood and
ivory, he sailed up a river in Africa to the point where Tamango
had conducted a large number of natives to be sold into slavery.
While they drank brandy together an agreement was concluded
for the purchase of 160 able-bodied slaves, but there still remained 30 children, old men, and women. At one bottle of brandy
for each, Ledoux agreed to accept 20 of the remainder. When he
refused to take the rest for a glass of brandy each, Tamango shot
one of them, the mother of three children. As he aimed at another,
his gun was deflected by his wife Ayché whom Tamango, besot-
ten by the brandy, then offered to Captain Ledoux.

Sobered up on the morrow, Tamango, in despair at the loss of
his beautiful wife, pursued the ship in his canoe. He mounted on

board demanding his wife, only to be taken prisoner. Persuading
Ayché to bring him a file concealed in a loaf of bread, Tamango
arranged with the slaves to file their chains, then seize and cut to
pieces their captors. Claiming that he was able to take them back
to their homeland, he suddenly reversed the helm, with the result
that the two masts broke off, covering the deck with death and
destruction. Helpless and derelict, the wrecked vessel drifted
aimlessly while the slaves tried to forget their misery in intoxication procured from the ship's stores of brandy. At last Tamango
persuaded them to launch the longboat and dinghy, abandoning
on board the weak and infirm. Heavily overloaded, the longboat
collapsed at the first onslaught of a wave, and only Tamango and
Ayché were able to make their way back to the ship. For lack of
food the blacks finally succumbed, last of all Ayché, until Tamango was left alone prostrate on his mattress.

Sometime later a British frigate, *La Bellone,* found this drifting
wreck, with only Tamango still breathing but so emaciated that
he resembled a mummy. With care from the surgeon he was re-
stored to health by the time the vessel docked in Kingston. Despite the pleas of planters that he be hanged as a rebellious Negro,
the governor decided to free him, since after all he had acted in
self-defense, "and since those he had killed were only Frenchmen"
(240). Working for the government at 6 cents a day and board,
he played the cymbals in the military band. But he was exces-
sively fond of tafia and rum, and died in the hospital from an
inflammation of the chest.

Tamango, almost twice the length of the preceding stories, has
consequently greater richness of scenes and events building up to
the final catastrophe. An even greater difference, however, is the
increase in subjectivity, expressed of course not in angry denun-
ciation but in irony—more acerbic and astringent perhaps than
any since Swift's *Humanitarian Proposal for the Disposition of
Babies in Ireland.* This irony is evident first of all in the name
given the slave trader—Captain Ledoux (Gentle) and to the slave
ship, *L'Espérance* (Hope). Captain Ledoux insisted that the
space between decks should be three feet and four inches, enough
to allow all slaves of average height to be comfortably seated, for
what good would it do them to stand up? "Once arrived in the
colonies they will remain only too long on their feet" (222). Since
a free space was left in the center of the vessel Ledoux conceived

the idea of filling it with an additional half-score of blacks, lying perpendicularly to the others. "In a pinch even more could be placed there; but one must be humane and leave a Negro at least five feet in length and two in width for a crossing of six weeks or more. For after all," said Ledoux to his ship owner to justify this liberal measure, "Negroes after all are men just as whites are" (222). The irons on the ship were called, for some inexplicable reason, "barres de justice." When the slaves were handed over to the French sailors, the latter hastened to remove the long wooden forks about their necks to substitute iron collars and handcuffs: "which shows clearly the superiority of European civilization" (225). When the slaves saw their oppressor, Tamango, a prisoner like themselves, Ledoux felt that they should chuckle heartily. "For the nonce they will see well that a Providence does exist" (228). Ledoux was already counting on his profits, since no contagious diseases had broken out on board. "Only twelve blacks, the weakest ones, had died from the heat; that was a bagatelle" (228). And after the irony of their liberation which had brought the slaves only a hopeless future, the crowning irony of the story is the laconic conclusion, Tamango's death in a hospital from heavy drinking.

Although presented to us first as a vain tyrant, made cruel by inebriation from the white man's fire water, Tamango later draws commiseration from the reader, both for his ignorance of nautical seamanship and for his willingness to sacrifice his last crust of bread for Ayché. Aside from the dramatic realism of the story, *Tamango* must have exerted an influence even greater than the humanitarian pamphlets and protestations in awakening the French public to the continuing scandal and horror of this illicit traffic in human souls.

V *Federigo*

This, the shortest of all his tales and probably the least well known, was published in the *Revue de Paris* for November, 1829, and was included in the first edition of *Mosaïque* but never in later editions during Mérimée's lifetime. In a footnote to the title he wrote: "This tale is popular in the kingdom of Naples. One observes in it, as in many other short stories originating in the same country, a strange mixture of Greek mythology with the beliefs of Christianity; it seems to have been composed near the end of the

Middle Ages." It is possible that Mérimée may have found it in
some old Neapolitan collection of folklore.

The hero Federigo, a handsome but dissolute young lord over-
fond of gambling, drinking, and womanizing, after having ruined
twelve sons of good family had finally lost all his wealth and retired to a small manor. One day three years later on returning
from the hunt he found thirteen guests knocking on his door for
hospitality—Jesus Christ and the twelve apostles. Federigo
roasted his last remaining kid in their honor, apologizing for the
mediocre quality of his wine. But Our Lord, having tasted it, pronounced it perfect and was confirmed in this judgment by Saint
Peter. Federigo himself, surprised by the delicious flavor, realized
that a miracle had occurred and that he was in the presence of the
Savior.

As his guests were ready to depart on the morrow, Jesus Christ,
charmed by Federigo's hospitality, offered to grant three requests.
Federigo, drawing out a pack of cards from his pocket, first asked
that he be allowed to win every time he used them. "So be it," said
Jesus, while Saint Peter whispered to Federigo that he ought to
ask for salvation. His second request, however, was that whoever
should climb up in the orange tree near the door be prevented
from descending without his permission. "Granted," said Our
Lord, while Saint Peter again urged Federigo to petition a place
in Paradise. For the third favor Federigo desired that whoever
should seat himself on the stool by the hearth not be permitted to
rise without his approval. After the departure of his guests,
Federigo hastened to test the new virtue of his cards, discovering
that without even trying he was able to win every game of
hombre from his tenant farmers.

Returning now to the city, he gathered about him all the gamblers who had caused his ruin, offered them a sumptuous dinner,
then proceeded to win back all the fortune he had lost through
their cheating, taking care to substitute an ordinary pack of cards
every three or four games in order, by losing, to avoid suspicion.
Remembering the twelve young nobles he had ruined, he realized
that they were the only honest gamblers he had ever encountered.
After giving a fête in which he completed the ruin of all his dis-
honest associates, he set forth into the world with his new jewels
and gold, gambling always with success, his conscience tormented, however, at the thought of his twelve honest victims.

On his way to Sicily he descended into the volcano, passed through the corridor guarded by Cerberus, and knocked on the door of Pluto, whom he challenged to as many games of cards as Pluto might desire, with the proviso that if he should lose a single one his soul would be forfeit to Pluto but that for every game won Federigo should have the right to carry off one soul from the infernal regions. In twelve games he succeeded in rescuing the twelve souls of his early victims, each one of which he deposited in his sack; then he returned to his manor.

Thirty years later when Federigo was sixty Death approached but was persuaded to climb up in the orange tree to bring him down one last bit of fruit so he could die content. Finding himself unable to climb down, Death realized he had been tricked; he offered to grant Federigo ten more years of life, but finding him a tough bargainer finally agreed to a hundred. At the end of a century Death appeared once more and, confident of his victory, agreed to wait on the stool near the fireplace until Federigo could receive absolution from a priest. Impatient after an hour of delay and finding himself unable to rise from the stool after Federigo started a fire which threatened to roast him, Death finally accorded the forty years of additional life demanded.

At the end of this respite Death carried off Federigo and his sack of twelve souls, flew with them to Hell where he was refused entrance by Pluto on learning the identity of Federigo, then to Purgatory only to meet a similar refusal, and finally as a last resort to Paradise where they were first denied entrance by Saint Peter. Reminded of the hospitality once granted him by Federigo, Saint Peter grudgingly agreed to call Jesus Christ to make a final decision. Filled with compassion, the latter agreed to let Federigo enter but refused the twelve souls taken from Hell. "What, Lord," replied Federigo, "when I had the honor to receive you in my house, were you not accompanied by twelve travelers whom I received, along with you, in the best possible manner?" (250). Jesus Christ then granted his request but asked him not to boast of this favor, which would set a bad precedent.

The irreverent and mocking wit of this amusing tale forms a striking contrast with the somber, blood-stained tragedies of the rest of this volume. The effect is that of frothy whipped cream placed on a cup of rich and variegated fruit. We shall never know why Mérimée removed this story from later editions of *Mosaïque*.

Could it be that the mature Mérimée, ambitious for a seat in the French Academy, may have felt this tale too licentious and irreverent to receive the approval of this august body? Perhaps Mérimée felt also that he had followed too closely an earlier folk tale for his work to be truly original; perhaps he realized that the lightness of touch in *Federigo* clashed too conspicuously with the grim and tragic atmosphere of the rest of the volume. After the literary success of such masterpieces as *Mateo Falcone* and *L'Enlèvement de la redoute, Federigo* does indeed seem of inferior stature. Yet few of us are so lacking in a sense of humor that we would applaud Mérimée's decision.

VI   *Le Vase étrusque*

Le Vase étrusque, first published in the *Revue de Paris* in January, 1830, differs in almost every respect from the short stories which preceded it and marks a new route the author will take in future tales—the psychological study of passion. It is the first and almost the last one also in which we may find a subjective analysis of the author's own personality and character.

As the story opens we glimpse the hero, Auguste Saint-Clair, leaving at daybreak the country home of his mistress, Countess Mathilde de Courcy. Convinced for the first time that she reciprocates his passion, he throws himself down on the couch of his country estate, entranced with thoughts of his ideal happiness, to sleep until time for him to join a luncheon with some of his aristocratic friends in Paris. As might be expected, the conversation of these young bloods soon turns to women and the masculine qualities most fitted to achieve amorous conquests. Alphonse de Thémines insists that a handsome face and elegant costume are more important in this respect than intelligence or wit. He tries to prove his point by insisting that three years before Mme de Courcy had been infatuated with the famous Massigny, handsome as Adonis and elegant as Beau Brummell but a stupid bore. Recalling with horror a certain Etruscan vase which Massigny had given the Countess on his return from Italy, Saint-Clair, consumed with jealousy, abandons the group and returns in torment to the couch on which he had earlier caressed dreams of felicity.

Though at first determined to give up his rendezvous with the Countess that evening, he finds himself unable to resist his passion. Observing that her only adornment is a simple rose replacing jewels and necklace, he is encouraged when he recalls that the day before he had brought her a beautiful engraving of the Duchess of Portland, adorned in this manner, and had told her that since jewels serve only to hide blemishes, she was too pretty to wear them. Before he leaves, the Countess returns to him his watch which she had broken and had repaired, with a lovely portrait of herself in the box. Saint-Clair's jealousy is revived, however, when she tells him that it was Massigny who had acquainted her with the painter. As he taps the Etruscan vase harder and harder with his key, Mathilde cries out: "Heavens, be careful, you're going to break my beautiful Etruscan vase" (265). Tortured by the thought that she must have once loved Massigny, instead of going home to sleep he rides frantically through the woods, where he is inopportunely joined by Thémines, the unconscious author of all his suspicions. Furious at this friend, Saint-Clair insults him and is challenged to a duel on the morrow.

When he arrives at his usual rendezvous next day, relieved at the thought of a duel in which death will end his jealous torments, Saint-Clair's strange gaiety worries the Countess who has had fatiguing dreams, one of which concerned Massigny. To his great surprise and pleasure, she relates a comic incident showing how she humiliated Massigny when he dared propose love to her. Saint-Clair, overcome with shame and remorse for having doubted her, confesses his ignoble jealousy, and as she breaks the valuable vase into a thousand pieces he feels himself once more the happiest of men.

The epilogue of this romantic tale is tragic indeed. Colonel Beaujeu, Saint-Clair's second in the duel, relates what happened: instead of drawing lots Saint-Clair insisted that Thémines fire first; he did so and Saint-Clair fell stone dead. As for the Countess, for three years she refused to leave her room. Finding her thin and pale as a corpse, her cousin Julie took her to the Riviera, where the Countess lingered three or four months before succumbing to a malady of the lungs.

Le Vase étrusque has great literary value in its combination of graceful charm and sincere passion which remind us of the short stories of Alfred de Musset. Here for the first time in Mérimée we encounter a number of philosophic epigrams, such as the following: "he who, without being asked, shares his secret with us, is usually offended not to learn ours. One imagines that there should

be reciprocity in indiscretion" (252). Or, for instance, this metallic gem: "A happy lover is almost as boring as an unhappy one"
(254). Yet its chief interest lies in its unusual subjective portrayal,
for seldom has the author so lifted his mask to reveal his own
character and personality, as in this famous passage so often
quoted by critics:

He [Saint-Clair] had been born with a tender and loving heart; but, at
an age when one acquires too easily impressions which last all his life,
his overflowing sensibility had brought him the raillery of his comrades.
He was proud, ambitious; he cared about opinion as do children.
Henceforth he endeavored to hide all the appearances of what he considered a dishonorable weakness. He attained his goal; but his victory
cost him dear. He was able to conceal from others the emotions of his
too tender heart; but, in locking them up within himself, he made them
a hundred times more cruel for him. In the world he acquired the sad
reputation of being unfeeling and careless; and, in solitude, his uneasy
imagination created for him torments all the more frightful because he
would not have wished to confide their secret to anyone. (251)

And a few pages later the portrait continues with equal verisimilitude.

After all Saint-Clair was a rather accommodating man. His faults in-
jured only himself. He was obliging, often amiable, rarely boring. He
had traveled greatly, and spoke of his travels and readings only when
asked to do so. Moreover he was tall, well proportioned, his expression
was noble and witty, almost always too serious; but his smile was full
of grace. (253)

The tortures of jealousy analyzed in Le Vase étrusque are too
poignant not to have been experienced by Mérimée in one of his
own love affairs. Indeed Martineau, after M. Levaillant, quotes
from a letter of Hortense Allart de Méritens to Sainte-Beuve in
1846: "I could not tell you yesterday evening that the lady in front
of you, to whom I went to speak, is the woman of Mérimée's Vase
étrusque, the one for whom he fought and the only one doubtless
whom he has loved; she is still very agreeable; she is a niece of
Mme Davilliers, a friend of Béranger, she is Mme Lacoste" (XX).
This is the same lady who served as the model for the heroine of
Mérimée's Chronique du règne de Charles IX, as we have seen.

As happened in Mérimée's duel with M. Lacoste, Mérimée had also insisted that his opponent fire first, and as a result had received a wound, serious but in his case fortunately not fatal. There are other elements in *Le Vase étrusque* taken from the author's own life, notably the dinner of the young aristocrats (in which M. Levaillant thought he could identify the real participants) and the confession of Saint-Clair's early love affair, at the age of sixteen, with a young seamstress.

VII *La Partie de trictrac*

The Backgammon Game, first appearing in the *Revue de Paris*, in June, 1830, is one of Mérimée's most original stories, for no one has succeeded in discovering any work which might have inspired it. Here Mérimée continues the psychological analysis of passion which we first observed in *Le Vase étrusque*, although this time not that of love but of remorse.

The reader is encouraged to feel that this tragic incident really occurred by the fact that it is related by one of the actual participants, now captain of a sailing vessel becalmed at sea, to one of the new officers. The latter, refused permission to borrow the captain's dagger for a game of mumbletypeg, hears this story to explain the captain's unwillingness to lend this weapon, sole remaining relic from his friend, the unfortunate Roger.

Roger, a lieutenant three years older than the narrator, as an ensign had been a witty and charming young man, generous to a fault, impulsive and susceptible, whose greatest weakness was his violent desire to be first in everything. While the navy was garrisoned at Brest, a pretty young actress named Gabrielle joined the town's theater, and it was not long before Roger became deeply infatuated with her charms. In an entr'acte he presented her with a bouquet of rare flowers in which was concealed a roll of 25 gold napoleons, all the money he possessed at this time. As long as she perceived only the flowers and the handsome young officer Gabrielle showed herself gracious and appreciative, but when she felt the weight of the coins she threw them scornfully at Roger's head, leaving scars for a week. Unable to forget his passion, Roger wrote the actress twenty letters a day until he discovered that she was giving them to the orange seller to wrap her oranges in them.

At this time an army regiment arrived at Brest, and the officers, unable to force Gabrielle to repeat a couplet, hissed and jeered her on her next appearance. Roger rose, challenged these officers to a duel one by one, and was joined by his naval comrades from a sense of solidarity. In the ensuing combat Roger fought successively against three officers, killing one and wounding the others without receiving a scratch. The narrator, less fortunate, received a serious wound in the stomach, which kept him in the hospital for two weeks. On his recovery he found his friend Roger living with Gabrielle in the greatest harmony and felicity.

A few weeks later there entered the port a Dutch vessel whose officers invited the French to dine and gamble with them, an invitation which was soon reciprocated. One Dutchman insisted on such high stakes that no one was willing to be his opponent until Roger accepted in order to uphold the honor of France. Little by little the household money of Roger and Gabrielle melted away; one night Roger was risking at backgammon his last 25 napoleons and only a throw of six and four with the dice would be able to win for him. He cast them with such force on the board that a candle was upset. After the Dutch officer had bent over to remove the wax from his new pantaloons he saw that the dice marked six and four. Roger, pale as death, received the money and, while playing carelessly as if anxious to lose, wound up the evening with a total of 40,000 francs. He tried to give back the money, but the placid Dutchman refused to accept it, but later that night he blew his brains out after drinking a bowl of punch.

From that day on Roger was so irritable and morose that Gabrielle said anyone who did not know him would think he had cheated. When he confessed that this was true, his mistress replied with bitter scorn that she would rather have had him kill ten men than cheat at gambling. Some weeks later, finding a stray letter from a midshipman thanking Gabrielle for her kindness, Roger accused her of accepting money from a sailor. "Why not?" the actress answered coldly. "Yes I would take money from a sailor but . . . *I would not steal from him*" (282). That evening the narrator found Roger writing a letter of farewell to Gabrielle. Another letter on the table, addressed to the narrator, announced his plan to commit suicide, since he was no longer able to bear her scorn and his own shame. If Gabrielle had not rushed in at that moment to proclaim her love and forgiveness, the narrator would have been unable to persuade Roger to seek a glorious death in battle at sea rather than commit self-destruction.

Soon after this Roger and the narrator were ordered to sea. After a few successful encounters their ship of thirty-eight guns was attacked by a British warship of fifty-eight cannons off the coast of Africa. Roger, unwilling to face captivity in the pontoons of Portsmouth, made the narrator promise to throw him overboard should he be only wounded. The superior firepower of the British *Alceste* smashed the French mainmast, and Roger received a terrible blast of grapeshot in the stomach. He reminded his friend of his promise. But just as the Captain had reached this point in his narrative, the cry "Whale on larboard side" sent him rushing to prepare to attack the whale and Mérimée (or the officer) was never able to learn how Roger died.

Taine felt that in the year 2000 people would still be reading *La Partie de trictrac* "to learn what it costs to be lacking in honor a single time." [12] Without detailed analysis and merely by narration of significant facts and dialogue, Mérimée has succeeded in portraying vividly Roger's remorse. When his friend tries to comfort him by telling him he is guilty not of cheating for 40,000 francs but only for 25 napoleons, Roger's mind is too lucid to accept this facile excuse. "So then," he cried with bitter irony, "I am a little thief and not a big one. I who was so ambitious. To be only a little rogue!" (282). And later when his friend consoles him with the assertion that his action had a noble motive—that of saving his beloved Gabrielle from abject poverty—Roger replies that he is only a cowardly rascal. "When I cheated this Dutchman I thought only of winning twenty-five napoleons, that was all. I was not thinking of Gabrielle and that is why I despise myself" (285). Unable to continue living without his own esteem, he renounced suicide only in hopes of finding an honorable death in combat against the enemy.

Typical of the author is the abundance in this story of violent emotion and bloodshed, recounted as usual in the impassive manner of the cold observer. Mérimée's studied restraint is evident from his unwillingness to conclude the story, a technique we have already observed in the *Chronique*. The characters are as primitive and elemental in their instincts as Mateo Falcone or the later Colomba and Carmen. While the picture of human nature is not a pleasant or idealized one, it must be admitted that Mérimée has given us here a remarkable study of the *point d'honneur*. It is perhaps this quality of the pure-blooded gentleman with respect for his honor at any cost which most truly has penetrated the armor of reserve under which Mérimée tried most often to hide his innermost nature from the world. It is still the *point d'honneur* of Roland, of Corneille's *Cid,* though shorn of its glamour by the cold gray light of modern realism.

VIII   *Evaluation of Mosaïque*

The stories included in *Mosaïque* mark one of the high points in Mérimée's literary career, to be equalled later but scarcely to be surpassed. If Mérimée had died at twenty-seven, he would still have achieved distinguished rank in the domain of the short story. Those two little masterpieces alone, *Mateo Falcone* and *L'Enlèvement de la redoute,* were sufficient to establish his solid reputation. Of the five others, two at least, *Tamango* and *La Partie de trictrac,* are included in school editions and are scarcely inferior to the two masterpieces. *Federigo* and *La Vision de Charles IX* may be of less value, although the latter has been highly praised for its mingling of supernatural fantasy and realism of vivid, significant detail. *Le Vase étrusque* remains a precious document for understanding the author's true nature.

In addition to its intrinsic literary value, this collection is noteworthy as marking a point of departure in Mérimée's artistic development—his realization of the path which he should henceforth pursue in the short story. In the great variety of subject matter and treatment we may perceive here all the traits to be exemplified in the best of his succeeding fiction: Romantic penchant for exotic scenes of bloodshed and terror, expressed with the precision of the Realists; preoccupation with the fantastic and supernatural; synthetic rather than analytic portrayal of elemental human nature; irony and impassive detachment. That Mérimée will be unable to remain consistently on this high level of achievement will be evident from a study of his next two comparative failures in the longer novella, before he rises once more to the perfection of *Colomba* and *Carmen.*

CHAPTER 7

Two Controversial Novellas

I La Double Méprise
(The Double Misunderstanding)

THE years from 1831 to 1834 were the least productive of Mérimée's mature life, spent as they were in idle dissipation which gained him a reputation of a cynical *viveur*, a reputation which remained unjustly throughout his later years. In contrast with the creative profusion we have observed in *Mosaïque*, *La Double Méprise*, a psychological novella, represents his only significant contribution in the first two of these years. As Mérimée himself confessed many years later, this work was dashed off "in haste." "It is one of my sins done to earn money offered to some one who was not worth very much," he confessed in 1858.[1] In order to give this novella the proportions of a novel it was necessary to resort to the artifice of printing it in very large letters, but as Martineau has pointed out, this was the first and only time in Mérimée's career that he subordinated his literary inspiration to financial needs.[2]

The title of this work, as well as the four lines in Spanish which precede it, come from Calderón: "Young lady, whiter than the flowers, blond with green eyes, if thou dost think to abandon thyself to love, since thou ruinest thyself, ruin thyself well." In the opening chapter we learn that Julie de Chaverny has been married for six years to a vapid, vulgar, and boring Marquis whose sensual nature is interested only in the delights of the chase, of the table, or of the boudoirs of his mistresses. Lazy because of increasing obesity, he prefers coarse amusements to more delicate pleasures; "for, to distinguish himself among the persons of his own taste, he needed no more effort than to shout more loudly than the others, which was not difficult with lungs like his" (290). His reputation was based on two solid accomplishments: he could drink more champagne than any ordinary man, and he could make his horse jump a four-foot barrier. It is not difficult for the reader to understand Julie's bored resignation, relieved only by feminine coquetry allied to a certain disdainful reserve which protected her virtue.

Among the young aristocrats dancing attendance on this attractive Marchioness is a handsome young Major Châteaufort, who on receiving a letter from Julie inviting him to bring his friend the old Major Perrin to dine, fatuously considers himself in line to become her lover. His distinguished elegance and courtesy at the dinner contrast sharply with the scandalous coarseness of Chaverny's manners and ribald conversation. This contrast is further enhanced one evening at the opera when Chaverny invites to their loge the Duke of H——, together with the latter's mistress, an overdressed, vulgar beauty who embarrasses Julie by becoming the cynosure of all eyes in the theater. As Julie reflects the following morning on the difference between the chivalrous attitude of Châteaufort and the boorish conduct of her husband from whom she plans to request a legal separation, the final touch to her disillusionment with marriage comes from the departure of the Marquis to spend four days hunting with the Duke of H—— and his mistress. She decides to drive four leagues into the country to ask the advice of her friend, Mme Lambert. Having read in the papers that day of the return to Paris of the young diplomat Darcy, with whom she had been on friendly terms before her marriage and his departure for Constantinople, she recalls his sympathetic commiseration on one occasion when to her great humiliation she had sung off key.

Arriving at the home of Mme Lambert, Julie is entreated to remain for a dinner to which had been invited among others Châteaufort, Major Perrin, and the friend of her girlhood, M. Darcy. The latter, urged on by the ladies, recounts at some length an adventure in Turkey during which he had rescued a Mohammedan slave girl from being thrown into the sea by her angry master. Then, to the annoyance of Châteaufort, Darcy pays Julie great attention until drawn aside by a young man interested in the statistics of the Ottoman Empire. When Julie calls for her carriage, she is somewhat piqued that Darcy allows Châteaufort to take leave of her, but as she starts out she observes that Darcy, pale and with sad eyes, is watching as if he desired a special greeting.

Her memory of their early comradeship revives her warm feelings toward him.

On the drive back to Paris a violent storm comes up, the horses stumble in the darkness, and the carriage is thrown into the ditch with one wheel broken. Fortunately, Darcy soon comes by and offers to take her back with him in his coupé. As he expresses his conviction that she must lead a happy life with her wealth, her friends, and her adoring husband, she bursts into uncontrollable tears, rests her head on his shoulder, and confesses her conjugal disillusionment. Darcy, apparently surprised by this turn of affairs, takes advantage of her emotion to make her his mistress. This scene reminds us of Flaubert's famous description of Mme Bovery's seduction by Léon in the cab at Rouen. Mérimée's summary is typically laconic: "She tried again to free herself from his embrace, but this effort was the last she attempted" (340).

As if he had now decided to change his project from a novel to a novella, Mérimée concludes his story in sudden haste. While Julie in anguished silence is overcome with remorse for her indiscretion, Darcy in his embarrassment rejoices at seeing Paris approaching. On their arrival at her home, Julie's dreams of flight with the man she loves are rudely shattered by Darcy's calm remarks which show he is contemplating only a convenient summer's liaison. Throwing herself on her bed without undressing, Julie in her self-pity and frustration is unable to sleep and on the morrow summons her maid to pack for a journey to her mother in Nice, leaving a brief word for her husband. In the midst of her preparations two gentlemen arrive, Châteaufort and Darcy. Though their arrival at the same time is purely fortuitous, she imagines that Darcy has made the other his confidant, and she refuses to receive either. Weakened by her fainting spell and effusion of blood, she sets forth in her carriage but by the following morning has such a fever that she has to be put to bed in a village inn, where a doctor is summoned. During a temporary respite from the fever Julie tries to write several letters, which she tears up and asks the maid to burn; on one of the fragments the maid notices the words: "Monsieur, you must despise me greatly" (349). Delirium resumes its sway, and next day she is dead.

The epilogue to this tragic story is ironic indeed. Chaverny arrived three days after the burial; unwilling to undergo all the formalities required for exhumation and transfer of the body to Paris, he ordered a simple but suitable tomb. Châteaufort, moved by this sudden death, "refused several invitations to balls and for sometime was dressed only in black" (330). Darcy never spoke of her and three or four months later contracted an advantageous marriage.

According to Billy,[3] this novella was inspired by the famous fiasco of Mérimée's one-night love affair with George Sand, but I see little resemblance except for the brief duration. La Double Méprise is certainly the most controversial of Mérimée's works; it has been attacked by some critics and fervently defended by others. Among its admirers mentioned by Billy are Bourget, Jaloux, Du Bos, Marsan, and (wrongly, I think) Faguet. Two recent biographers, Baschet and Raitt, agree with Billy. Baschet, for example, considers it a masterpiece: . . . He practices with mastery "the art of the psychological miniature. In this novella he needs only a few lines to sketch out an epicurean and refined ideal of life whose Stendhalian resonance does not escape those familiar with the author of the treatise De l'amour."[4] Raitt is even more enthusiastic, reminding us that a committee of French writers and critics recently voted it one of the twelve best novels of the nineteenth century.[5]

The detractors of this novel are no less numerous or impressive. Faguet for example feels that it would have been much more successful developed at greater length as a novel, rather than compressed as a novella: "In order not to fall into the ridiculousness of his time, which was eloquence, he falls into the opposite defect, which is a little dryness, the lack of development necessary to be understood. La Double Méprise is a very fine, very delicate psychological novel which needed for full effect a more deeply examined study of the two principal characters. He has decided to treat it as a novella, reducing to a minimum the investigation of the moral complexion of his two personages, leaving us to do it ourselves."[6] Though Billy mentioned only Paul Souday among the detractors of La Double Méprise, he might have cited many others, among them the usually sympathetic Filon who found it spoiled by Mérimée's "dandyism" at this period and who considered it certainly not one of his good works: "It is the beginning of a novel which is aborted and reduced to the minute psychology of a feminine character. Moreover this psychology is neither very clear nor very lifelike. The dénouement is too unexpected to be moving and one feels that the author does not believe in it." [7] Buffum calls this work one of Mérimée's poorer stories, and Martineau in his scholarly *Préface* contrasts unfavorably the minutely detailed analysis of the first part with the breathless speed of the conclusion, which "relates events with the dryness of a police report." [8]

I have presented these conflicting evaluations of *La Double Méprise* at some length so that the reader may judge for himself. As for my own reactions, I must agree with the less favorable critics, all the more so since the mature Mérimée would undoubtedly join them: "It is one of my sins made to earn money." Conceived first as a novel, its slow development at the beginning is out of proportion for a novella. The detailed portraits of Châteaufort, Major Perrin, and Marquis de Chaverny the husband are somewhat superfluous, although that of the latter does help explain his wife's revulsion and her ultimate seduction by Darcy. The long-drawn-out, twice-repeated story of Darcy's rescue of the Greek slave, a tale within a tale, occupies eight of the sixty pages, an amount more appropriate in a novel. The character of the heroine, Julie de Chaverny, is not really convincing. Portrayed first as an ironic observer of society, something of a coquette but at the same time filled with reserve and disdain toward masculine admirers, she puzzles us by her decision that she has loved all these years the companion of her childhood, even more by her excessive remorse for a moment of weakness. Billy has explained her melodramatic death from an "inflammation of the chest" or congestion of the lungs as a concession to Romantic tendencies of the age, reminding us that the same tragic end came to Mme de Courcy in *Le Vase étrusque*. We might reply that this malady in the latter story required three years, not three days as in *La Double Méprise*, an example of "galloping consumption" which must make medical history. And though the background of fashionable society is much the same in both stories, the sincere pathos of *Le Vase étrusque* contrasts strongly with the cold sophistication of this novella, which leaves this reader unmoved and unconvinced.

There is, however, one aspect of *La Double Méprise* which should interest even its detractors: the extent to which we may discover the character of the author at this time in the person of Darcy. The latter, like Mérimée, had possessed too little income as a young man for him to think of matrimony. What first brought him together with Julie before her marriage was their mutual fondness for satirizing their acquaintances. "A little misanthropic and caustic he took great pleasure . . . in making fun of the ridiculousness and pretensions of other young men" (311). We may glimpse the author also in his physical description of Darcy: "He was a tall, pale young man whose features expressed calm, but a calm which seemed to come less from the habitual state of his soul than from the restraint which it had succeeded in gaining over the expression of his face. . . . Darcy was very simply dressed but with that elegance which indicates the habits of good company and indifference in regard to a matter which occupies the attention of so many young men" (318). Like Mérimée, Darcy had a habit of drawing sketches. Like Mérimeé also, Darcy was too modest to accept any reputation as knight-errant for saving the life of the Greek slave. His independence of social formality is shown by his remark: "I have never known how to act in friendly manner with people I did not like" (331). Like Mérimée, Darcy was fond of foreign languages, having studied Greek and Turkish (332).

Like the author, Darcy seemed incapable of deep passion. "He had met with pleasure a pretty woman who recalled happy memories and whose acquaintance would probably be agreeable to him for the winter he was going to spend in Paris" (32). While Darcy obviously had not planned a seduction of Julie in his carriage, he was too much a man of the world to resist the opportunity when it presented itself; "he was polite and politeness often takes the place of more respectable sentiments. The first moment of rapture having passed, he declaimed to Julie tender phrases which he composed without too much difficulty and which he accompanied with numerous kisses on her hands which spared him as many words" (340). We may find Darcy a little cold and fatuous in his reaction to his amorous conquest: "Darcy got back into his coupé and had himself driven home while whistling with an air of a man very well satisfied with his day" (342), before putting on his Turkish robe and carpet slippers to enjoy a placid pipeful of Latakia tobacco while caressing in his mind his good fortune. The conclusion after Julie's death may seem almost too cynical. When he made an advantageous marriage three or four months after her decease and was congratulated by Mme Lambert with the phrase that only poor Julie could have suited him as well, his only reply was to smile "with that ironic smile which was habitual to him" (350).

In the light of these quotations it is not difficult to agree with Faguet. "It seems to me that he [Mérimée] has painted himself twice; in the Saint-Clair of *Le Vase étrusque* in flattering himself a little, in showing himself a sensitive person who represses himself; in the Darcy of *La Double Méprise*, in blackening himself slightly and making himself out a Valmont; the truth seems to me to lie somewhere between these two." [9]

II *Les Ames du Purgatoire*
(*The Souls of Purgatory*)

This modernization of the Don Juan legend was first published on August 15, 1834, in the *Revue des Deux Mondes;* it was republished with *Colomba* in book form in 1841. Written shortly before his departure from Paris in his new capacity as inspector general, this irreverent and licentious tale might be considered Mérimée's farewell to his life of dissipation. We recall that on his first visit to Spain in 1830 Mérimée had made the acquaintance of Mme de Teba (later de Montijo) who may well have suggested some of the incidents in the life of Don Juan. He had observed that in Seville there seem to have been several Don Juans, the most distinctive of whom were Don Juan Tenorio and Don Juan de Maraña whose histories paralleled and mingled except for the denouement—in the case of the latter, remorse, conversion, and salvation. In Seville Mérimée had been impressed by the Church of Charity, with its tomb of Don Juan de Maraña and its inscription: "Here lies the worst man who ever existed in the world." As far as possible, Mérimée says in his introduction, he will endeavor to separate the legends of the two Don Juans, restricting himself to the adventures of Don Juan de Maraña.

The subject of the Don Juan legend was very much in vogue during the early 1830's. Molière's famous play continued of course to be well known, and Byron's poem *Don Juan,* of which Mérimée himself had written a review in 1830, was extremely popular. Furthermore, Mozart's opera was revived in Paris in 1833 and was playing at the Opéra and the Théâtre Italien simultaneously. Martineau reminds us also that Mérimeé's friend Stendhal had devoted several pages to Don Juan in his treatise *De l'Amour.*[10] It is easy to understand why this subject should have attracted Mérimée, first for the opportunity to paint with precision the scabrous details of this adventurous lover, second for the effect of the fantastic and supernatural in bringing about the unexpected conclusion.

Only son of Don Carlos de Maraña, Don Juan has left Seville to complete his studies at the famous university of Salamanca. There he becomes the friend of another student, Don Garcia Navarro, who soon introduces him to the debaucheries of student life. Since Don Garcia is intent on making the conquest of the noble Fausta, he persuades Don Juan to court her younger sister Teresa. One evening their serenade before the balcony of these two young ladies is interrupted by the arrival of a rival, Don Cristoval, accompanied by friends and musicians. Refusing his impudent demand to leave, Don Juan kills Don Cristoval in a duel, then flees with Don Garcia to escape the police, leaving his broken sword behind. As Don Juan remarks sadly to his friend, "It is a very sad thing to kill one of our fellow men," the greater sophistication of Don Garcia is apparent in his reply: "There is something still more sad, that is to have one of your fellow men kill us, and a third thing that surpasses the other two in sadness, is a day passed without dining" (372).

The two friends succeed in their amorous conquests of Fausta and Teresa, but, after a few weeks of happiness, boredom and satiety ensue, and Don Garcia suggests that they exchange mistresses. Fausta, far from accepting Don Juan to avenge herself on her faithless lover, arouses the household against him; in the ensuing confusion, her father shoots Fausta with a blow intended for Don Juan, who in turn slays the father while making his escape. It being too dangerous to remain in Salamanca, Don Garcia suggests that they join the Spanish army fighting the Dutch near Brussels. Here they take service under brave Captain Gomare, who is soon killed in battle, leaving his whole fortune of 60 gold pieces to Don Juan with a request that he have masses said for the repose of his soul. As an impious freethinker, however, Don Garcia persuades his friend to devote this money to gambling, with the result that nothing is left to carry out the Captain's dying request.

About this time a new recruit joins the company, an intrepid young man but so mysteriously aloof from drinking and carousing that he acquires the nickname of Modesto. One night during the siege of Berg-op-Zoom an arquebus shot rings out, apparently from the ranks of the besiegers, and Don Garcia falls mortally wounded. Modesto makes his escape in the darkness. Don Juan is overcome with grief at the loss of his dearest friend and, receiving shortly news of the deaths of his father and mother, decides to return to Seville for the inheritance.

Here he gathers about him a group of debauched young nobles and devotes his vast fortune to dissipation and amorous conquests. During his convalescence from a brief illness he amuses himself by drawing up a list of his mistresses in one column and that of the deceived husbands in another. When he showed this list to a friend, with the pope heading the group of cuckolds opposite the name of one of the pope's mistresses, his friend remarks that the list is incomplete without God on it. This gives Don Juan the idea of seducing a nun, who turns out to be his former mistress Teresa, who after the deaths of her father and sister had taken the veil. Despite her remorse, her passion is still so strong that she finally agrees to his scheme for escape from the convent. Returning to the Maraña château two days before the date arranged for the elopement, Don Juan is fascinated by the picture he had seen so often in his boyhood, portraying the torments of purgatory and a man being devoured by a serpent. Back in Seville an hour before the signal to be given Teresa, Don Juan sees defile before him a procession of penitents with wax tapers, preceding and following a coffin covered with black velvet, to the accompaniment of funereal chanting. Each time he inquires concerning the identity of the man in the coffin, he receives the reply, "Count Don Juan de Maraña." Entering the church he perceives the horrible apparition of Don Garcia and Captain Gomare, together with a gigantic serpent which seems about to enter the bier. Don Juan falls on the pavement in a faint.

On recovering his senses, he calls for a confessor and vows to spend the rest of his life in a cloister. He sends Teresa a letter explaining his diabolical scheme and his conversion; the latter, exclaiming over and over "He never loved me," dies a few days later from a broken heart. Dividing his wealth among his poor relatives and the pious foundation of a hospital, Don Juan now devotes himself to a life of austerity and self-mortification. One day while spading in the garden he is accosted by a young man, the former Modesto, who reveals that he was the brother of Fausta and Teresa whom Don Juan had killed, and challenges him to a duel. Unwilling to have another murder on his conscience, Don Juan offers himself humbly as a victim, but when he receives a slap from the young man, his proud temperament reasserts itself. He accepts the proffered rapier, and in the violent duel which follows he leaves Don Pedro dead at his feet. When the superior hears his anguished confession, he arranges with the *corregidor* to hush up the affair so as not to bring disgrace on the order. For his penance Don Juan lives the rest of his life with Don Pedro's sword at the foot of his bed to remind him of his crime and every morning receives a slap from the cook of the monastery, never failing to turn the other cheek and thank him for the humiliation. Asking to be buried under the threshold so that everyone would step on him at entrance, he dies, venerated as a saint. Considering his request excessive, the officials agree, however, to the inscription he had asked on his tomb—"Here lies the worst man who was ever in the world"—but they place it near the high altar of the chapel he had founded, together with a eulogy of his conversion. His hospital and chapel are visited by foreigners passing through Madrid, and Murillo adorned the wall with several masterpieces, later to be found in the gallery of Marshal Soult.

This second novella, like *La Double Méprise,* has been the subject of much contention among critics. Earlier commentators have given it rather a low rating: Faguet, for instance, found it "without interest," [11] and Filon was even more contemptuous, remarking "what tediousness, what boredom, what a complication of insipid adventures, and how the story drags until the dénouement." [12] More recent critics have tended to react against this interpretation and evaluate the work more favorably. Baschet, for instance, finds here a singular power of suggestion, praising in particular the scene of the procession of souls, which in his view "counts among Mérimée's successes in the fantastic tale." [13] Billy likewise, reminded agreeably of Anatole France, considers this novella "a model of the well-constructed tale, of skillful diction, of well-assimilated erudition, of clever and delicate transposition, on a background of skepticism expressed only by barely perceptible reflections." [14]

This time I find myself in hearty agreement with Mérimée's recent and more favorable critics. The recital of Don Juan's amorous adventures sparkles with ingenuity, freshness, and variety of incident. The atmosphere of sixteenth-century Spain is vividly evoked, especially in the antagonism between town and gown, citizens and students—of particular interest for us today as we think of parallels on campuses throughout the world. From the viewpoint of technique there is an admirable contrast between the rollicking adventures of the youthful Don Juan and the somber, mysterious procession of penitent souls which brings about his conversion. Despite the licentiousness of their conduct, there is a touching bond of loyalty and brotherhood between the two friends, Don Juan and his mentor, the diabolical Don Garcia. Martineau was the first, perhaps, to point out the relationship here to the long friendship between Mérimée and his elder, Stendhal.[15] This can be observed in the fact that the two nobles, en route to Flanders, first sailed from Spain to Civitavecchia, a city Mérimée could have chosen only because Stendhal had been stationed there for many years as French consul. Then, at the death of Don Garcia, Don Juan expresses his grief and admiration in a paragraph obviously reminiscent of the almost filial respect held by Mérimée for his master, Stendhal.

To sum up, it seems fair to state that if *Les Ames du Purgatoire* does not rank among Mérimée's masterpieces, it remains nevertheless a work of great interest, not lightly to be dismissed as the failure Faguet and Filon would have us believe.

CHAPTER 8

The Golden Decade: 1837-1847

I La Vénus d'Ille

WE have seen that after the rich harvest of short stories written by Mérimée in the period of fourteen months 1829–30 there ensued a comparative desert of seven years, caused at first by his worldly successes in Parisian society, then by his travel throughout France in his new capacity as inspector general of historical monuments. From one of these excursions into Southern France and the Pyrenees he brought back the setting if not the inspiration of one of his finest works, La Vénus d'Ille, first published in the Revue des Deux Mondes of May 15, 1837, and later in book form with Colomba in 1841. With this publication begins a glorious decade of literary activity consisting of works on art, literary criticism, history, and fiction, the latter including many of the masterpieces most appreciated today.

In regard to the direct sources of inspiration for La Vénus d'Ille, the problem is complicated and confused. Billy found the legend in the Historia Regum Britanniae of William of Malmesbury of 1125.[1] The legend of the statue of Venus coming to life and crushing the man who deceived her was a favorite in the folklore of Europe dating back to the Middle Ages. Filon claimed to find its origin in a Latin chronicle of the tenth century, reproduced in Eckhardt's Corpus Historiarum published at Leipzig in 1723, observing here all the elements of Mérimée's modern tale: "the tennis match, the ring slipped on the statue's finger, the nocturnal visit of the goddess."[2] More perplexing is the fact that Mérimée himself has given us two different explanations. In a letter to Eloi Johanneau of November, 1847, he wrote: "The Venus d'Ille never existed. . . . The idea of this story came to me while reading in Fischer a legend of the Middle Ages. I took some features also from Lucian, who speaks of a statue which used to beat people." But in a later letter to Francisque Michel, August

10, 1851, he gave an entirely different version of his sources. "I read in Pontanus . . . the story of a man who had given his ring to a Venus of marble or of bronze, but that was so long ago I no longer have too much idea who Pontanus was." In any case, Mérimée by his artistry has so adapted the legend to a contemporary, more sophisticated audience as to render it a purely original work.

Descending the slopes of Canigou Mountain toward the village of Ille in order to visit M. Peyrehorade, a local antiquary, the author is told by his guide that his prospective host is about to marry off his son to a wealthy heiress. The guide informs him also of the recent discovery in Ille of a bronze, Roman statue of Venus, which in falling had broken the leg of Jean Coll, one of the excavators. Mérimée is received with great cordiality by the antiquary and is introduced to his wife and to the son whose marriage is planned for Friday (*vendredi*, day of Venus), two days later. After a succulent repast he is conducted to his room, from which he has a beautiful view of the mountain in the moonlight, and he catches a glimpse of the statue of Venus. At this moment, two young peasants are heard uttering threats against the statue; one of them throws a stone which rebounds from the metal, wounding him in the head.

On the following morning Mérimée is taken by the antiquary to visit the statue, a beautiful example of ancient Roman art and with an expression of ferocity which made it appear almost human.

This expression of infernal irony was enhanced perhaps by the contrast of its eyes encrusted with silver and very brilliant with the patina of blackish green which time had given the statue. These shining eyes produced a certain illusion which recalled reality, life. I remembered what my guide had told me, that it caused the eyes of any onlooker to drop. That was almost true and I could not restrain a movement of anger against myself from feeling ill at ease before this figure of bronze. (418)

A discussion ensues concerning the inscription *Cave Amantem* which the author says may be translated in two ways: "beware of him who loves thee," or "beware if she loves thee." In the afternoon the son shows Mérimée with great pride the carriage he had bought for his fiancée and the bridal ring, a family heirloom en-

crusted with diamonds worth 1,200 francs. That evening they dine
at the home of the bride-to-be, a charming young lady whose delicate contours contrast greatly with the coarse appearance of the
bridegroom.

On the wedding morning some visiting Spaniards are in the
process of badly defeating a local team at handball. Oblivious of
his wedding finery, M. Alphonse enters the game to retrieve the
honor of the natives. Bothered by the weight of the huge ring, he
runs to place it on the finger of Venus, then defeats the foreign
team decisively, offering to give his opponents a handicap next
time. A young Spaniard, furious at such condescension, responds
in bitter rage: "Me lo pagaras" (You'll pay me for this).

Arriving at Puygarrig for the wedding, M. Alphonse suddenly
realized he had left the dimond ring behind on the hand of the
statue, but rather than send back for it he decides to use a plain
ring he had once received from a mistress in Paris. After the civil
and religious ceremonies, a copious luncheon and an afternoon of
dancing on the lawn of the château, the wedding party returns to
Ille for another wedding feast. In the midst of the licentious mer-
riment, the bridegroom whispers in Mérimée's ear that he feels
himself bewitched, unable to remove the ring from the finger of
Venus. Thinking that Alphonse is probably intoxicated, rather
than go out in the rain Mérimée proceeds at midnight to his room.

At dawn he is awakened by footsteps and the moaning of Alphonse's mother in the bridal chamber. On entering he sees a
tragic sight. The young man, livid and motionless, is lying half-
dressed across the bed, his father rubbing his temples with eau de
cologne in a fruitless effort to revive him, his mother weeping beside him, his bride in terrible convulsions on a couch.

I approached the bed and raised the body of the unfortunate young
man; it was already stiff and cold. His clenched teeth and his blackened face expressed the most terrible anguish. It was apparent that his
death had been violent and his agony terrible. But there was no trace
of blood on his clothes. I pushed aside his shirt and saw on his chest a
livid imprint prolonged on his ribs and back. One would have said that
he had been crushed in a circle of iron. My foot struck against something hard on the carpet; I bent down and saw the diamond ring.
(432–33)

Deciding that assassins must have made their way into the room,
the author goes down into the garden to search for footprints, but

the only ones he can find, proceeding from the house to the statue and back to the house, must have been those made by Alphonse when going to try to retrieve the ring.

By noon the young bride has become calm enough to relate her story to the examining magistrate. Soon after going to bed she heard the door open and first thought it was her husband. The bed creaked under an enormous weight, and her hand felt the contact of something cold as ice. Soon the door was opened a second time by someone who called out "Bon soir, ma petite femme." The person in bed with her sat up, stretched out her arms, and she saw her husband on his knees beside the bed in the arms of a greenish giant which she recognized as the bronze Venus. When she recovered consciousness, she heard the cock crow, saw the statue drop the corpse, then she rang for help. During his examination by the magistrate Mérimée testifies to the threat uttered by the Aragonese, who is then summoned. He explains that he meant by his remark only that he would seek revenge in a later contest; his footprints are found not to match those in the garden, and since he enjoys a good reputation in the countryside he is set free with apologies for his arrest.

M. de Peyrehorade dies a few months after his son. Mérimée learns later that the statue of Venus no longer exists, for the antiquary's widow had it melted down to serve as a bell for the church of Ille. Since this bell has been ringing the vines have twice been frozen—which shows the evil power that the bronze still exerts.

Mérimée considered *La Vénus d'Ille* his masterpiece.[3] Billy does not agree, asserting that Mérimée is not particularly gifted for the fantastic.[4] Most other critics, among them Pierre Richard, Baschet, Martineau, and Raitt, rank it very high indeed, an opinion with which I am in full accord. Mérimée might have been amused, had he been able to foresee the various interpretations it has had. Valéry Larbaud, for instance, in the preface to his edition of the story, asserts that "the statue punishes the young man for having treated lightly the love of Parisian women who gave him another ring." Equally misleading in my opinion is the conclusion expressed by Billy in the discussion cited above: "*La Vénus d'Ille* is . . . a testimony to the fundamental idea which Mérimée had of woman, malevolent being par excellence." If the warm friendships which Mérimée enjoyed with Jenny Dacquin,

Mme Delessert, Mme de la Rochejacquelein, Mme de Montijo and her daughter Eugenia were not sufficient to refute this statement, a closer reading of the story itself would do so. Mlle Puygarrig, the fiancée, is presented as a charming and delicate person, with an air of kindness not exempt from a slightly mischievous touch, and who is overcome with emotion at parting from her beloved old aunt. What a contrast with the earthy materialistic bridegroom, more interested in the rich dowry than appreciative of his lovely bride. "I thought of this young girl, so beautiful and so pure, abandoned to a brutal drunkard" (431). Never perhaps has Mérimée protested more fervently against a *mariage de convenance* and come out in favor of a union marked by true love.

If Mérimée has succeeded better here than in the earlier *Vision de Charles XI* in making the reader fall under the spell of the fantastic and supernatural it is because he has so artfully prepared us, through touches of precise realism, to accept the truthfulness of his narrative. First, the author himself is part of the action; the milieu of the little village on the slopes of Mount Canigou is so real; the language of his peasant guide is so natural and colloquial; the ribald conviviality of the rustic wedding, the characters of the antiquary, his devoutly superstitious wife, and egotistical son are so vividly delineated. Whether the pompous and pedantic antiquary is a satire of a local archeologist and professor of Perpignan who had criticized Mérimée's *Voyage dans le Midi,* or whether he is rather a synthetic portrait of all the vain and pompous antiquaries Mérimée encountered during his travels as inspector general matters little. The author's irony here is more genial than acerbic, and the portrait is one of the most diverting in the gallery of Mérimée's creations.

To put us in the proper frame of mind to accept a miraculous denouement, the author has proceeded with the deft touches of a great artist. First we are impressed by the malevolent character of the statue, which in falling broke the leg of the town's famous athlete. Then we have the description of the glittering eyes which gave it the illusion of being alive and caused the onlooker to lower his eyes in confusion. Next comes the inability of the bridegroom to remove the ring from the statue's finger, bent back over the ring as if she felt it sealed her marriage to M. Alphonse. On hearing this account from the bridegroom, the narrator felt a sudden shiver and for an instant gooseflesh (430). Then on the morrow, to corroborate the vision of the gigantic, greenish Venus seen by the frantic bride, there was the circular imprint of a metallic embrace on the ribs and back of the corpse, and the diamond ring on the floor.

Yet there is a new element here in the author's technique, the introduction of a choice between two possible solutions to the enigma—one supernatural, the other purely materialistic. It was the author himself, we remember, who called to the attention of the authorities the threat uttered by the Aragonese athlete after his humiliation at the hands of M. Alphonse. Did not his own words of disculpation testify to the violence of his nature? "If I had thought that M. Alphonse had wished to insult me, I would have thrust my knife at once into his belly." In this unwillingness to impose either a realistic or a mystical conclusion on the reader, Mérimée anticipates the method of some of his later stories and one of Maupassant's favorite techniques. One of the fascinations of this story for the reader is this tantalizingly difficult choice; for if we have brought ourselves to prefer the idea of purely human revenge, how shall we account for the continued malevolence of Venus the jilted bride, even when melted down as a church bell, as shown by the successive frosts which ruined the vineyards?

II *Colomba*

While *Mateo Falcone* was composed by Mérimée merely from his reading of treatises and stories about the Corsica he had never seen, *Colomba* with its greater complexity and vividness is the result of Mérimée's visit to this island in his capacity of inspector general from August 16 to October 17, 1839. Six months later appeared his *Notes d'un voyage en Corse* and on July 1, 1840, *Colomba* in the *Revue des Deux Mondes,* before its publication in book form in 1841. In Paris Mérimée had met a Corsican consul, Orso Carabelli, who in his home at Fozzano introduced Mérimée to his sister, Colomba, famous *vocatricero,* or composer of funeral ballads. Her beautiful daughter Catherine, thirty-one years old but in appearance not more than twenty, served Mérimée for the physical portrait of his heroine, but for the rest he drew on her mother, whom he rejuvenated by thirty years. From her he had heard the story of the mortal vendetta between the Carabelli and Durazzo familes: in the bloody climax in 1833 two of the Duraz-

zos had been killed and another wounded; the aggressors, Michel
Bernardini and Colomba's son, François Bartoli, also perished. Although peace between the two houses had been signed in 1834,
Colomba, inconsolable for the loss of her son, was still unwilling
to forgive. While crossing Corsica to visit its churches and monuments, Mérimée met several bandits and was entertained with
cordial hospitality in the homes of the natives, one of whom was
the original for the famous *coup double* with which Orso killed
both of his antagonists in Mérimée's novel.[5]

Since *Colomba* has been published as a school text in innumerable editions, a brief résumé of the action should be sufficient.
The retired English Colonel Sir Thomas Nevil and his attractive
daughter Lydia, somewhat bored by their recent tour of Italy,
have learned from a British captain they met in Marseilles that
Corsica is still a country untouched by banal civilization where
the hunting is superb. On the little ship taking them from Marseilles to Ajaccio they meet a young Corsican lieutenant, Orso Antonio della Rebbia, like the Colonel in retirement after the Napoleonic Wars, whose father had been slain in ambush some two
years before. From a ballad sung by one of the sailors, Miss Lydia
learns of the feud between the Barricini and della Rebbia families
and fears that the young lieutenant is returning to Corsica to exact
a bloody vengeance. After a few days in Ajaccio they are visited
by Colomba, who has come to accompany her brother Orso to
their native village of Pietranera, where she hopes to convince
him that their father had been slain not by the bandit Agostino
but by the rival family Barricini, which had been cleared of the
murder by a judicial investigation. In hopes of terminating this
old feud, the Prefect brings to Orso's home the old mayor Barricini and his two sons Orlanduccio and Vincentello for a reconciliation. He offers as proof of their innocence a deposition from a
thief, Tomaso Bianchi, now in prison at Bastia, which stated that
he had forged the letter that caused Agostino to murder della
Rebbia. Colomba, however, produces a witness who had been in
prison with Tomaso and who testifies that Orlanduccio had come
several times to visit the latter, bringing him money and delicacies
to persuade him to give this false testimony. At this, the attempted reconciliation fails, and a battle between Orso and the
hated Orlanduccio is barely averted by the Prefect. That night
Colomba slips into the garden and slits the ear of her brother's

black horse, to arouse his indignation further against the Barricini, whom he blames for this dastardly deed.

Receiving a letter from Lydia telling of their projected visit,
Orso sets off next morning to meet the Nevils on the way and to
warn them of the danger from the renewed vendetta. He is ambushed by the brothers, one shot striking him in the arm, the other
in the chest but fortunately blunted by the medal which Lydia
had given him. Despite his pain, he manages to fire twice with the
big English gun received as a present from the Colonel, each time
killing a Barricini son. He is taken by friendly bandits to hide in
the maquis until he can establish his innocence. By noon the
Colonel and Miss Lydia arrive at Colomba's castle. They have
seen no trace of Orso but report that they heard two shots, followed twice by the deeper boom which must have been made by
Orso's English gun. Their anxiety over Orso's fate is finally relieved by the arrival of little Chilina, niece of the bandit Brando-
laccio, who informs them that Orso is only wounded in the arm
and has killed both the Barricini brothers in self-defense.
Colomba takes Lydia to the wounded Orso, and they confess their
mutual love. An investigation by the Prefect, thanks largely to
Colonel Nevil's testimony concerning the two shots, absolves Orso
from shooting the two brothers first.

In the epilogue we find Colomba, Colonel Nevil, and the young
married couple traveling in Italy near Pisa the following April.
While Orso and Lydia are sketching, the other two repair to an
adjacent farmhouse to enjoy strawberries and cream. Urged by
the farmer's wife to say a few words in Corsican to a pitiful old
invalid from that land who has but little longer to live, Colomba
finds herself face to face with the father of the slain Barricini lads.
At the sight of Colomba great tears roll down his cheeks as he
sobs, "Why both of them? . . . You should have left me one." "I
had to have them both," Colomba said to him in low voice and in
the Corsican dialect. "The branches are cut off; and if the stump
were not rotten, I would have torn it out. Well, don't complain;
you don't have long to suffer. *I* suffered two years" (563). After
Colomba left the farm, the farmer's wife remarked to her daughter: "You see that pretty girl, well I'm sure she has the evil eye."

Colomba, the longest of Mérimée's works of fiction except *La
Chronique,* is nevertheless one of the shortest of novels, hardly
more than a novella in fact. It is perhaps the most perfectly pro-

portioned and broadly human of all Mérimée's stories. The main action of the novel is rapid and vigorous and the final epilogue of the encounter with old Barricini gives a final touch of perfection. Although there is as much treachery and bloodshed as in *Carmen,* the general impression of the book is, strangely enough, cheerful, owing partly to our sympathy with the chief protagonists and partly to the genial humor evident in the creation of the English aristocrat and of the bandit "curate" whose chief diversion was the perusal of Horace.

No work of Mérimée has received more nearly universal approbation by critics from his day to ours. Several have remarked indeed that its only fault is in being almost too perfect—a reference perhaps to the fact that it has become such a classic in school editions that few beginners in French literature have escaped exposure to it. Filon, in fact, makes the astounding assertion: "It is the only work of Mérimée in which the most austere Puritan can find nothing to criticize and that one can place without hesitation in the hands of the young." [6] (Filon must have forgotten such masterpieces as *Mateo Falcone, L'Enlèvement de la redoute, Tamango,* and *La Vision de Charles XI.*)

The perfection of *Colomba* may be explained by the fact that it represents the most perfect fusion of the author's Romantic and Classical tendencies. It is Romantic, of course, in its exotic setting and in Mérimée's fascination with savage, primitive human nature, a preoccupation we have glimpsed as early as his *Théâtre de Clara Gazul* and *La Guzla.* It is Classical, on the other hand, in the unity of its theme of vengeance and in its psychological study of the patient effort of Colomba to counteract the influence of Lydia's moderation and the civilizing effect of Orso's long stay in Europe, in order to arouse in him a hereditary passion for vengeance. One of the few unenthusiastic commentators on *Colomba,* Mr. Raitt, finds its antitheses and balance too artfully contrived and criticizes Mérimée's too manifest predilection for local color. "Not even Mérimée's immense technical skill can quite disguise the fact that the whole work exists to excite us about Corsica; it may be the best of guide books, but in essence a fictionalized Baedeker is what is remains." [7] Raitt comes to this conclusion perhaps from a letter Mérimée wrote to his friend Etienne Conti on November 12, 1840, thanking him for his eulogies of *Colomba*: "I tried to make a mosaic with the tales I gathered right and left on your country. . . ." [8]

But if *Colomba* gives the reader an astonishing sensation of acquaintance with life on the island of Corsica, it is not because Mérimée was much impressed with its monuments or scenery but rather with the picturesque and exotic nature of its inhabitants whom he had come to know at first hand. Even the secondary characters are sketched in vivid outlines, among them the poetic and fairylike creation of little Chilina, her bandit uncle willing to accept donations of bread and gunpowder but bristling with anger when offered money, and his scholarly bandit-colleague, popularly known as "the curate," because of his early studies in theology and his fondness for Latin quotations. We might indeed question the realism of this character did we not know that such a personage had actually been encountered by the author. Orso himself, the hero, is a less striking and well-defined character, but we recall that his Corsican inheritance had been weakened by his long stay in Europe; the gradual crumbling of his rational skepticism concerning the guilt of the Barricini, under the relentless assaults of his primitive sister, is analyzed with precision and realism. Perhaps the only weakness to be found in the characters of *Colomba* is in the somewhat conventional painting of the English Colonel and his daughter Lydia, together with the sentimental romance between her and Orso. In the author's defense, however, one might point out that Colonel Nevil, in his testimony concerning the timing of the four shots, becomes a necessary participant in the freeing of Orso, and that the love of Orso for Miss Lydia forms the basis for his opposition to Colomba's efforts to convert him to an avenger. This conflict, indeed, furnishes the psychological battle which intrigues us throughout most of the novel.

Yet the triumph of Mérimée here must always remain the character of Colomba herself, who overshadows all the others to become one of the immortal figures of French fiction. Her appearance captivates Miss Lydia at first glance.

The remarkable beauty of the woman attracted Miss Nevil's attention at once. She appeared to be about twenty years old. She was tall, blond, with dark blue eyes, rosy mouth, teeth like enamel. In her expression one read at the same time pride, uneasiness and sadness. On her head she wore that veil of blue silk named *mezzaro,* which the Genoese introduced into Corsica and which suits a woman so well. Long plaits of chestnut hair formed as it were a turban around her head. Her costume was neat but of the greatest simplicity. (418)

Brought up isolated from civilization she nevertheless possessed a natural gift for poetry and song, as she proved by her serenata "The Young Girl and the Dove" which she sang for her English friends, and later by the funeral ballad she composed and sang extemporaneously at the wake of Pietri. In the letter to Conti quoted above, Mérimée explains a change he had made in his first version of *Colomba* in which he had emphasized family ambition.

Her father avenged, I wanted to show her occupied in assuring the fortune of her brother and I made her organize a sort of ambush to oblige the English heiress to marry him. Perhaps it was truer that way. A lady [Mme Delessert] to whom I showed this end said to me: "up to here I have understood your heroine, now I no longer understand her. The combination of noble sentiments with self-interested views seems to me impossible." I have much respect for this lady's taste and I made the change you have seen, leaving Mlle Colomba's designs vague. However I had some uneasiness concerning this reproach of baseness and selfish views, and for that reason I have exaggerated in the final scene the passion of the vendetta. Yet remember that in her eyes the old man is the most guilty, and it seems to me one hardly pardons in your country.[9]

Patient in the unfolding of her plan to convert Orso, she tactfully refrains from persuasion until she has got him back to his native home, then shows him the revolver, the bloody shirt, and the bullets which murdered their father. Guided by her instinct, she scorns the trumped-up evidence which seems to exonerate the Barricini, proving by her father's papers the falsity of Tomaso's deposition. So intent is she on preventing a reconciliation that she is not above cruelty and trickery in slashing the ear of Orso's horse to make him think it had been done by their enemy. Her passionate anguish at the thought of Orso's possible ambush shows the depth of her affection for her brother. Her fanatic bravery is evidenced by her appearance in front of the Barricini partisans whom she scornfully defies to fire on her. It is true that in the epilogue she appears softened at first by European civilization to the point of wearing jewels and fashionable hats and dresses. Yet she reverts to type in her cruel disdain for the old lawyer Barricini, so pitiful in his grief for the loss of both sons. In this moment of her triumph Mérimée has approached tragic grandeur. It is no wonder that critics like Sainte-Beuve have compared Colomba to the figure of Sophocles' Electra.

III *Arsène Guillot*

As the story opens, the wealthy and charitable Mme de Piennes was attending mass at Saint-Roch when she saw entering the church a pretty young woman of twenty-five, pale from suffering or malnutrition, dressed in a rather incongruous mixture of negligence and coquetry and obviously of a lower social order. At her timid request concerning directions for buying a wax taper to burn for Saint-Roch, Mme de Piennes showed her the janitor, to whom the girl handed a 5-franc piece, obviously the only one in her purse. Impressed by this piety, Mme de Piennes followed her from the church and saw her enter a bakery and emerge with a four-pound loaf of bread. On the following days Mme de Piennes encountered the girl from time to time, ever more pale and fragile, and one day was present at a funeral in the church at which the coffin was accompanied by a single mourner, apparently a concierge, who explained that one of his lodgers had died, a Mme Guillot, leaving a daughter as only relative.

As Mme de Piennes was leaving her home the next day, she saw the young girl dressed in mourning, her features contracted, her great black eyes haggard, her face marked with a desperate resolution. On returning from her errand Mme de Piennes noticed a crowd clustered about an adjacent house, pointing to the fourth-story window from which a girl had jumped to the pavement. Dr. K., after examining the victim, reported that thanks to an awning which obstructed the fall the girl had only bruises and a few broken bones. Mme de Piennes sent a mattress and a comfortable bed and at the doctor's suggestion visited the wounded girl, whose name was Arsène Guillot. She explained her suicidal attempt as being due to her feeling of loneliness after her mother's death and her sorrow over the loss of a lover. She had been an "extra" in the Opéra ballet, supporting her mother through a life of prostitution until her physical charms had faded. Her dedication of a taper to Saint-Roch, far from being the act of piety Mme de Piennes had imagined, was only a response to her mother's insistence that such an act would be bound to bring her a lover within a week. Mme de Piennes, shocked at this revelation, nevertheless determined to rescue this lost soul and bring her to repentance and Christian resignation.

Soon after this event Mme de Piennes receives a visit from a friend, Max de Salligny, just returned from a two-year voyage. After an early period of dissipation Max has apparently settled down, and Mme de Piennes has hopes of making his reform permanent since she is conscious of his affection for her. A fortnight later, after visiting and admonishing the invalid, Mme de Piennes is writing in Arsène's antechamber when she is astonished by the arrival of Max, whose passionate reception by Arsène proves that he is the lover of whom she had previously spoken. Interrupting his visit, she sends him away, then pleads with Arsène to forget such passionate reminders of her past. She agrees to accept from Arsène the bouquet of flowers Max has sent, leaving her only the camellias. At this Arsène protests violently, asserting that camellias remind her of the only quarrel she has ever had with Max, when she had tried to make him give her a red camellia which he had evidently received from a woman he loved. Mme de Pienne then remembers an occasion on which she had taken from her coiffure a red camellia and given it to Max. Finding Max at her home, she is about to reprove him for his responsibility in Arsène's misfortunes when he begins an eloquent defense. Insisting that he had not seduced Arsène since she was already a courtesan, he explains that on his part the affair had been only a temporary infatuation to console himself for a hopeless love and that Arsène, feeling no great grief at their parting, had taken up with a Russian lover. Max had sent her money on one occasion but then had lost track of her whereabouts, since she was evidently too proud to appeal again for his aid.

Mme de Piennes, sensing an opportunity to reform Max, agrees to let him visit Arsène daily but only in her presence. She realizes that Max has loved her without daring to reveal his passion and that she herself has been using the pretext of reforming him to account for her own affection for Max. Her confusion is further increased when Max announces that he plans to enlist in the Greek army to fight the Turks.

As days go by the condition of Arsène becomes more and more

hopeless, and the end is near. When Max leans over her apparently lifeless body to say, "Poor child, what happiness has she had in life?" Arsène opens her eyes one last time to murmur with a sad smile, "I have loved."

Unlike those other novellas of Parisian society life, *Le Vase étrusque* and *La Double Méprise*, *Arsène Guillot* is completely free from any trace of dandyism or cynical sophistication on the part of the author. It is indeed unique in Mérimée's fiction, for it is the only story in which he betrays his personal emotion and sympathy with his characters, though he checks himself at the end as if ashamed of this temporary lifting of the mask. Filon has compared this work with the manner of Balzac,[10] but it seems to me to be much closer to Musset, not only in its choice of a heroine from the *grisettes*, but also in its impatience with conventional piety and its triumphant conclusion of the sanctity of love. Perhaps we can account for this more personal accent by the fact that Mérimée did not at first intend publication but presented it to Mme Delessert with whom his liaison commenced in 1836. According to Martineau, Mme Delessert had expressed some umbrage at Mérimée's earlier liaison with a ballet dancer from the Opéra, Céline Cayot (Arsène Guillot) whom Stendhal had also known and later portrayed in his novels *Lamiel* and *Lucien Leuwen*. Martineau quotes Parturier, recent editor of *Arsène Guillot* and of Mérimée's *Correspondance*, as proof of Mérimée's intention: "The entire passage in which Max de Salligny explains the nature of his love for Arsène Guillot has manifestly the tone of a pleading in which Mérimée defended himself for having loved Céline Cayot. To whom would he excuse himself thus? Unless to the woman whom he always wished to please by his writings."[11] That this story was first written as a personal document is shown also by the frequent intervention of the author to speak to a listener, "Madame," whose weariness at the end affords the pretext for not completing the denouement. Evidently, Mme Delessert was pleased with the novella, for she persuaded several friends, among them Mme de Boigne and Mme Lenormant, to organize a group of ladies for a reading, who in turn persuaded Mérimée to have it published, with the resulting scandal we have seen.

The character of Arsène the courtesan, which caused such shocked outcries among the pious Conservatives of Mérimée's day, is deeply moving to a modern reader for her artless sincerity,

humility, and efforts at repentance. Less attractive is Mme de
Piennes, in spite of her very real kindness of heart, charity, and
preoccupation with saving the souls of both Arsène and of Max.
The author's attitude toward Mme de Piennes can be guessed
from this passage: "A strong conviction makes one almost insensi-
tive; and as a surgeon applies fire and iron to a wound without
listening to the cries of the patient, Mme de Piennes pursued her
task with pitiless firmness" (592). It is to the credit of Mme
Delessert that she was apparently not offended by Mérimée's
shrewd analysis of Mme de Pienne's real motivation in trying to
salvage the soul of the little courtesan.

Mme de Piennes was proud of having vanquished the perversity of a
courtesan, of having destroyed by her eloquence the barriers that
twenty years of seduction had raised around a poor abandoned soul.
And then must one say, perhaps? to the pride in this victory, to the
pleasure of having done a good act there was mingled this feeling of
curiosity which many a virtuous woman experiences in knowing a
woman of a different species. (579)

As for the role of Max de Salligny, there can be no doubt that
he represents that of Mérimée himself in this whole affair. Not
that we have here a psychological portrait of the author, such as
we found in the Saint-Clair of Le Vase étrusque or the Darcy of
La Double Méprise; Max is quite different from the author in his
happy-go-lucky effervescence and his outgoing personality and
charm. Yet there are many traits and occurrences in the life of
Max which parallel closely those of Mérimée himself. Just as Max
sometimes misspelled Arsène's name, writing Guyot for Guillot, so
Mérimée, M. Parturier tells us, had often written Caillot for Cayot
in corresponding with Céline. Max, like Mérimée, had acquired
the reputation of "bad actor," "gambler," "man-about-town." Like
the author, Max had returned from a voyage to Germany, Italy,
and Greece, where he had been interested in paintings and in
excavations as an antiquarian. His mention of having dined at the
Rocher-de-Concale with "ces vauriens" (586) recalls the dissi-
pated group Saint-Clair (Mérimée) frequented in Le Vase
étrusque. When Max asks Arsène what became of her Russian
lover, M. Parturier reminds us that Céline Cayot had indeed consoled herself for the rupture with Mérimée by accepting the at-

tentions of a Russian. We have already referred to Max's impassioned defense of his affair with Arsène, so obviously an attempt of Mérimée to gain the sympathetic understanding and pardon of Mme Delessert.

As with *La Chronique* and *La Partie de trictrac*, Mérimée leaves us with the story unfinished, and we can only imagine what will happen to Max and Mme de Piennes in their undeclared passion for each other. Yet in this regard we may be aided by the Greek quotation from Homer which precedes the story and which may be translated as follows: "Thou art valiant but Paris and Phoebus Apollo will cause thy downfall before the gates of Scées." Most commentators have interpreted this to mean that "in spite of her virtue Mme de Piennes will succumb before Max de Salligny, aided by the devil, or by love." [12] To appreciate the sincerity and pathos of this novella it is not necessary to know the circumstances of its conception; yet these explain in large measure the exceptional character of this work, the only one which expresses the personal emotion of Mérimée.

IV *Carmen*

As we have seen, in 1840, ten years after his first trip, Mérimée was back in Spain, now more interested in history and archeological research as we learn in the opening pages of *Carmen*, again a guest of Mme de Montijo in her palace at Madrid. It was to her that he owed by his own admission the inspiration for his novella. We have seen that in 1843 Mérimée had begun a *History of Don Pedro I, King of Castile* on which Mme de Montijo had encouraged him. According to an apocryphal legend, this king was supposed to have had a bohemian as a mistress, and this may well have been the origin of Mérimée's interest in bohemians. Among the writers whom he consulted, the most influential was doubtless the British missionary George Barrow (*The Zingali* and *The Bible in Spain*) whom he accused however of "lying like a tooth-puller" in ascribing chastity to all his Gypsies. As for his heroine's name, this may well be a reminiscence of a certain Carmencita, a *gitana* with whom he had flirted in 1830 near Granada and whom he had described in his *Lettre sur les sorcières* as "a very pretty girl, not too swarthy," whose portrait he sketched in his album. Some critics have suggested, however, that Carmen is really a portrait of the author himself—just as Flaubert had insisted "Mme Bovary, c'est moi"—a reflection of his amorous flirtations with Mme Lacoste and Mme Delessert.

The story of *Carmen* is a familiar one since it has inspired the libretto of the most popular of all operas, though many liberties were taken by the librettist with Mérimée's text. The author first encounters Don José in a pictureque gorge near Córdoba, and, despite the obvious hesitation of his guide, shares a bountiful picnic lunch with the bandit, then rides with him to a modest *venta* (inn) to spend the night. Finding that his guide has ridden off to summon the constabulary and thereby win the reward placed on the bandit's head, the author wakens Don José and allows him to escape. A few days later in Córdoba Mérimée encounters a vivacious Gypsy girl who seems fascinated by his "repeater" watch; she invites him to her dwelling to tell his fortune. As she prepares the cards, Don José enters the room, speaks harshly to the girl, then forces Mérimée to leave. On undressing he notices that his watch is missing but decides to make no complaint to the authorities. After several months of archeological and historical research in Andalusia, en route back to Madrid he stops once more in Córdoba, where he learns that his watch has been recovered and that the thief, convicted of several murders, is awaiting execution. On visiting Don José in his cell, he learns from him the tragic story leading up to his incarceration and death sentence.

Forced to leave his native Basque village in Navarre, Don José had joined the dragoons. He was promoted to corporal and assigned to guard duty at a tobacco factory in Seville. Hearing a loud commotion in the factory, he entered with two soldiers, found that Carmen had slashed a cross on the forehead of one of her companions who had insulted her, and carried her off to prison. En route she whispered to him that she would give him a magic stone if he would allow her to escape, and, fascinated by her youthful charm, he permitted her to break loose. Punished for this laxity by a sentence of thirty days in prison and reduction to a private's rank, he received a present of a loaf of bread containing a file and some money, but he was still too honest and naïve to think of escaping. After serving his sentence he met Carmen at the restaurant of Lilas Pastia where, to show her gratitude, she agreed to become his *romi*, or wife. Stationed a few days later as guard at the city gate, he was approached by Carmen and was persuaded to allow her band of smugglers to pass through with the contraband. On another occasion finding Carmen with a young lieutenant, José from jealousy sought a quarrel, in which he killed the officer and received a serious head wound. Carmen arranged a safe hiding place, bandaged his wound, and soon persuaded him to join her band of smugglers, under the leadership of Le Dancaïre. Soon they were joined by an ugly monster, Garcia the One-eyed, whom, as Carmen's first *rom,* or husband, she had managed to free from prison.

After various escapades and armed robberies in the mountains, Don José learned that Carmen went often to the bullfights in Granada and was often seen in the company of Lucas the picador. On his discovery that Carmen planned to attend a bullfight in Córdoba, Don José followed her there and observed that Lucas plucked the *cocarde* from the bull and carried it to Carmen who put it in her coiffure. On Carmen's return at two in the morning Don José made her ride off with him and, offering to forget the past, asked her to accompany him to America. At her refusal to say that she still loved him he went to a nearby monastery to ask a priest to pray for a soul about to appear before its Maker. Returning to the lonely gorge where he had left Carmen he pleaded desperately for her love, but she said she could no longer live with him and threw his ring into the bushes. He struck her twice with his knife; she died without uttering a cry. Remembering that Carmen had often said she would like to be buried in a wood, he dug her grave there, placing her ring at her side and a little cross above. Then he rode to Córdoba to confess his murder of Carmen, but he refused to give the location of her body.

After this thrilling recital of violence and passion the reader is treated to a six-page learned discussion of bohemian customs in various countries, climaxed by an eloquent disquisition on forms of the preterite tense as they differ between German and Spanish Gypsies.

Critics have not always agreed on the rank to asign *Carmen* in the list of Mérimée's fiction. Filon considers it "the least well-composed of all Mérimée's tales, the most confused and the least homogeneous." [13] More recent critics have tended to go to the opposite extreme: Raitt, for instance, calls *Carmen* "one of the world's finest tales"; [14] Saintsbury, "one of the dozen finest short stories of the world." [15] He is full of admiration for the marvelous precision of its sixty pages, one-fourth the length of *Colomba*. It is true of course that the reader's interest is almost quenched by the soporific discussion of archeology which precedes it and by the irritating pedantry concerning the Gypsy dialect in the conclusion, though as Saintsbury suggests, the latter may be as easily removed as an appendix.

A more serious criticism, perhaps, is that the rapid variation of incident leaves the fascinating character of Carmen something of an enigma. For all the brilliance of color and atmosphere which make an indelible impression on the reader, he may be tempted to agree with Sainte-Beuve in his preference for that eighteenth-century Carmen, Manon Lescaut, more naïve and human.[16] Like Colomba, Carmen testifies to Mérimée's fondness for primitive, savage types, but except in her refusal to compromise her sincerity even to escape death she is perhaps a less moving character for the reader. And Don José, called by Filon one of the least convincing bandits of this period, is a weakling, easily swayed from his duty by Carmen's slightest whim.

As for the author's own evaluation of his novella, his modesty, as so often excessive with him, is revealed by his suggestion at the opening and close that the story may have a temporary interest but that we must return to more serious matters, such as archeology and philology. His real preoccupation at this time was the serious *History of Don Pedro the Cruel,* and if we are to take him at his word his purpose in writing *Carmen* was purely financial. On September 17, 1845, returning from a long inspection trip in southern France, he wrote to his friend Requien, "Poverty, inevitable result of a long voyage, made me consent to give Carmen to Buloz" [Editor of the *Revue des Deux Mondes*]; and on September 21 he wrote to Vitet, "You will be reading soon a little trifle [*drôlerie*] of your humble servant which would have remained unpublished if the author had not been obliged to purchase some trousers."

If we are unable to accept Raitt's and Saintsbury's ecstatic praise for *Carmen* we shall find on the other hand, I believe, that Mérimée is far too modest and Filon far too severe. It was perhaps fortunate for Mérimeé that his heroine has been immortalized in the magic melodies of Bizet's greatest work. Yet even in the original prose version this savage and seductive character, capricious and passionate, superstitious and heroic, can stand on her own feet as one of the most vivid creations of all French fiction.

V *L'Abbé Aubain*

L'Abbé Aubain, a short story in letter form, was published anonymously in the *Constitutionnel* of February 24, 1846. When Mérimée sent a copy to Mme de Montijo he called it "a little story I made without signing it because it is only necessary for me to speak of priests to have all the old devout women cry out against irreligion." [17] Though he added that the adventure really happened and he could name the personages, no one to this day has been able to discover the key. Martineau, however, after M. Parturier, has made several interesting suppositions: the heroine resembles Jenny Dacquin in regard to her interest in German and Latin, Mme Delessert in her obvious coquetry.[18] It is possible also that Mérimée may have heard the story from one of the many priests he encountered on his trips through the provinces as inspector of monuments.

In the first five letters from Mme de P. to her friend Sophie we learn that a rascally stockbroker has brought the family so close to ruin that they are obliged to leave the luxury of Paris to bury themselves in their somber country manor in the little village of Noirmoutiers in the Vendée. Apparently there is little love lost between husband and wife, and the only refuge from boredom is conversation with the young priest, Aubain, "a very gentle young man although he has arched, bushy eyebrows and great black eyes like a hero of melodrama" (668). Each letter to her friend indicates rather subtly a growing interest in the young priest, who is prevailed upon to give Mme de P. lessons in Latin and botany. On one occasion while visiting him in his humble parsonage she notices a bouquet of dried flowers, and her romantic imagination is confident that a love story is connected with it. Indeed, after some hesitation the priest confesses that nine years earlier he had become engaged to a girl in N—— who had promised to wait for him while he prepared himself for the teaching profession, giving him this bouquet as a pledge of her fidelity. One year later, just when he was about to attain the coveted position in a *collège*, he learned that his fiancée had married a notary of N—— and in despair he had entered the church. Having finished his confession he threw the dried flowers into the fire, thanking Mme de P. for having separated him from a memory ill-befitting his clerical profession. By the fifth letter Mme de P. has become so fascinated with the attractive young priest that she easily persuades herself she has made an amorous conquest. Rather than causing this young man unhappiness, she must break off the affair at once by removing him from the village. Though Father Aubain protests that he is happy in his little parish, Mme de P. persuades her uncle the Bishop of N—— to name the young priest curé of Sainte-Marie in that city.

What renders the story so ironic and amusing is the surprising denouement, found in the sixth letter, this one from l'abbé Aubain to his former professor of theology. Rejoicing in his beautiful city parish, he is now "curé of a great church, well built, well kept up, of magnificent architecture, sketched in all the albums of France. The first time I said mass before an altar of marble, all resplendent with gilding, I had to ask myself if it was really I" (677–78). He explains to his friend this sudden improvement in his fortunes: a Parisian lady, bored by her seclusion in the provinces, had become infatuated with his society, laden him down with gifts, plunged with enthusiasm into the study of Latin and botany at his feet. One day she presented him with a new book on Abélard and he was embarrassed by the realization that she was evidently casting herself in the romantic role of Héloïse. Learning that the curé of Sainte-Marie had died, she had dashed off to her uncle the bishop to persuade him to name Father Aubain priest of this magnificent parish where he was happy to have escaped from the claws of this lioness. And he closes the letter with the hope that soon he will have the opportunity to talk philosophy with his old teacher "each in a good armchair, in front of a fat hen and a bottle of bordeaux . . ." (679).

Most critics have taken as lightly as Mérimée himself this amusing *boutade* of a dozen pages. Yet technically, within its modest framework, it is a little masterpiece, particularly in the trick or surprise ending. It is delightful also in the psychological contrast between its two protagonists. On the one hand, we have the astute little priest, who appears to Lady Bountiful so modest and contented with his humble station but who in reality, knowing her to be the bishop's niece, adroitly takes advantage of her infatuation to achieve, like l'abbé Troubert in Balzac's *Curé de Tours,* the accomplishment of his worldly and materialistic ambitions. On the other hand, by her own naïve admissions we see unfolding the vanity of Mme de P. taking comfort in her "sublime" martyrdom for her decision to rebuild the family fortunes by seclusion in the provincial manor—on 10,000 crowns a year! With a smattering of superficial culture, she reads Byron while taking strolls along the ocean shore. With mingled pleasure and remorse, she confesses her *naïveté de coquetterie* in attracting the young priest. We chuckle when she confides to her friend that l'abbé Aubain is as good a counselor as she, and more "impartial," for he always takes her side against her husband. She admits a brief feeling of pride in her triumph: "A conquest at my age [thirty years] an innocent conquest like this. . . . It is something to excite such a passion, an impossible love! . . . Fie then, this naughty feeling left me very quickly" (676). A final satisfaction with her removal of the priest from the danger of falling in love with her is shown by her martyrlike insistence that "it must be." Already she is contemplating her reentry into the Parisian world of fashion in three years and wondering whether at thirty-three she will still need to worry about other loves. Rarely has Mérimée drawn with such subtle strokes the portrait of a coquette, merely by her own unconscious revelation of character.

With *L'Abbé Aubain* Mérimée said farewell to his production of fiction for twenty years. The reason for this long abstention, as we have seen, was the growing coolness shown him by his confidante Mme Delessert whose approbation meant so much to him.

CHAPTER 9

Two Closet Dramas

ON September 16, 1848, Mérimée wrote to the actress Augustine Brohan to thank her for her interest in his *Carrosse du Saint-Sacrement*, but he also gave her several reasons to discourage her from reviving his comedy, ending his letter with a disclaimer of his ability to write for the stage. "Unfortunately I am quite unable to aid you in making anything presentable out of it. I am not in the slightest accustomed to the stage and I feel myself particularly inept at writing for the theater." [1] When despite his warning *Le Carrosse* was presented at the Comédie Française in 1850, Mérimée must have felt his forebodings justified by its failure at this time, for it had to be withdrawn after only four performances.

I *Les Deux Héritages*

Convinced that he had none of the qualities requisite for dramatic success, Mérimée wrote his last two plays in the form of dialogued closet drama. In reading them we would do well to follow the advice of M. Marsan in his recent edition: "Take the two dramas as tales all of whose narrative portion is omitted, leaving only a dialogue, so marvelously accurate that it is enough. Do that, put yourself in that disposition of mind, forget the stage, accept the fact that it concerns two evenings under the lamp, and you will see." [2]

The Two Inheritances, a comedy in six tableaux subtitled *Don Quixote, Morality with several Characters*, read to a group of ladies on April 1, 1850, at the home of Mme Delessert's sister, Mme Bocher, was published in the *Revue des Deux Mondes* on July 1, 1850. The only reference to it that I can find in Mérimée's correspondence is a letter to Adolphe de Circourt, thanking him for his friend's appreciation of "ma petite drôlerie. It has the defect of our time which is to be neither pathetic nor gay, but I am happy you found a little truth in it." [3] Mérimée's low opinion of this comedy seems to have been shared by most later commentators, with the exception of Eugène Marsan who wrote an enthusiastic preface for his recent edition in which he takes issue with the fact that the play has reminded many of Dumas and Scribe. Far closer to Musset than to Scribe, I think, are the delightfully drawn protagonists, in particular the young heroine, Julie, who is altogether charming with her playful witticisms, her scorn for convention and hypocrisy, and her infatuation with heroism and romance.

The young bachelor Louis de Saqueville is carrying on three projects at once as the play opens: a rather sordid affair with a dancer of the Opéra, a courtship of Julie de Montrichard, and especially a political campaign for deputy from Brittany in which he has assured himself the support of a wealthy capitalist by promising him the coveted ribbon of the Legion of Honor. Louis' uncle, Colonel Saqueville, newly arrived on furlough in Paris after thirteen glorious years with the French army in Algeria, highly approves his nephew's approaching engagement to Julie, and we are given to suspect a long-smoldering attachment of the Colonel to Julie's mother. When Louis and his uncle arrive at the country home of the Montrichards, we are soon introduced to the occupants: Julie's mother, a widow occupied only with her authorship of conventional tracts; Sévin, a youthful Tartuffe who has ingratiated himself into Madame's confidence through flattery and subservience; and Julie, a lovely, spirited girl of nineteen, whose playful effervescence scarcely conceals her boredom with the constant moralizing of her mother, of Sévin, and of the prissy Miss Jackson, her English companion.

Julie, falling into the garden canal, is impetuously rescued by the quadragenarian Colonel, with whom she soon is enamoured by his chivalry, his frankness and honesty, and his heroic background. Later ensue two charming scenes which only a Musset could have equalled, first when Julie bares her heart to Miss Jackson, second when she timidly but forthrightly confesses her love to Colonel Saqueville. The latter is overwhelmed by this avowal, and now the reader has come to understand the real situation: Julie is the daughter of the Colonel and Mme de Montrichard through an affair before the latter's marriage; the Colonel had returned to France hoping to marry the widow after keeping his love silent for all these years. Discouraged by the widow's cold reserve and alarmed by Julie's romantic infatuation, the Colonel decides to return to Algeria, leaving half his fortune to the *spahis* of his regiment, half to his nephew if he marries Julie.

And now Mérimée winds up this realistic comedy of manners by a conclusion as breathtakingly fantastic as any imbroglio of Scribe. The ballerina-mistress of Louis informs him that her early English "protector" has died, leaving her a bequest of almost 900,000 francs to allow her to become an "honest woman"; Mme de Montrichard breaks off all relations with Louis after discovering his plan to marry the daughter of the millionaire Breton for her money; Sévin has persuaded the latter to accept him for a son-in-law by explaining that it was he, not Louis, who had obtained for him the Legion of Honor; and the Colonel, now aware of his nephew's perfidy and greed, tears up the donation of half his fortune he had planned to give Louis. Thus the latter, as a reward for all his scheming, has now lost both inheritances, that of his uncle and that of the Breton's dowry. But wait—not all is lost. By a sardonic touch at the end Mérimée shows us Louis starting off on a honeymoon with his mistress of the chorus, whom he will now marry in order to share her recent legacy.

It will be evident from this synopsis that this comedy, so loosely constructed, so lacking in dramatic realism, could never have been a success on the stage. If, however, as Marsan suggests, we read this not as a play but as a story in dialogue, we shall find in it much realism of character development, as well as delightful satire of many features of French life at midcentury which Mérimée despised. Among these are political chicanery, religious hypocrisy and cant, and shameless pursuit of wealth. Contrasting with the representatives of such decadent morality—Louis, Mme de Montrichard, and Sévin—we see on the other hand two of the noblest characters Mérimée has ever created. We can understand the subtitle *Don Quichotte* as we note the bravery and naïve candor of the heroic Colonel, true for so many years to the woman he had lost and idealized, who scorned wealth and glory and sought solace in the comrades of his beloved regiment. Julie also, disgusted with the mechanical charities and smug austerity of her mother and Sévin, quick to appreciate honesty, courage, and true chivalry in the Algerian Colonel and above all so sparkling, ebullient, and charming in the freshness of her vivacity—Julie is surely one of the most attractive heroines Mérimée ever created. No masterpiece certainly, yet in my opinion this play is the most underrated of Mérimée's work.

II *Les Débuts d'un aventurier*

In the letter quoted above to M. de Circourt thanking him for his appreciation of *Les Deux Héritages,* on July 11, 1850, Mérimée added that for some time he had been doing research on the false Demetrius, pretended son of Ivan the Terrible. As Mérimée tells us with dry humor in his introduction to his closet drama, *Les Débuts d'un aventurier,* referring to his imprisonment in the Conciergerie as a result of his intervention in the *Libri* case, he was "forced to spend a fortnight in a place where he was in no wise bothered by the sunshine" and where he "enjoyed profound leisure." It was here that he read all the correspondence of his hero and decided to write "a second edition of the historical work I had just finished" and present a romanticized summary of his research in which he will attempt to explain the reasons for his hero's masquerade. As the title of this closet drama indicates, Mérimée carries the career of this false Demetrius only to the point where he is ready to confront Boris Godunov with a challenge for power. In Filon's words, "it is scarcely anything more than the prologue of the drama of which Démétrius was to be the hero . . . yet this prologue, like a true drama, has its unity, its progression, its moral significance." [4]

As the drama opens, the young Cossack Yourii is bidding farewell to his mortally wounded protector Gheraz Evanghel who leaves his young protégé 120 ducats and a gold cross set in diamonds, with the inscription "To Demetrius, son of the Tsar Ivan." While Yourii is burying his friend he is joined by Choubine, a rich merchant of Ouglitch, whom he accompanies back to the latter's hospitable home. Among the guests here are the drunken monk Grégoire Otrepief and Prince Gustave of Sweden, who relates the fantastic story of his escape into exile despite all the efforts of his royal uncle to kill him. The latter predicts a glorious future for Yourii, and everyone notices the wen under Yourii's right eye, similar to that of the child Tsarevitch, son of Ivan the Terrible, who had been killed ten years earlier by the Prime Minister, Boris Godunov, to enable him to usurp the throne. Choubine gives Yourii a golden seal, once the property of the murdered prince, which he had received from the latter's secretary as he fled to Siberia. The dead prince's nurse Jdanova, now gone mad, believes that her ward is still alive and is convinced that Yourii is the true Tsarévitch.

Almost persuaded by these coincidences that he is the rightful heir to the throne, Yourii goes to Moscow. A young monk sends out secret notices to the court, warning them that the real Demetrius is still alive and will later come to overthrow the usurper Boris, who by this time has alienated most of his people by his tyrannical acts. Yourii then goes to Poland, receives protection from Prince Adam after his remarkable feat of taming a wild horse who up to now had thrown every rider, and is later discovered receiving letters from Russia addressed to Demetrius. The monk Grégoire, convinced that Yourii is indeed the lost Démétrius, has gone to the Ukraine to arouse the Cossacks in his behalf, and Prince Adam is about to put a Polish army at his service. The drama ends at this point, now that everything is ready for the confrontation between Boris and the false Demetrius.

Critics agree in general that this colorful closet drama is far more original and creative than Mérimée's somewhat prosaic and conventional *History of the False Demetrius*. In the preface to his edition, Marsan has admirably summarized Mérimée's play: "He has shown how a twenty-year-old Cossack was able to desire and gain a throne, by what conjunction of insidious proofs of appearances so well knit together that the adventurer himself may have believed at times in his own right. The inexplicable is thus explained, in a manner which satisfies the reason." [5]

CHAPTER 10

Mérimée under the Empire: 1853–1870

I   *Mérimée and the Empress Eugénie*

BY an overwhelming plebiscite (7.5 out of 8 million votes)
Louis Napoleon had become president for ten years, then, by
the coup d'état of December 2, 1852, Emperor of the French. As
early as 1848 or 1849 he had begun to notice the charm of Eugénie who with her mother the Countess de Montijo spent the
winters in Paris. Enthused by the stories of the first Napoleon
which Stendhal used to tell her and despite the forebodings of
Mérimée who at first took rather a dim view of Louis Napoleon
and of the stability of his regime, Eugénie showed herself dazzled
by his wooing. On January 15, 1853, the emperor formally asked
Mme de Montijo for her daughter's hand. The marriage was celebrated January 30 in the cathedral of Notre Dame which had
been decorated by Viollet-le-Duc. In March, Mérimée was
charged by the emperor with accompanying Mme de Montijo as
far as Poitiers on her return to Spain, a return in all likelihood
suggested by Napoleon, who found her too tempestuous and dom-
inant.

When Eugénie informed Louis Napoleon that Mérimée was her
best friend, the emperor promptly offered him the important position of keeper of the imperial archives which he politely declined.
As he wrote later to Véron: "I begged him to leave me to my old
monuments where I was more free. The Empress then said to me
in Spanish. 'We shall give you something else, if you do not accept, you are our enemy.' That is how I lost my old liberty." [1] It
was not long before he discovered what this "something else"
turned out to be. On June 23 he was appointed by imperial decree
Senator of the Empire, with an annual salary of 30,000 francs, a
sinecure which removed all financial worries and still left him free
for his archeological pursuits. The minister Fould asked him to
continue as inspector general of historical monuments, a position

Mérimée accepted on condition that it would be henceforth without salary. With his accustomed irony Mérimée wrote his friend Mme de Boigne concerning the dramatic change in his fortunes:

Just one year ago they sent me to prison for having taken up the defense of a poor man victim of an enormous injustice; today I am rewarded for having moralized and saved from punishment a pretty lady whom I knew as a charming child. . . . It's the Emperor who whispered my name yesterday in the ear of the Empress. She made a little cry . . . and embraced her husband *con amore*. That gives me more pleasure perhaps than the positive side, which has however its poetry all the same. Since I've been living alone with a cat and a tortoise, I am happy to feel myself loved.[2]

A letter to Lagrené the same day expressed the same gratitude to his dear friend the Empress, who he knew was responsible for his nomination as senator. "The Emperor whispered to the Empress that he had signed the decree. She uttered a little cry, rose to her feet and embraced him. This little detail gives me more pleasure than the appointment itself." [3] A year later in the letter to Véron quoted above Mérimée gave a picturesque summary of the miraculous change which had come about in his position, together with his insistence that he would never try to profit from his new position at court:

You know my story as well as I do. As chance would have it, I once went to Spain where I found some good and likable people who received me well. I found there a little girl to whom I told stories; I requested pardon for her when she didn't know her lesson, and later, I gave her serious sermons for I am not very indulgent toward youth. One day this little girl told me that she was going to marry the Emperor. I asked her to make me swear never to ask her for anything. After a discussion she had me make the aforesaid oath in a very solemn manner.[4]

Mérimée always kept his promise as far as he was personally concerned, for the only requests he ever made the Empress were for charitable bequests to the needy.

II   *Final Break with Valentine*

In the summer of 1853 Mérimée went to Spain to visit Mme de Montijo and her charming nieces at Madrid and her country home of Carabanchel. He was able to relax from his duties as inspector and enjoy himself fully, since he had a presentiment that this might be the last happy year he would ever know. The countess tried to arrange a marriage for him, but, still under the spell of his affection for Valentine, he returned to Paris in the late autumn. Although the Delesserts through Mérimée had become friends of the Montijos, as fervent Orléanistes they did not approve Mérimée's reconciliation with the empire. Long before the final rupture, Mérimée had been conscious of a growing hostility on Valentine's part, for in May, 1853, he had confided his anxiety to Mme de Montijo: "I have endured every possible misfortune—I mean of the heart, for my life is running most smoothly on the material side." [5] By June, 1854, he was becoming desperate, for he wrote to the countess: "If a sorcerer had told me, ten years ago, that I would be in 1854 as free as air, I would have taken him for a great fool. I am the biggest one for having made happiness consist of finding a white blackbird, an infinitely rare bird." [6]

Finally Mme Delessert, tired of dissembling and urged on no doubt by her secret lover Maxime Du Camp, decided on an open break, requesting the return of her letters and presents, under a very slightly veiled pretense which she must have known Mérimée could see through. Thus on New Year's Day, 1855, Mérimée wrote the following heartbroken letter to Mme de Montijo:

Three days ago I received from Valentine a package containing a certain number of old letters, along with a few little objects I had given her, all of this accompanied by a letter friendly enough as regards its form, in which she said that in view of death which might occur at any time she had wished to put her affairs in order and leave nothing which could surprise her heirs. I confess to you that this shocked me very much. I asked her how I had deserved to be treated with this distrust. If the objects, which basically are not in the least compromising, seemed to her to be so, why not destroy them instead of sending them back to me thus. [7]

Incredible as it seems, Mérimée does not appear to have suspected for a moment that he had been displaced in Valentine's affections by a rival, for the letter continues: "I am cudgeling my brains to understand what makes her act like this. Sometimes it seems to me that she hates me, but I can't guess why. There is no

trace of the priesthood in this affair. Although for several years I
have had to steel myself for this, I cannot tell you how much pain
it has given me."

To those who may have considered Mérimée cold, blasé, ironic,
and lacking in emotion, the poignant letter he wrote his friend
Mme de Montijo a fortnight later should be a revelation of the
real Mérimée behind the mask.

Since my last letter I haven't been able to explain to myself the
brusque parcel of which I spoke to you. I am just about certain that
there is no religious instigation in it. Perhaps something in the nature
of remorse. What seems to me certain is that for several years she has
been feeling for me a growing hatred, or if you prefer, repulsion. I
can't tell you how afflicted I am. . . . It is very difficult for me to find
her alone, and she shows great art in depriving me of any opportunity
to speak to her at length. The result of a liaison of more than twenty
years makes me despair and I have come to the point of distressing
myself for the past and of thinking that all the happiness I have had
was false.[8]

The coming of February 16, 1855, brought with it new anguish
because of its association with the beginning of their intimate liaison.

It is a dream which is over. The reawakening is rather sad. The only
consolation I have is the thought that I have done nothing for which
to be treated in that way. . . . Yesterday it was just eighteen years
ago that this had begun. Every year the sixteenth of this month I used
to give her a little souvenir and she would give me one.[9]

For many months Mérimée remained in a state of prostration. His
health, never too sound, was worsened by his suffering, particularly in regard to his bronchial trouble and difficulty in breathing.
In 1856 for the first time he consulted a doctor, from whom he
received a rather discouraging report. Time, which usually dulls
all sorrow, brought Mérimée no relief for several years. Almost
two years later, November 9, 1856, he unburdened himself to
Mme de La Rochejaquelein:

I shall tell you that you have not understood what I meant by *mon
ennemi*. Add a mute e. If that is not clear enough, that is what I call
a woman I loved, whom I still love, and who no longer loves me, who

perhaps has never loved me. The result is that I must cut off fifteen years of my life, not only lost, but the memory of which is poisoned for me. I do not regret the time lost . . . but there are memories which were a superhuman world for me, to which I used to have access and which is now closed for me.[10]

If so much space has been devoted to Mérimée's love affair with Valentine, it is because it was perhaps the most important event in his life, the one most closely connected with his literary production. It explains why for two decades he refrained from the writing of fiction and sought refuge from boredom in history, occasional articles, and translations from Russian literature. How many masterpieces like *Colomba* and *Carmen* we may have lost because of Valentine's defection! We may find confirmation of this in innumerable remarks by Mérimée himself. Thus, for instance, he wrote an English friend, Mrs. Senior, July 29, 1855: "When I used to write I had a goal. Now I no longer have one. If I wrote, it would be for myself and I would bore myself even more than I am doing." [11] And the following year he wrote to Mme de La Rochejaquelein: "I would like to write and I cannot. . . . For fifteen years I had an aim which was to please someone. That made me happy and it seemed to me I was successful. I never in my life wrote anything for the public, always for someone. I no longer write novels since I have no longer been in love." And finally, if any doubt is left concerning the catastrophic effect of this break with Valentine on Mérimée's writing, we have this decisive letter to his friend Turgenev, January 27, 1865: "What most of all kept me from writing is a rather stupid motive. When I used to write, it was to amuse a beautiful lady. When she was no longer amused with me, I did nothing." [12]

III *Reconciliation*

Fortunately, this tragic affair was to have a somewhat consoling ending. Apparently it was not until 1857 that Mérimée learned the real cause for the rupture, the fact that Valentine had taken on as a lover Maxime Du Camp. At this discovery, Mérimée felt more pity than anger and blamed himself for his own stupidity. Writing to Mme de Montijo on April 11, 1857, Mérimée admitted that time has its effect for good as well as evil, expressing his surprise that his love had gone out like a lamp lacking in oil. It was a decade later that a final reconciliation occurred. When Maxime Du Camp's novel *Forces perdues* was published in 1866, Valentine was furious at having been too visibly portrayed as the heroine. Apparently this anger was sufficient to make her seek a reconciliation with Mérimée, for we read in one of his letters to her:

The last time I saw you, you gave me a great happiness. You have given back to me, I like to believe, a friendship which was very precious to me and which I sometimes doubted with the greatest sorrow on my part. It seemed to me that you removed a thorn from my heart. Let's talk no more about that, Madame, permit me only to thank you for it.[13]

Baschet suggests that in the restraint Mérimée shows in expressing his joy in this passage he has never been closer to his hero Saint-Clair of the *Vase étrusque*.[14] It is certainly no coincidence that Mérimée will now return to works of fiction, although the first of these *La Chambre bleue* was written for the Empress Eugénie shortly before this final reconciliation.

IV   *Mme de La Rochejaquelein*

In 1854 Mérimée had met at a ball a certain Mme de La Rochejaquelein, an ardent Catholic and Royalist from la Vendée. A few days later he received a mysterious box containing a silver medal of the Virgin. Apparently this lady had conceived her mission to be the conversion of this famous agnostic. The loneliness of Mérimée after his break with Valentine was consoled to some extent by the friendly interest of this noble lady, for their visits and letters continued for the next decade. Mérimée showed his appreciation by helping to secure funds for the restoration of historic monuments dear to his friend, in la Vendée. That her efforts at conversion were without avail, however, can be seen from this letter he wrote her in January, 1855:

I have the misfortune of being a skeptic, but it is not my fault. I have tried to believe but I do not have faith. Although I am not insensible to poetry, I have never been able to write verse. I am too much *a matter of fact man*. That comes not from my education but from my organization. . . .Many things please me in the Christian religion and in the Catholic one in particular. I like it less in France.[15]

Indeed, the latter comment is symptomatic of Mérimée's constant suspicion of the clerical party, which he feared equally with the growing power of socialism (*les rouges*), for he always remained a man of the middle, convinced that only a strong central government was suitable for France.

V *Mérimée and the Empire*

Mérimée's attachment to the empire was due at first only to his affection and veneration for Eugénie, with whom he remained on the closest terms throughout two decades. He was especially fêted by the empress when he returned from his trip to Spain, bringing her news of her mother the countess. Likewise, in his frequent letters to Mme de Montijo he kept her informed of her daughter's health. It was only gradually that he came to modify his early rather unfavorable opinion of Napoleon III, partly as a result of the close cooperation which developed between them from 1860 to 1865 as a result of Napoleon's preoccupation with his *Life of Caesar,* for which he utilized Mérimée's early notes and gave Mérimée many commissions to look up historical references for him. Mérimée became a great favorite at the court, whether it met at the Tuileries, Saint-Cloud, Fontainebleau, or in the early autumn at Biarritz. He wrote and acted in many charades, masked balls, and other extravaganzas. It was at Biarritz in August, 1866, that he wrote for Eugénie his first fiction in many years, *La Chambre bleue,* signing it facetiously "the jester of her majesty the Empress," and it was at Saint-Cloud in 1869 that he read to the Empress and her ladies in waiting his *Lokis* before allowing it to be published by Buloz in the *Revue des Deux Mondes.*

Mérimeé never traded on his popularity at court to accept public office, though on two occasions, through the intervention of Eugénie, he was offered the post of minister of public instruction. His career as senator was not particularly brilliant: it was marked only by three rather ineffectual speeches: in favor of Mme Libri's petition to have her husband's case reopened; in defense of artists' rights and against a law exempting musical instruments from copyright restrictions; and against a petition denouncing materialism. In 1861–62 Mérimée served as secretary of the Senate. In 1860 he had resigned his active duties as inspector of historical monuments, though continuing in an honorary capacity, as well as vice-president of the Commission of Historical Monuments. From

1850 to 1868 he made fourteen trips to England, staying in those later years as guest of his close friend Panizzi, director of the British Museum. Without any official position Mérimée was of great assistance to Napoleon on these trips, gathering material to help reorganize the Imperial Library (now the Bibliothèque Nationale) along lines pioneered by the British Museum, serving as one of the judges at the Universal Exhibition of Arts and Crafts in London, and, perhaps most important of all, acting as informal liaison between the French and British governments through his contacts with such British statesmen as Palmerston, Gladstone, and Lord Russell. Another member of Parliament, Edward Ellice, became a warm friend of Mérimée, whom he entertained at his vast estate of Glenquoich in Scotland. On August 14, 1866, Mérimée was promoted to the post of Grand Officier de la Légion d'honneur.

VI   *Illness and Winters in Cannes*

Mérimée performed many good deeds during these last years, among them editing the letters of his late friend Jacquemont to aid his relatives financially, selling autographs to furnish support for Stendhal's poverty-stricken sister, and appealing to Eugénie on many occasions in regard to pensions for various penniless widows. He was saddened by the deaths of so many friends: Béranger, Charles Lenormant, Alfred de Musset, his American friends the Childes, later his British friends Ellice and Lord Ashburton, in 1867 both Achille Fould and Victor Cousin, and in 1869 Sainte-Beuve. From 1856 on he was afflicted with physical ailments: difficult breathing, neuralgia, lumbago, emphysema, and asthma. His letters to his friends are full of these afflictions, expressed, however, with his usual wit and humor.

In the winter of 1856 he went for the first time to visit the Ashburtons in Nice, then went on to Cannes, which for the rest of his life was to become his favorite winter residence. Usually he sent his elderly English companions, Miss Lagden and her sister Mrs. Ewer, on ahead to procure a suitable dwelling. In letters to his friends in Paris or to Ellice or Panizzi in London he described with almost lyrical fervor the charms of this earthly paradise— azure skies, snow-capped mountains in the distance, profusion of flowers and orange trees, with the Mediterranean calm and unruffled almost beneath his window. Some years, of course, there were tempests and frosts, making him consider taking refuge in Egypt or other tropical climes. He remained faithful, however, to Cannes, where he amused himself studying biology or, armed with the bow and arrow prescribed for him to strengthen his chest muscles by Dr. Maure (what an ironic name for a doctor, he said, since it was pronounced "mort") with which he shot down pine cones for the fire in his grate. Here in Cannes he received visits from his friends in Paris, from Panizzi from London, and on one occasion from King Ludwig of Bavaria. His special delight was his conversations with his old teacher, the philosopher Victor Cousin, whose painful death in 1867 caused him great sadness and depression. Usually in late February or early March he would return with great reluctance to Paris for meetings of the Senate or the French Academy, journeys which often resulted in a return of the ailments the warm climate of Cannes had alleviated.

VII *Tragic End of the Empire and of Mérimée*

On June 1, 1870, Mérimée arrived in Paris from Cannes for the last time. Returning from the Senate in a state of collapse, his feet and legs so swollen that he could walk only a few steps at a time, he spent the month of June in extreme suffering. The empress sent him a comfortable bed and fruits from the garden at Saint-Cloud; she would have come herself had he not protested that it was unseemly for his sovereign to mount the stairs to his apartment. Learning of the Prince of Hohenzollern's candidacy to the Spanish throne, Mérimée was confident that there would be no war with Prussia unless Bismarck wished it "absolutely." After Bismarck's falsification of the telegram of Ems which led to the French declaration of war on July 19, he was much depressed but soon felt encouraged by the wave of patriotic enthusiasm sweeping over all sections of the nation. After the defeats of the French army in the first week of August he realized, however, that all was lost, for the empire as well as for France. On August 16 and 20 he made his way in carpet slippers to the Tuileries for last visits with the Empress, whom he found "like a saint" and "firm as a rock," while she later affirmed that this was the only time she ever saw Mérimée lose control of himself. He also went to see his old friend Thiers to implore his backing for the imperial family but received only a suggestion for their abdication.

After the revolution of September 4 and Eugénie's flight to

England, Mérimée allowed his two old English ladies to take him back to Cannes on September 10. Here he was met by faithful Dr. Maure who describes his appearance in carpet slippers, house jacket, bent over, his face ravaged by suffering and eyes full of tears. From Cannes Mérimée wrote to Mme Beaulincourt these moving lines:

All my life I have tried to free myself from prejudices, to be a citizen of the world before being French. But all these philosophic mantles serve for nothing. I bleed today from the wounds of these imbecile French; I weep for their humiliations and, however ungrateful and however absurd they may be, I love them still.[16]

On September 23, two hours before his death, he wrote his last letter, to Jenny Dacquin. "I am very sick, so sick that it is difficult to write. There seems to be a little improvement. Go to my house in Paris and get the *Lettres de Mme de Sévigné* and a *Shakespeare*. I should have taken them to you before I left. Adieu. Je vous embrasse." [17]

In his will Mérimée had asked to be buried by a Protestant minister. Why he felt this way, a lifelong agnostic, we do not know, but perhaps it was out of deference to those old Anglican ladies, Mrs. Ewer and Miss Lagden, who had watched over him faithfully for so many years. He left the bulk of his property, some 365,000 francs, to Fanny Lagden who, since her death in 1879, lies buried beside him in the cemetery of Cannes, under an English inscription ending with the words "Dwell in safety." Eight months after Mérimée's death the *pétroleuses* of the Commune soaked his house in gasoline and burned it to a shell, including all his books, paintings, letters and papers—no doubt in vengeance for Mérimée's long association with the empire. The only things later recovered from the ashes were his Turkish pipe and a little bronze fawn.

CHAPTER 11

The Last Stories (Dernières Nouvelles)

I   *Il Viccolo di Madama Lucrezia*

WHEN the posthumous publication of Mérimée's last four stories appeared in the 1873 edition, *Dernières Nouvelles,* only one of these, *Lokis,* had previously been published. The first of these, *Il Viccolo di Madama Lucrezia,* dated by the author April 27, 1846, was originally written for Mme Odier, sister of Valentine Delessert. Why did Mérimée decide against publication? M. Lemonnier in his edition of *Les Dernières Nouvelles* suggests that Mérimée may have felt his story had too close a resemblance with the *Inès de la Sierras* of Nodier, who had already accused Mérimée of plagiarizing him in *La Guzla.*[1] A more probable reason is that when he had received it back from Mme Odier and shown it to Valentine to get her opinion concerning publication, her negative response made him decide to keep it in his drawer. Mérimée had probably found the background for his story on his visits to Italy in 1839 and 1841. The direct inspiration for his tale may well have come from an adventure which happened to his father, for he wrote in a letter to Paul Lacroix, already quoted: "The only romantic adventure I know of my father . . . was at Rome where he narrowly missed being assassinated at the same time as Basseville. He was saved by a Roman lady whom I met when she was very old, and who received me in Rome with great affection."[2]

At the age of twenty-three the narrator of this tale sets out for Rome, armed with a letter of recommendation from his father to a former lady friend, the Marchioness Aldobrandi. As he is examining in her palace a portrait of Lucrezia Borgia by da Vinci, the Marchioness enters, receives him warmly, apologizes for the absence of her elder son the Marquis, and introduces her younger son, Ottavio, a pale and melancholy young man whom she is preparing, much against his will, for the priesthood. During the following day, the narrator is conducted by Ottavio, always accompanied by his mentor, Father Negri, to visit the art galleries and monuments of Rome.

One evening at dinner in the Aldobrandi mansion the guests relate various tales of supernatural events which prepare the reader for the mystery about to occur. On his return home the young Frenchman, wandering through the *viccolo* (alley) of Madama Lucrezia, observes a rose falling at his feet from a second-story window and at once decides that he must have made the conquest of some unknown beauty. "I believed piously in the inflammability of German, Spanish and Italian ladies at the mere sight of a Frenchman" (687). Finding the door of this dwelling padlocked, he waits five minutes, throws pebbles against the window to no avail, wondering if "Roman ladies imagine that one carries ladders in one's pocket. No one had informed me of this custom" (687).

On the morrow he gives his hair a fastidious brushing, puts on his new frock coat and yellow gloves, and returns to number thirteen, which by daylight seems to be a rather dilapidated two-story dwelling with a chalked inscription "House for sale or for rent." Unable to extract any information from the neighbors, the narrator discovers in a dark cellar "an old woman whom one could suspect of sorcery, for she had a black cat and was cooking something in a caldron" (689). She agrees to produce a key to the padlock but is unable to make the rusty key turn. "However, by means of three oaths and as many grittings of my teeth, I succeeded in turning the key" (689). The rooms on the ground floor, covered with spider webs, showed traces of fifteenth-century elegance, and the windows opened on a rose garden. The second floor was in better condition and contained as sole furniture a large armchair in black leather, which strangely was not covered with dust. Seated in this chair our narrator listens to a fantastic legend which the old woman relates: once this belonged to Madama Lucrezia, a voluptuous woman who used to call up handsome passersby from the street, then have them assassinated by her servants so that they could not tell of their night of love. One night in the darkness her own brother mounted and after his departure and assassination, when she discovered his identity through a handkerchief he had left, she hanged herself in despair.

For the next three or four nights the narrator waits in vain in front of this house of mystery, though once at midnight he hears a woman's laughter behind the closed shutter. Another evening after visiting Ottavio he is persuaded to borrow the latter's mantle against the cold and on the sidewalk is handed a piece of paper with the written warning: "Don't come this evening or we are ruined. They know everything except your name, nothing can separate us. Thy Lucrezia." Returning to number thirteen he sees a human form in the open window and in calling out "Lucrezia" he is struck by a bullet, which is deflected by his heavy mantle, so that he is only bruised. Dragging himself along the wall to safety, he is joined by Ottavio and is taken in a cab to his hotel.

When he announces to the Marchioness his plan to leave Rome for Florence within two days, Ottavio takes him to his room, pleading desperately to go along disguised as his servant, to escape ordination into the priesthood set for the near future. Departure by coach is arranged for three o'clock in the morning. On returning to his hotel at two o'clock after saying farewell to the Roman families that had befriended him, he is astonished to find in his room a beautiful young lady who asks him if he is Ottavio's friend. "At this word everything becomes clear. The young woman, in spite of her pallor, had in no way the appearance of a specter. She lowered her eyes, which ghosts never do" (700). At this moment Ottavio arrives, and we learn that he has fallen in love with this girl of a lower social class whom his family would never have allowed him to marry, even if he had not been destined for the priesthood. The resemblance between our narrator and Ottavio was so great—"Some slanderers who had known my father in Rome claimed that there were reasons for that"—that Lucrezia had mistaken the Frenchman for Ottavio when she dropped the rose, and later he had been handed the warning note intended for Ottavio. The jealousy of Lucrezia's brother had been responsible for the shot.

Unlike most of Mérimée's stories, the conclusion is a happy one. On arrival in Florence, Ottavio marries Lucrezia before setting off with her to Paris where she receives the same warm welcome from the narrator's father that the narrator had received from the Marchioness. With some difficulty a reconciliation is arranged with the latter; Marquis Aldobrandi dies very opportunely from a fever; Ottavio inherits the title and fortune; and our narrator becomes the godfather of the couple's first child.

If we tried to determine in what category to place *Il Viccolo di Madama Lucrezia* we would be undecided between stories of mystery and fantasy and those of sophisticated society life. The novella, while inferior to Mérimée's masterpieces, is nevertheless a charming blend of intriguing mystery and graceful, nonchalant, and sparkling humor, of which several examples have been given in the quotations. The entire ambiance of Roman social life at the time is romantically rendered, and the lighthearted touch of the narrator is a welcome relief from the cynicism of *La Double Méprise* and of the somber savagery of so many of his other tales.

II *La Chambre bleue*

La Chambre bleue, the first story written by Mérimée in twenty years after *Il Viccolo,* was dedicated to Mme de la Rhune. The Rhune was a mountain in the Pyrenees which was visible from the imperial mansion in Biarritz, and was the name used in Mérimée's correspondence with Empress Eugénie, whom he also called "la dame de Biarritz." On September 1, 1866, Mérimée joined the train taking the empress and her suite to Biarritz. In a letter to Jenny Dacquin, on November 5, of that year, Mérimée states that he wrote this little tale at the request of the empress one night when he had absorbed some very strong tea. The imperial household had just been discussing "the difficult situations in which one can find oneself, as for instance Rodrigue between his papa and Chimène, mademoiselle Camille between her father and Curiace." [3] His reading of this story to the emperor and empress came to the attention of the Grand Duchess Marie, daughter of Tsar Nicholas, who was vacationing in Biarritz.

Shortly thereafter I receive the visit of a policeman, claiming to have been sent by the Grand Duchess. . . . "I come on behalf of her imperial highness to ask you to come this evening with your novel to her home."—"What novel?" "The one you read the other day to her Majesty." I replied that I had the honor to be her Majesty's buffoon and that I could not go to work *en ville* without her permission; and I ran at once to relate the affair to her. I expected that the result would be a war with Russia and I was a little mortified that not only did I receive permission, but also that I was urged to go that evening to the home of the Grand Duchess, to whom they had given the policeman as factotum.[4]

Mérimée had signed this tale "P. Mérimée, fou [jester] de S. M. l'Impératrice." When the story was found in the library of the Tuileries after the flight of the imperial family and the proclamation of the Third Republic, this comical signature was sufficient to arouse political passions and puritanical protests against the frivolity of the imperial court and the servility of the author who had contributed such a shockingly immoral tale (one which seems to us today quite innocuous). Although the story was already being printed its publication was considered undesirable, and all but six copies of the proofs were destroyed. When a Belgian paper, *L'Indépendance Belge*, published it in its issues of September 6 and 7, 1871, "the virtuous and republican papers of Paris judged it a very smutty work." [5] In 1873 it was first published in France in the collection *Dernières Nouvelles*.

In the opening pages we witness in a Paris railway station the meeting of a young man disguised with blue spectacles and a young woman in black with a thick veil. From their passionate embrace they must be lovers, for they exhibit "those poignant emotions for which I [the author] would give a hundred years of a philosopher's life" (703). Ensconced in a first-class coach, they are disturbed by the arrival of a man who, when they begin to converse in English, informs them in a much purer British accent that he is an Englishman. From a glimpse at his thick wallet of bank notes, they conclude that he is very rich. Dismounting from the train at the little town of N—— they see the Englishman accosted by a young man who calls him uncle, but who is handed a few papers and ordered angrily to be off.

At the hotel in N—— the lovers are given the best room, since "in France a traveler who has the good fortune to have a well-dressed woman on his arm is sure of obtaining the best room in all hotels; thus it is established that we are the most polite nation in Europe" (705). The room was called "la chambre bleue" because the two armchairs were upholstered in blue velvet of Utrecht. The walls were covered with wallpaper depicting a view of Naples, together with many persons, male and female, on whom unfortunately previous occupants had added mustaches and pipes. Léon, "not lacking in good sense although a lover" (706), goes to the kitchen to order dinner in a private room, learning with consternation that some officers of the *hussards* are giving a dinner to

some officers of the *chasseurs* in the public dining room adjacent
to theirs. In the room next to theirs through an open door they
perceive the Englishman at a table with a glass and bottle. Just as
the young couple are about to enjoy the felicity of their reunion,
alas "The devil always finds a way to pour his drop of absinthe
into the cup of happiness" (707). The officers relate in loud voices
the most scabrous anecdotes "quite foreign to strategy and tactics," until a cooler head persuades them to have regard for "the
newlyweds" next door, though at midnight they leave serenading
the couple with a martial air with twenty-four trumpets plus a
number of trombones. The Englishman shouts in the corridor for
another bottle of port (which the innkeeper concocts with a mixture of rum, cheap wine, and brandy). Calm having been re-
stored, the young couple enjoy the moonlight from their window
until they perceive the nephew of the Englishman walking in the
garden.

Late in the night they are awakened by a sound from the Englishman's room which seemed to be that of a heavy body falling,
followed by a stifled cry, then a door opening and a stealthy tread
in the corridor. While the young woman goes back to sleep, Léon
is assailed by horrible suspicions of a tragedy—no doubt the
nephew, aware of the thick bank notes carried by his uncle, must
have entered his room and killed him. This foreboding is soon
increased by the sight of a reddish liquid, apparently blood, flowing from a crevice in the door into their room. Léon is seized by
the dilemma: whether to announce the murder in hopes that the
assassin can be apprehended, or to escape from the hotel and
catch an early morning train to Paris in order to avoid an embar-
rassing confrontation with the police involving an explanation of
his illicit rendezvous. In defense of his hero Mérimée writes: "I
shall add respectfully, but with firmness, that, if it is wrong to let
an Englishman die next door, it is not praiseworthy to sacrifice for
him a woman sleeping with her head on your shoulder" (711).
When Léon explains the situation to his *inamorata*, they are convinced that they will be found guilty of the murder and promise
to die together and "as they were not sure that they would be
allowed to embrace on the scaffold, they smothered each other
with kisses, vying with each other in sprinkling the other with
their tears" (713).

Paying their bill next morning, they are astounded to hear a servant call out "Quick, some hot water for milord's tea. Bring a sponge also. He broke his bottle and the whole room is inundated" (715). Needless to say, the couple decide to postpone their departure until the two o'clock train and order a good luncheon for noon.

La Chambre bleue, that "bluette," or literary trifle as Mérimée called it, must be included, I suppose, with his tales of mystery and fantasy, yet the light witty tone, of which I have tried to give some examples, is scarcely conducive to a feeling of terror on the part of the reader. As Mérimée admitted in a letter to Augier, his story had the fault of a change in the denouement. He had originally planned on a tragic ending but "naturally" had related it in a jesting manner and therefore had to give it a comic conclusion. As for the prudish charge of immorality which caused the destruction of the first proofs under the Third Republic, modern readers will find the story quite innocuous. Mérimée's own comment in the letter already mentioned to Jenny Dacquin is full of delightful irony. "The thing is very moral at bottom, but there are details that might be disapproved by Monsignor Dupanloup. There is also a begging of principle necessary for the development of the plot: two persons of different sexes go off to an inn; that has never been seen, but that was necessary for me." [6]

The chief interest for us in this *bluette*, of course, is the fact that it marks Mérimée's return to imaginative fiction after an absence of two decades. As for the royal nature of this inspiration, M. Martineau has made an interesting comparison with a greater predecessor in the seventeenth century. "If he took up again, after twenty years, his pen as a novelist, it was only at the solicitation of the Empress Eugénie, just as some two centuries earlier it had required almost a royal order for Racine to write his last two tragedies, after an equally rigorous interruption." [7]

III *Lokis*

Although *Lokis* was not published in the *Revue des Deux Mondes* until 1869, its subject had occupied Mérimée's attention since 1867. It was in May of that year that his friend the Polish Countess Przezdziecka (the other *Inconnue*) had interested him in a study of the Lithuanian language. M. Castex has pointed out that one of the properties of the countess was famous for raising bears. It was to her that Mérimée owed acquaintance with the person who became his hero, Count Szemioth, in whose family an occurrence similar to the one in his story had taken place.[8] When Mérimée told his story to Jenny Dacquin, on September 3, 1868, he quite correctly suspected that she would be shocked, for "this gentleman is the illegitimate son of this badly raised bear."[9] Jenny Dacquin proposed an important modification: let it be the mere glance of the bear which made the hero's mother insane and gave her son his sanguinary instincts. With some reluctance, Mérimée accepted her suggestion: "It shall be done according to your wish. I have always found your advice excellent; but this time you take advantage of my permission."[10] Martineau feels that the story gained greatly from this advice: "We are able to think that the cruel instincts of the hero come to him merely from the terror experienced by his mother and from the delirious and panicky ideas to which she was a prey during the whole period of pregnancy. The work gained thus in verisimilitude as well as in humanity."[11]

The first reading of Lokis in public took place before the empress and her entourage in the palace of Saint-Cloud in July, 1869. After having completed the reading in his usual indifferent voice, he turned to Filon, preceptor of the imperial prince and later Mérimée's biographer, to ask if he had understood it. Without giving him time to reply, he concluded: "You have understood nothing. That's perfect." Mérimée realized that he had succeeded in writing a scandalous tale without anyone being shocked.[12] To Buloz, who had asked Mérimée to let him have Lokis for the Revue des Deux Mondes, Mérimée had answered on October 17, 1868, "I am entering the period of my second childhood and if I still have the weakness of writing novels, I have the good sense to show them only to my friends. If my bear is ever licked [polished] enough to be shown to friends I shall be charmed to read it to you . . . but I shall never publish it."[13] Nevertheless, Mérimée later relented, and Lokis appeared in the Revue des Deux Mondes of September 15, 1869.

To complete this discussion of the circumstances surrounding the writing of Lokis, we should add that at this time Mérimée was reading a great deal in the Polish writer Mickiewicz from whom he borrowed details for local color, and that the first idea of the story may have come from a similar tale by Bandello, as M. Pierre Martino has suggested. More important perhaps was the influence of Mérimée's good friend Turgenev to whom he had sent the story for revision and suggestions. In addition to changes in the background of Lithuanian customs, Turgenev suggested that in place of Mérimée's original title "Le Trouveur de miel" [The Finder of Honey] the word "Lokis," Lithuanian for bear, should be used.

As for the narrative itself, it is supposedly his Journal for the year 1866 which the German Professor Wittembach is reading aloud to two friends. Having pointed out to the Bible Society that their recent translation of the Scriptures into Lithuanian could not be read by the peasants of Samogitie who speak only *jmoude*, the learned professor of philology has been commissioned by the society to make a translation of Saint Matthew into that dialect and has therefore decided to visit this province to learn the vocabulary from a study of popular folklore and legend. Writing to Count Szemioth, who possessed such a collection in his library, Professor Wittembach received from him a cordial invitation to be his guest.

On his arrival at the château, he was informed that a bad migraine confined the Count to his room but that the professor could dine with Doctor Froebel. Soon a carriage drew up, containing an elderly lady with long white hair who was seized by three feminine attendants and carried despite her protests to her room. Doctor Froebel, the doctor of the Countess, introduced himself to the professor and related the strange tale of the madness which had possessed the Countess for twenty-seven years. It seems that while on a hunting expedition two days after her marriage to the young Count's father, she had been carried off by a bear which fortunately was shot by one of the valets. Although her face had been scratched and one leg broken, the Countess was still alive but had apparently lost her reason. Doctors predicted that as soon as she gave birth to her child she would recover her sanity, but alas, when this event took place, she cried out "Kill him, kill the beast" and was only with difficulty prevented from wringing the baby's neck.

After Professor Wittembach retired for the night he heard a noise in the branches of a tree next to his window, saw a human head in the foliage, then a body hanging from a limb and quickly dropping to the ground. Next morning the young Count presented himself to apologize for his indiscreet curiosity of the night before. The following day, the Count invited the Professor to accompany him through the forest on horseback to visit a tumulus famous as the rendezvous of sorcerers in ancient times. Here they encountered an old woman begging for alms. Her basket was full of mushrooms, some of which the Professor recognized as poisonous; but when he tried to remove these from the basket, she called out "Pirkuns," the name of a divinity corresponding to Jupiter among the peasants, and the head of a serpent rose from the basket. Then the old woman cryptically advised the Count not to go to Dowghielly, a château he was accustomed to visit to call on the young *châtelaine*. Disturbed by this warning, the Count nevertheless allowed his horse to choose the direction, and soon they found themselves welcomed by the vivacious and coquettish Ioulka and her aunt. Joined later by other guests they were regaled by a picturesque folk dance and a copious dinner. The Professor then recounted an experience in South America when, without food or drink for three days, he had been obliged to follow the example of the Indians in bleeding his horse and drinking the blood. Prevailed upon to spend the night, the Count astonished the Professor by locking up his firearms in the cupboard, explaining that once he had pulled the trigger while asleep, barely missing the head of a comrade.

Back at home the next day there ensued a curious psychological discussion concerning the "duality" or "duplicity" of human nature in which the Count averred that sometimes we are assailed by horrible temptations, such as jumping off a high tower or assassinating one's best friend—temptations one might not always have time for sane judgment to reject. One day the Count returned from a visit to Dowghielly castle in very bad humor, protesting that he was not in love with the capricious Ioulka, whose only attraction was her white skin. "Her skin is marvelous! Mr. Professor, the blood which is under this skin must be better than that of a horse?" (749).

After the Professor had been gone for two months continuing his research on the folklore and patois of Samogitie, he was astonished to receive a letter from the Count requesting him, in his capacity as Protestant minister, to perform the nuptial ceremony between the Count and Ioulka. He found the château in full celebration. At noon a carriage drew up, containing Ioulka, her aunt, and the Count. As they dismounted, the horses, frightened by the shower of petals from the guests or by the fear which the Count always seemed to inspire in animals, reared and started to pull the carriage against the landing; fortunately, the Count was able to seize his fiancée and carry her to safety. "Suddenly a tall, pale, thin woman, her clothing in disorder, her hair disheveled, and all her features contracted by terror, appeared at the top of the landing, without anyone knowing whence she came. 'Get the bear!' she cried in a loud voice; 'get the bear! Guns! He is carrying off a woman. Fire! Fire!'" (752–53). It was the old Countess, and those in the gathering who were superstitious felt this to be an evil omen.

After the marriage ceremony the numerous attendants regaled themselves with dining and drinking champagne until late in the evening. Waking at three o'clock, the Professor thought he saw a heavy body pass before his window and fall with a dull thud in the garden. Returning to the salon at eleven the next morning, he found the company worried because neither the Count nor his bride had yet appeared. On receiving no answer to their knocks, they broke into the bridal chamber and saw a terrible sight: "the young Countess was lying dead in her bed, her face terribly lacerated, her bosom open, drenched with blood. The Count had disappeared and no one has had any news of him since then" (756). Examining the horrible wound, the doctor observed that it had been made, not by a steel blade, but by a bite.

As in the sanguinary story of *Carmen, Lokis* begins with a learned philological discussion and ends with the pedantic dissertation of Professor Wittembach on the meaning of "Lokis," the Lithuanian name for "bear," and a comparison with Sanskrit, Greek, Latin, German, and Old French. Unlike *Carmen,* however, the dramatic events in *Lokis* are interrupted from time to time by the linguistic preoccupations of the erudite narrator. Whether Mérimée is influenced by his lifelong interest in comparative philology and newfound enthusiasm for Lithuanian studies, or whether he intends by these interpolations to express the modesty of a discreet man of the world toward his own achievements in fiction, it must be admitted that this technique interferes at times with the tragic intensity of the narrative. Because of the gruesome, morbid, and almost unbelievable nature of the theme, critical evaluation of this novella's rank in Mérimée's fiction has been somewhat varied, ranging from the hyberbolic acclaim of Marsan to the more guarded reaction of Billy and Raitt.

On one point, however, there can be no disagreement, namely with the skill Mérimée manifested in preparing the reader to accept the fantastic denouement as realistic and possible. In *Lokis,* as in *La Vénus d'Ille,* we are given two possible interpretations, one fantastic and mysterious, the other more prosaic and rational; is the half-ursine, half-human nature of the young Count due to his birth as illegitimate son of the bear, or are his animalistic tendencies merely the result of his mother's shock and insanity from her terrible experience? In any case, the ursine character of Count Szemioth is prepared with many subtle suggestions, the first being his proclivity for climbing trees. This is followed by the fear he inspires in dogs and horses, in his ability to direct himself unfailingly in the forest, in the advice of the old sorceress to make himself ruler of the animal kingdom, in the dark fuzz under his arms, in his questioning of the Professor concerning the best place to bleed horses in order to drink their blood, and finally in his fascination with the white skin of his fiancée.

In a letter to the young writer Edouard Delessert on February 1, 1848, Mérimée had written: "And then one must not forget that when one relates something supernatural, one cannot multiply too much the details of material reality. That is the great art of Hoffmann in his fantastic tales. . . . Try in a few words to fix the place of the scene." [14] Nowhere better than in *Lokis* has Mérimée followed his own prescription. It is this careful preparation, along with many exotic details of the story's setting in the barbarous world of northern forest and marshland, which make *Lokis,* if not one of Mérimée's masterpieces, at least the most important of his *Dernières Nouvelles.*

IV *Djoûmane*

Djoûmane, a dream sequence, written for the Empress at Fontainebleau about the same time as *Lokis* and finished later, has its scenes laid in Algeria during the colonial wars about 1843. Though he had long planned a trip there, Mérimée had never visited this colony; he had been frustrated each time by some unexpected development. In 1860 he had documented himself on this country through the works of General Daumas and had tried to draw information from Jenny Dacquin, at that time in Algeria with her brother, concerning Moslem women.[15] The story appeared first in the *Moniteur Universel* of January 9, 10, and 12,

1873, to whose director, Paul Dalloz, the author had handed it before his death.[16] It was included as the last of four stories in *Dernières Nouvelles*.

A French battalion has just returned to barracks from an expedition of several months against dissident Arabs when they are informed that they must set out again to cut off the retreat of the Arab leader, Sidi-Lala. Before dining the narrator and other officers watch a curious spectacle in the courtyard where an old sorcerer is making an incantation to the music of two flutes and three drums while a band of mountebanks performs dances. A charming little girl of fourteen or fifteen makes her way through the crowd, dropping a basket from which emerges a big serpent which bites her on the ankle, causing her to fall backward in tears, rolling in the dust, her lips covered with a white foam. The officer-narrator calls upon the military doctor to go to her aid, but the latter is quite aware that all this is part of the ceremony. Indeed, the old magician puts the snake back in the hamper, cures the little girl with a pinch of white powder and an incantation, and soon she is collecting coins from the audience.

As the squad under the narrator's command sets off for the ford in the gorge to cut off Sidi-Lala, the description of the moonlit fog making all objects unreal prepares the reader for the fantastic adventures to follow. Finding a lone Arab horseman, Sidi-Lala, taunting them from the other side of the gorge, the narrator crosses to meet him in hand-to-hand combat, plunges a saber into him, then falls with him and the horses from the precipice into the water. Seeking to grasp a root, he finds it is a big serpent; then he sees a woman holding a torch in one hand and filling a jug with the other. He follows her through a labyrinth of tunnels in the cliff until he sees below him the old magician with a great multitude bearing torches and at his feet the little girl he had seen that afternoon. Twenty bystanders pull off the lid of a well, filled with a muddy liquid, from which at the oft repeated cry "Djoûmane" rises the enormous head of a serpent, livid gray with phosphorescent eyes. While the narrator averts his eyes in horror, he hears the splash of a body and, looking down, perceives the sorcerer all alone and the little girl's kerchief floating on the muddy water. Then all the torches are suddenly extinguished.

Making his way painfully along the walls, the narrator comes to a tapestry lighted up from within. Crossing the corridor he enters, through an open door, a room furnished in Oriental splendor with silk, velvet, and gold, permeated with a voluptuous, delicate perfume. A lovely young woman, her hair black as a raven, welcomes him to a seat beside her on a divan, pouring out for him a café mousse.

"Shall we not have a morning nip, my lieutenant?" At these words I opened my eyes wide. That young woman had enormous mustachios, she was the very portrait of sergeant Wagner. Indeed Wagner was standing in front of me and handing me a cup of coffee while, lying on my horse's neck, I was watching him quite dumfounded. "It seems we have been taking a snooze, all the same, my lieutenant. Here we are at the ford and the coffee is boiling." (768)

According to M. Raoul Roche, Mérimée has given us here an authentic dream almost without modification. In his Freudian interpretation, M. Roche sees here a reflection of Mérimée's fondness for a young Jewish girl.[17] In support of this interpretation Raitt suggests that not only is the *mane* of Djoûmane the phonetic equivalent of the termination *mann* common in Jewish names, but that the first syllable *Djoû* is almost a transcription of the English word "Jew."[18]

In any case *Djoûmane* is notable for the skill with which Mérimée glides from the realistic and picturesque opening of the story to the only slightly more exotic and colorful scenes of the dream, so that the reader is quite unaware of the transition. The story also shows that Mérimée has lost none of his power for vivid, hallucinating description—first in the atmosphere of this magic nocturnal ride, then in the horror of the little girl's immersion in the black liquid surrounding the serpent, contrasted with the later voluptuous richness of the Oriental boudoir. *Djoûmane* may be compared also to *La Chambre bleue* in its trick ending, typical of Mérimée's ironic bent.

In summary, we may say of these last three tales—for *Il Viccolo di Madama Lucrezia* belongs after all in composition to a period two decades earlier—that with the possible exception of *Lokis* they add little to Mérimée's reputation and are inferior to the very great stories of *Mosaïque* and the masterpieces which followed. Yet they are well written and interesting, and proof that old age had occasioned no significant falling off in his powers as a literary craftsman.

CHAPTER 12

Conclusion

THE mask of cynicism and wordly sophistication which Méri-mée wore during his lifetime except before his most intimate friends has been pierced for recent readers, revealing the real Mérimée which lies beneath it. Once considered a purely objective and coldly impersonal writer, Mérimée, as we have seen, transformed episodes of his own love affairs into the artistic stuff of fiction: Mme Lacoste into the Diane of *La Chronique* and the Mme de Courcy of *Le Vase étrusque*. In both of these works we find duels paralleling his own. Twice he has given us a "portrait of the author," slightly flattered perhaps as Saint-Clair, slightly blackened as Darcy. At least once in his fiction he has given vent to personal emotion in the heartrending pathos of *Arsène Guillot*.

But it is above all in the many volumes of correspondence collected and annotated so carefully by M. Parturier that the true Mérimée appears—witty, skeptical, but generous to a fault. A devoted son, he was capable of lifelong masculine friendships, among them of course his alter ego Stendhal, and also Albert Stapfer, Jacquemont, Requien, Victor Cousin, Musset, Sainte-Beuve, the American Childe, and in England Sutton Sharpe, Ellice, and Panizzi, director of the British Museum. Yet his real genius for friendship lay in his appreciation of the feminine sex, among whom we might mention Mme de Montijo and her daughter Eugénie, the *Inconnue* Jenny Dacquin, Mélanie Double (Mme Libri), Mme de Boigne, Mme de Lagrené and those elderly English ladies, Mrs. Ewer and Fanny Lagden. On at least two occasions we know that he lost control of his steely reserve to break into tears—on the departure of his beloved Valentine Delessert into temporary exile and on his final interview with Empress Eugénie before her flight to England. But perhaps the most humanly appealing revelation of the real Mérimée, up to this time the blasé cosmopolite ever on guard against chauvinism, is the

heartbreaking letter he wrote Mme de Beaulincourt at the downfall of his beloved country. To complete this picture of the true
Mérimée gained from his correspondence we should add his
sturdy independence and refusal to profit personally from his
friendship with the imperial family, his readiness on all occasions
to aid those in distress, and above all his passionate devotion to
the one great love of his life, Valentine Delessert.

It is seldom one encounters a writer as broadly versed in so
many fields as Mérimée. To his devoted efforts as archeologist
through two decades we owe, more than to any other man, the
preservation of France's priceless architectural heritage of the
past. Art and literary critic, linguist and philologist—he spoke flu-
ently English and Spanish besides his knowledge of German, Russian, Italian, Latin, and Greek and Gypsy dialects—he thought of
himself chiefly as a historian, remaining always the amateur in
fiction and drama. As a critic of his own fellow countrymen, he
was frequently unjust to his Romantic contemporaries, full of
scorn for the lyric effusions of Lamartine, Vigny, and Hugo, later
unappreciative of Flaubert, his only favorites being Musset, Augier, and Sainte-Beuve. In the domain of foreign literature he was
more perspicacious; his essays on Spanish literature—Calderón,
Lope de Vega, Moratín, and Cervantes did much to increase
French interest in this field. But it was especially in Russian literature that he was a pioneer; if he lacked a full appreciation of
Gogol and Dostoevsky, his essays and his translations of Pushkin
and Turgenev did much to assure their reputation in France.

Mérimée would probably have been surprised to have been
told that his creative works in drama and fiction together with his
correspondence rather than his historical works would be most
highly esteemed today. As in the case of the novelist Stendhal he
has had to wait till this century for a full appreciation of his dramatic works, at least two or three of which have now become
classics and with Musset's plays have become the jewels of French
Romanticism. Mérimée's short stories and *nouvelles*, even his one
venture into historical fiction, have maintained their rank and
even gained in popular favor. Like his friend Stendhal, he was a
forerunner of Romanticism before laying the foundation for the
Realism which followed. If Mérimée is lacking in lyricism and
broad epic sweep, he is rivaled only by Maupassant—who owes
much to his predecessor—as a master of the French short story

whose standing he did so much to establish. He has become a model for concision of description blending with elements of fantasy and mysticism, and for synthetic depiction of character, primarily among primitive and passionate natures. His style, akin to that of French Classicism and the eighteenth century, is so simple, unpretentious, and pellucid that his stories are read today with a freshness and naturalness which make them seem as if written only yesterday.

Notes and References

(Place of publication Paris unless otherwise noted)

Chapter One

1. Mérimée, *Correspondance générale* (hereafter referred to as CG) Vol. III, 2ᵉ série, établie et notée par Maurice Parturier, Toulouse, Privat, pp. 4, 5.
2. *Ibid.*
3. *Ibid.*
4. *Ibid.*
5. *Ibid.*
6. Augustin Filon, *Mérimée.* (Hachette, 1898; second edition, 1922), hereafter referred to as Filon, pp. 9–10.
7. Robert Baschet, *Du Romantisme au Second Empire. Mérimée,* hereafter referred to as Baschet (Editions Latines, 1959), p. 15.
8. Quoted by Baschet, p. 23.
9. C. G. VI, 1ᵉʳᵉ série, p. 348.
10. Stendhal, *Souvenirs d'égotisme* in *Oeuvres intimes,* Bibliothèque de la Pléiade, 1961, p. 1466.
11. P. Trahard, *La Jeunesse de Prosper Mérimée,* hereafter referred to as Trahard, (Champion, 1925), Vol. I, p. 142.
12. *Ibid.,* pp. 143–44, citing the *Journal* of Delécluze, pp. 223–24.
13. Filon, p. 22.
14. C. G. I 1ᵉʳᵉ série, pp. 1–3.
15. Sylvia Lyon, *The Life and Times of Prosper Mérimée,* hereafter referred to as Lyon (New York: The Dial Press, 1948), p. 38.
16. In 1669 the Marquis de Chamilly, a French officer in Portugal, had translated five letters supposedly written by a Portuguese nun. Nine years later these were translated into English as *The Letters of of a Portuguese Nun* by Sir Robert L'Estrange, member of Parliament for Winchester. Miss Lyon suggests that it was in this version Mérimée had found the name. Lyon, p. 42.
17. Filon, p. 26.
18. Quoted by Yovanovitch, *La Guzla de Prosper Mérimée* (Hachette, 1911), hereafter referred to as Yovanovitch, p. 191.
19. C. G. VIII 2ᵉ série, p. 82.

20. Filon, p. 28.
21. C. G. I 1ère série, pp. 375–79.
22. Baschet, p. 51.
23. A. W. Raitt, *Prosper Mérimée*, hereafter referred to as Raitt (London: Eyre and Spottiswoode, 1970), pp. 69–70.
24. C. G. I 1ère série, pp. 24–25.
25. *Ibid.*, pp. 25–26.

Chapter Two

1. C. G. I 1ère série, pp. 4–5.
2. *Journal* of Delécluze, pp. 262–63, quoted by Baschet, p. 32.
3. Fr. Michel, "Stendhal et Mérimée" in *Nouvelles Soirées du Stendhal Club, Mercure de France*, pp. 159–70, quoted by Baschet, p. 31.
4. Trahard, Vol. I, p. 219.
5. Baschet, p. 30.
6. F. Baldensperger, "Le Moine de Lewis dans la litt. fr." *Journal of Comparative Literature* (July-September 1903).
7. Trahard, I, p. 208.
8. Quoted by Baschet, p. 23.
9. Quoted by André Billy, *Mérimée*, hereafter referred to as Billy (Flammarion, 1959), p. 34.
10. *Ibid.*
11. C. G. V 1ère série, p. 90.
12. C. G. V 1ère série, pp. 392–94.
13. Trahard, II, p. 108.
14. *Ibid.*, pp. 122–23.
15. P. Poujet, *Notice* to Classiques Larousse ed. of *Le Théâtre de Clara Gazul*, p. 9.
16. Trahard, II, p. 169.
17. Trahard, I, pp. 171–224, II, pp. 107–27.
18. Baschet, p. 31.

Chapter Three

1. Yovanovitch, pp. 247–52.
2. *Ibid.*, p. 249.
3. *Ibid.*, p. 279.
4. *Ibid.*, pp. 287–88.
5. *Ibid.*, p. 293.
6. *Ibid.*, pp. 298–99.
7. *Gazette de France*, September 19, 1827, quoted by Yovanovitch.
8. Yovanovitch, pp. 303–7.
9. *Ibid.*, p. 320.
10. *Ibid.*, pp. 338–39.
11. *Ibid.*, pp. 340–41.

12. *Ibid.*, p. 356.
13. *Ibid.*, pp. 371–80.
14. *Ibid.*, pp. 384–90.
15. *Ibid.*, p. 397.
16. Mérimée, *Avertissement* to 1842 ed. of *La Guzla.*
17. Yovanovitch, p 449, corrects Mérimée's boast, asserting that Gerhardt made no such statement in his modest preface but only availed himself of his acquaintance with true Serbian poetry to achieve these rhythms.
18. Yovanovitch, pp. 456–58.
19. Quoted by Filon, *Mérimée et ses amis* (Hachette, 1894), p. 40.
20. Filon, *Préface à La Guzla* by Yovanovitch, pp. x, xi.
21. Yovanovitch, p. 533.
22. Trahard, I, pp. 291–93.

Chapter Four

1. Trahard, I, p. 322.
2. *Ibid.*, p. 307.
3. *Ibid.*, p. 311.
4. *Ibid.*, pp. 313, 319.
5. *Ibid.*, p. 306.
6. *Ibid.*, pp. 317–18.
7. *Ibid.*, p. 333.
8. E. Marsan, Introduction to Divan ed. of *La Jaquerie*, p. ii.
9. H. Martineau, preface to Pléiade ed. of Mérimée's *Romans et Nouvelles* (hereafter referred to as Martineau), p. xiii.
10. Filon, p. 35.
11. Trahard, II, pp. 50–56.
12. *Ibid.*, pp. 36–37.
13. Quoted by Baschet, p. 55.
14. Trahard, II, p. 61.
15. Raitt, p. 97.
16. Martineau, pp. xiv, xv.

Chapter Five

1. C. G., I 1ère série, p. 33.
2. *Ibid.*, p. 184.
3. Raitt, pp. 76–78.
4. Trahard, II, p. 169.
5. C. G., I 1ère série, p. 82.
6. *Ibid.*, pp. 254–55.
7. Raitt, p. 106.
8. Quoted by Baschet, p. 80.
9. Alphonse Lefèbre, *La Célèbre Inconnue de Prosper Mérimée*, Bib.

Internationale d'Edition, B. Sansot et Cie., 1908, preface by Félix
Chambon, p. 28.
   10. C. G., I 1ère série, p. 275.
   11. Raitt, p. 153.
   12. Filon, p. 84.
   13. P. Léon, *La Vie des monuments français*. Picard, p. 200, quoted
by Raitt, p. 154.
   14. Baschet, p. 95.
   15. C. G., II 1ère série, p. 8.
   16. *Ibid.*, p. 60.
   17. *Ibid.*, pp. 288, 290.
   18. *Ibid.*, p. 289.
   19. C. G., III 1ère série, p. 408.
   20. *Ibid.*, pp. 456–57.
   21. C. G., IV 1ère série, p. 62.
   22. *Ibid.*, pp. 66–67.
   23. *Ibid.*, p. 70.
   24. *Ibid.*, p. 239.
   25. C. G., IV 1ère série, p. 294.
   26. Baschet, p. 136.
   27. Raitt, p. 218.
   28. C. G., IV 1ère série, p. 441.
   29. *Ibid.*, p. 422.
   30. Raitt, p. 224.
   31. C. G., V 1ère série, p. 264.
   32. Filon, p. 145.
   33. Raitt, p. 284.
   34. C. G., VI 1ère série, p. 344.

Chapter Six

   1. Gustave Charlier, "La Source principale de *Mateo Falcone*,"
Revue d'Histoire Litt. de la France (July-September, 1921).
   2. Pierre Richard, Notice to Classiques Larousse ed. of *Mateo Falcone et Colomba*, p. 17.
   3. W. Pater, "Prosper Mérimée" in *Miscellaneous Studies* (New
York: Macmillan, 1895), p. 45.
   4. Pierre Richard, *op. cit.*, p. 20.
   5. Martineau, p. xvii.
   6. Billy, p. 44.
   7. Pierre Richard, Notice to Classiques Larousse ed. of *Carmen,
L'Enlèvement de la redoute et La Vénus d'Ille*, p. 6.
   8. Filon, p. 44.
   9. E. Faguet, *Etudes litt. sur le 19è siècle* (hereafter referred to as
Faguet), p. 337.

10. Léon Vignots, "Les Sources de Tamango," *Mercure de France,* December 15, 1922, cited by Martineau, p. xviii.

11. Billy, p. 44.

12. H. Taine, *Derniers Essais de critique,* Hachette, p. 225. This essay on Mérimée is also found as the preface to *Lettres à une Inconnue,* Lévy, 1874.

Chapter Seven

1. Billy, p. 77.
2. Martineau, p. xxii.
3. Billy, p. 77.
4. Baschet, p. 80.
5. Raitt, p. 176.
6. Faguet, p. 342.
7. Filon, p. 55.
8. Martineau, p. xxii.
9. Faguet, p. 328.
10. Martineau, p. xxii.
11. Faguet, p. 328.
12. Filon, p. 56.
13. Baschet, p. 87.
14. Billy, p. 78.
15. Martineau, p. 802 note 2, and p. 803 note 1.

Chapter Eight

1. Billy, p. 105.
2. Filon, pp. 62–63.
3. C. G., II 1ère série, p. 244.
4. Billy, p. 106.
5. C. G., II 1ère série, pp. 462–63.
6. Filon, p. 68.
7. Raitt, pp. 190–91.
8. C. G., II 1ère série, pp. 462–63.
9. *Ibid.*
10. Filon, p. 70.
11. Martineau, p. xxvii.
12. Martineau, Pléiade ed., p. 816.
13. Filon, p. 72.
14. Raitt, p. 196.
15. Saintsbury, *A History of the French Novel,* Vol. II (London, Macmillan), p. 238.
16. Sainte-Beuve, *Mes Poisons* (Les Oeuvres représentatives, 1926), pp. 98–99.

17. C. G., IV 1ère série, p. 422.
18. Martineau, p. xxix.

Chapter Nine

1. C. G., V 1ère série, pp. 392–93.
2. Marsan, preface to *Les Deux Héritages et Les Débuts d'un aventurier* (Divan, 1928), pp. xi, xii.
3. C. G., VI 1ère série, pp. 74–75.
4. Filon, p. 146.
5. Marson, *op. cit.*, p. xiii.

Chapter Ten

1. C. G., 1 2e série, p. 303.
2. C. G., I 2e série, p. 78.
3. *Ibid.*, p. 76.
4. *Ibid.*, p. 303.
5. *Ibid.*, p. 60.
6. *Ibid.*, p. 312.
7. *Ibid.*, p. 412.
8. *Ibid.*, p. 417.
9. *Ibid.*, p. 426.
10. C. G.., II 2e série, p. 165.
11. C. G., I 2e série, p. 441.
12. C. G., VI 2e série, p. 346.
13. C. G., VII 2e série, p. 302.
14. Baschet, p. 195. He also points out pp. 189–90 that Flaubert in his *Education sentimentale* takes traits of Valentine for Mme Dambieuse, of Du Camp for Frédéric Moreau, and even of Mérimée.
15. C. G., I 2e série, p. 426.
16. C. G., IX 2e série, p. 170.
17. *Ibid.*, p. 172.

Chapter Eleven

1. Léon Lemonnier, preface to *Dernières Nouvelles* (Champion), cited by Baschet, p. 141.
2. C. G., III 2e série, pp. 4, 5.
3. C. G., VII 2e série, pp. 278–79.
4. *Ibid.*
5. Martineau, p. xxxi.
6. C. G., VII 2e série, pp. 278–79.
7. Martineau, p. xxx.
8. Baschet, p. 249.
9. C. G., VIII 2e série, p. 233.
10. *Ibid.*, p. 255.

11. Martineau, p. xxxii.

12. Billy, p. 262.

13. C. G., VIII 2ᵉ série, pp. 270–71.

14. C. G., V 1ᵉʳᵉ série, pp. 237–38.

15. Billy, p. 269.

16. Martineau, p. 830.

17. Raoul Roche, "Un rêve de Mérimée," *La Grande Revue* (October, 1928).

18. Raitt, p. 335.

Selected Bibliography

PRIMARY SOURCES

(Place of publication Paris unless otherwise noted)

1. Literary Works

Romans et Nouvelles, ed. by H. Martineau. Bibliothèque de la Pléiade, N. R. F. (Gallimard), 1951.

Romans et Nouvelles, ed. by M. Parturier. Garnier, 1967. In addition to his fiction there is a ten-volume edition by Le Divan with excellent prefaces by E. Marsan, published from 1927 to 1931, containing the following: *Contes russes* with four stories Mérimée translated from Pushkin: "La Dame de Pique," "Les Bohémiens," "Le Hussard"; "Le Coup de Pistolet"; also four by Turgenev, "Le Juif," "Petouchkof," "Le Chien," and "Apparitions"; and the following:

La Guzla.

La Jaquerie.

Les Deux Héritages and *Les Débuts d'un aventurier.*

Les Mécontents (included in *Mosaïque*).

Théâtre de Clara Gazul.

2. Historical Works

Épisode de l'histoire de Russie. Les Faux Démétrius. Lévy, 1852.

Histoire du règne de Pierre le Grand, ed. by Mongault and Parturier. Conard, 1947.

Histoire de Don Pèdre 1er roi de Castille, ed. by G. Laplace. Didier, 1961.

3. Correspondence

Correspondance générale. The first six volumes ed. by Parturier, Mallion, and Josserand published by Le Divan in Paris, the next eleven of the 2e série ed. by Parturier, published by Privat in Toulouse. Begun in 1941, this *Correspondance* was completed in 1964.

SECONDARY SOURCES

1. Books

These are limited to those found helpful in the preparation of this study. For a more complete bibliography see Trahard and Josserand, *Bibliographie des oeuvres de Prosper Mérimée* (Champion, 1929), or the more recent Raitt, A. W., *Prosper Mérimée* (London: Eyre and Spottiswoode, 1970).

BASCHET, R. *Du Romantisme au Second Empire, Mérimée*. Nouvelles Editions Latines, 1959. Well balanced both for biography and literary criticism, perhaps the best work in French on Mérimée.

BILLY, ANDRÉ. *Mérimée*. Flammarion, 1959. A good solid work, perhaps better for biography than literary evaluation.

BOWMAN, F. P. *Prosper Mérimée, Heroism, Pessimism and Irony*. Berkeley and Los Angeles: University of California Press, 1962. A very detailed analysis of Mérimée's heroes and of Mérimée's own attitude toward religion, politics, love, friendship, death, and fate, illustrated from his fiction, drama, and correspondence. Also a very perceptive description of Mérimée's technique as a writer.

DALE, R. C. *The Poetics of Prosper Mérimée*. The Hague and Paris: Mouton, 1966. A scholarly study of Mérimée's comments on literary theory as found in his letters and essays on Russian literature, rather than an analysis of his own practice. These comments are limited to fiction, particularly the supernatural tale.

FILON, A. *Mérimée*. Hachette, 1898. Long a standard work, by one who knew Mérimée at the imperial court. Still very useful though many of its literary judgments have been reversed by recent scholarship.

IBROVAC, M. *Claude Fauriel et la fortune européenne des poésies populaires grecque et serbe*. Didier, 1966. Contains a discussion of Mérimée's friendship with Fauriel and the latter's influence on young Mérimée's interest in Serbian folk poetry.

LEFÈBRE, A. *La Célèbre Inconnue de Prosper Mérimée*. Sansot, 1908. A detailed account of Jenny Dacquin's life and her influence on Mérimée.

LÉON, P. *Mérimée et son temps*. Presses Universitaires Françaises, 1962. Excellent study by one who, like Mérimée, was employed in the conservation of historical monuments, of Mérimée's relation to his period, particularly under the Second Empire, to which almost half the book is devoted.

LYON, SYLVIA. *The Life and Times of Prosper Mérimée*. New York:

The Dial Press, 1948. Somewhat superficial but highly entertaining and readable.

RAITT, A. W. *Prosper Mérimée*. London: Eyre and Spottiswoode, 1970. The best book on Mérimée which has appeared so far in English, both for his life and for his literary work. Excellent bibliography.

TRAHARD, F. *La Jeunesse de Prosper Mérimée*. Vols. I and II. Champion, 1925.

————. *Prosper Mérimée de 1834 à 1853*. Champion, 1928.

————. *La Vieillesse de Prosper Mérimée 1854–1870*. Champion, 1930. This four-volume work is considered the standard one on Mérimée. Scholarly but a little pedantic, excellent for the sources of Mérimée's plays and fiction, it is sometimes, in my opinion, a little harsh in literary judgments.

YOVANOVITCH, V. M. *La Guzla de Prosper Mérimée*. Hachette, 1911. This remarkable doctoral dissertation by a Yugoslav is the definitive work on Mérimée's *La Guzla*.

2. Articles in Books or Magazines

Excellent prefaces to Mérimée's works already listed: by H. Martineau, to Pléiade edition of *Romans et Nouvelles;* by E. Marsan, to the ten volumes of the Divan edition.

FAGUET, E. *Dix-neuvieme siècle*. Boivin, 1887. Pp. 235–51. An early but still valuable essay on Mérimée, though perhaps too insistent on his impassivity.

GEORGE, A. J. *Short Fiction in France 1800–1850*. Syracuse University Press, 1964. Pp. 102–35. He finds no two of the nineteen stories alike, yet Mérimée's ironic point of view makes his stories monotonous.

————. "Prosper Mérimée and the Short Prose Narrative," *Symposium*, Vol. X (Spring, 1956), pp. 1–31. Contains a brief history of the short story in France before the nineteenth century; compares Nodier and Mérimée and concludes that Mérimée's experimentation gave great impetus to short prose fiction among his successors.

JOURDA, P. Introduction to *Colomba*. Droz, 1947. Excellent documentation of Mérimée's sources for this novel.

MAUROIS, A. *Lélia ou la vie de George Sand*. Hachette, 1952. Pp. 172–74, 196. Discusses the brief liaison between Mérimée and George Sand.

PATER, WALTER. "Prosper Mérimée" in *Miscellaneous Studies*. New York and London: Macmillan, 1895. First delivered as a lecture at Oxford, November, 1890, and appearing in the *Fortnightly Review*, December, 1890. One of the best, if not the very best, of the essays on Mérimée in English. Covers all his literary work, particularly eulogistic of the *Chronique* and *Colomba*. Emphasis is on Mérimée's impeccable construction and style, by this master of style.

RICHARDS, P. "Introduction" and "Notice" to Classiques Larousse ed. of *Mateo Falcone, Colomba*, pp. 7–20 and 29–47. Discussion of differences among the *roman, nouvelle*, and *conte* and analyses of Mérimée's technique and influence on later writers.

SAINTE-BEUVE. *Portraits contemporains*. Didier, 1846. Vol. III (on *Colomba*)

————. *Causeries du lundi*, VII. Garnier. Pp. 371–89. Detailed and favorable commentary on Mérimée's history *Les Faux Démétrius* followed by an interesting comparison of Carmen with l'abbé Prévost's *Manon Lescaut*, then by a very perceptive contrasting of Mérimée and Musset in their short stories.

SAINTSBURY, GEORGE. *History of the French Novel to end of nineteenth century*, Vol. II. London: Macmillan, 1917. Pp. 238–51. Rather harsh on *the Chronique* but eulogistic of the short stories, especially of *L'Enlèvement de la redoute* (which he calls *La Prise de la redoute*).

SMITH, MAXWELL A. "Introduction to *La Partie de trictrac*" in *Short Stories by French Romanticists*. Boston: D. C. Heath, 1929. Pp. 153–56. Discussion of Mérimée as Romanticist, Realist, and Classicist; comparison with Vigny; emphasis on *le point d'honneur* in *La Partie de trictrac*.

TAINE, H. Preface to *Lettres à une Inconnue*. Michel Lévy, 1874. Also reprinted in his *Essais de critique et d'histoire*, 1874, and *Derniers essais de critique*. Hachette. Vivid description of Mérimée as he appeared to a contemporary, the great critic Taine. One of the earliest and best analyses of Mérimée's work.

Index

87415